The Neoliberal Subject

The Neoliberal Subject

Resilience, Adaptation and Vulnerability

David Chandler and Julian Reid

ROWMAN & LITTLEFIELD
INTERNATIONAL

London • New York

Published by Rowman & Littlefield International, Ltd.
Unit A, Whitacre Mews, 26-34 Stannary Street, London SE11 4AB
www.rowmaninternational.com

Rowman & Littlefield International, Ltd. is an affiliate of Rowman & Littlefield
4501 Forbes Boulevard, Suite 200, Lanham, Maryland 20706, USA
With additional offices in Boulder, New York, Toronto (Canada), and London (UK)
www.rowman.com

British Library Cataloguing in Publication Information Available
A catalogue record for this book is available from the British Library

ISBN: HB 978-1-7834-8771-4
ISBN: PB 978-1-7834-8772-1

Library of Congress Cataloging-in-Publication Data

Names: Chandler, David, 1962- author. | Reid, Julian (Julian David McHardy), author.
Title: The neoliberal subject : resilience, adaptation and vulnerability / David Chandler and Julian
    Reid.
Description: London ; New York : Rowman & Littlefield International, [2016] | Includes bibliograph-
    ical references and index.
Identifiers: LCCN 2015044202 (print) | LCCN 2016004665 (ebook) | ISBN 9781783487714 (cloth :
    alk. paper) | ISBN 9781783487721 (pbk. : alk. paper) | ISBN 9781783487738 (Electronic)
Subjects: LCSH: Neoliberalism. | Liberalism.
Classification: LCC JC574 .C4825 2016 (print) | LCC JC574 (ebook) | DDC 320.51/3--dc23
LC record available at http://lccn.loc.gov/2015044202

∞™ The paper used in this publication meets the minimum requirements of American
National Standard for Information Sciences Permanence of Paper for Printed Library
Materials, ANSI/NISO Z39.48-1992.

Printed in the United States of America

Contents

Introduction

The Neoliberal Subject

Resilience is becoming the key term of art for neoliberal regimes of governance. Across and throughout international relations, practices are being reshaped around the need to develop the capacities of humans, individually and collectively, for resilience. Resilience is currently propounded by neoliberal agencies and institutions, especially, as the fundamental property that peoples and individuals worldwide must possess in order to become full and developed subjects. We are writing this book to address the political and philosophical implications of this shift. It is the first study of the implications of neoliberal discourses of resilience for theories and practices of human subjectivity.

In spite of its claims to make humans more adept and capable in their dealings with the world, the promotion of resilience requires and calls forth a much degraded subject, one defined by much diminished capabilities for autonomy and agency, so crucial to the formation of human subjectivity. Rather than enabling the capacities of peoples and individuals for autonomy so that they can make their own decisions as to how they wish to live, the discourse of resilience understands autonomy as a threat to life. The resilient subject is one that has been taught, and accepted, the lessons concerning the danger of autonomy and the need to be 'capacity-built' in order to make the 'right choices' in development of sustainable responses to threats and dangers posed by its environment. Thus the process of constructing resilient subjects requires divesting peoples and individuals of any belief in the possibility of determining their own conditions for development and security, and accepting instead the necessity of adaptation to the 'realities' of an

1

endemic condition of global insecurity and to the practice of 'sustainable development' instead.

In drawing out the theoretical assumptions behind the drive for resilience and its implications for issues of political subjectivity, we are writing this book to establish a critical framework from which discourses of resilience can be understood and challenged in the fields of governance, security, development, and in political theory itself. In place of resilience we will argue, in our individually distinct and contrasting ways, that we need to revalorize an idea of the human subject as capable of acting on and transforming the world rather than being cast in a permanent condition of enslavement to it.

UNDERSTANDING NEOLIBERALISM

Neoliberalism is, according to current orthodoxy, best understood as a theory of political economic practices proposing that human well-being can be advanced by the development of entrepreneurial freedoms within an institutional framework characterized by private property rights, individual liberty, unencumbered markets, and free trade (Birch and Mykhnenko 2010; Chomsky 1998; Harvey 2005; Saad-Philo and Johnston 2004; Steger and Roy 2010; Touraine 2001). It is about the growth of 'consumer sovereignty' and the shift from ideological political contestation to the use of market-based tools and techniques to achieve political and social goals (see, for example, Lipshutz 2005: 750), or the rationalisation of the market as the 'site of truth', in the critical language of Foucauldian economic theorists (Jaeger 2013: 34). In contrast we believe neoliberalism is better understood more fundamentally as a theory and practice of subjectivity. We stake the claim that we cannot understand how neoliberalism is able to function as a socioeconomic program, and most especially how it has gained the global hegemony that it has today, without addressing how it problematizes human subjectivity. It is the interpretive capacities through which human beings reflect upon the nature of their world, their relations with themselves, each other, and their environments that are seen as being of crucial issue for the legitimation of neoliberal practices of government.

Doing this necessitates breaking from the existing understandings of what liberal subjectivity entails. Within the disciplines of political theory and international relations, the liberal subject is still identified with the idealized figure of *Homo Economicus* (Kiersey 2009) founded as that figure was in its supposedly unique capacity for reason and knowledge, its potential to achieve sovereignty over nature, and its pursuit of security and autonomy. In contrast, we will show how neoliberalism is based upon a fundamental rejection of the figure of *Homo Economicus* and the promotion of a subject neither rational or autonomous nor empowered or secure in its relations with nature. We will argue that the form of subjectivity inculcated through neoliberal discourses of risk, security, and governance today, presented as essential to bear the institutionalization of markets, private property rights, and free trade, is not the rational, sovereign subject of mythic representations of the liberal tradition, but a resilient, humble, and disempowered being that lives a life of permanent ignorance and insecurity. The account of the world envisaged and constituted by neoliberalism is one that presupposes the unknowability of the world, and likewise one which interpellates a subject that is permanently called upon to live in accordance with this unknowability; a subject for whom the bearing of risk and its responsibilization is a required practice without which he or she cannot grow and prosper in the world.

The critique of the human subject was, for much of the twentieth century, the provenance of the political right rather than the political left. The left propounded optimism concerning the potential for progress, an increase in human knowledge and transformational capacity, understanding the market as a barrier to human control and emancipation. The critique of universalizing views of progress as 'imaginary' was largely undertaken by ideologues of the right, concerned with explaining away the gap between liberal promises of progress and social realities: the crisis of the market and the inequalities perpetuated by it, both domestically and internationally. This work was largely undertaken in the sphere of economic theorizing, which sought to extend and transform economic understandings of individual choice-making to explain inequality and difference and its reproduction in terms of institutional blockages to the perfect operation of the market.

During the Cold War, the neoliberal framing of the human subject was not clearly and overtly articulated in policy or related discourses, nor was the critique of the human subject central to mainstream thinking. In fact, neoliberalism in the 1980s and early 1990s referred to the temporary confidence of conservative advocates of market-based policy-making, emboldened by the decline of socialist alternatives, and ideologically intent on the rolling back of the state. Policy debates of the 1980s and early 1990s illustrated the shared assumptions of both the Cold War left and right in that both sides shared an understanding of the capacity of the human subject to autonomously organize and act in pursuit of its rational interests. The difference was in the form in which autonomous action could be best developed—through more free play of the market or through more intervention at the level of the state. That shared understanding of the capacity for autonomy of the subject meant that the Cold War essentially froze the promise of modernist thinking—through making the future (replete with promises of control and progress) the object of ideological contestation between liberal and communist forces. The fact that neoliberal thinking developed on the margins of the policy process and that some neoliberal perspectives were drawn upon, particularly by governments of the right, such as Margaret Thatcher's and Ronald Reagan's, should not blind us to the fact that the dominant framing of left/right debates on the relationship between states and markets was dominated by a modernist understanding of the human subject, replete with universalizing assumptions of rationality and capability for autonomy.

We want to explore the resurgence of neoliberal framings of the human over the last two decades, and consider how its diminished understanding of the human have come to be hegemonic in framings of risk, vulnerability, contingency, insecurity, conflict, development, and the proposed policy-solutions in terms of resilience, capacity-building, adaptive efficiency, and good governance. Today, neoliberalism operates as the guiding rationality for understanding the world we live in and for informing governing policy-practices. Examining how that has become the case, we will trace how neoliberalism came to preach the sickness of the human, the hubris of ideals of autonomy and security, the 'illusion' of sovereign freedom, and our vulnerability as a species to the unique events and unpredictable risks and drastic economic and social transformations said to be inherent in our complex, interdependent, and globalized world, along with a growing awareness of the catastrophic capacities of the biosphere on which we depend for life.

As we will show, the diminished view of the human, which neoliberalism insists on, has transformed and undermined the role and possibilities of politics (see Thaler and Sunstein 2008; IfG 2009). Politics requires a subject capable of conceiving the transformation of its world and the power relations it finds itself subject to. In contrast, the neoliberal subject is a subject that must permanently struggle to accommodate itself to the world. Not a subject that can conceive of changing the world, its structure and conditions of possibility; but a subject which accepts the unknowability of the world in which it lives as a condition for partaking of that world, and which accepts the necessity of the injunction to change itself and adapt in order to cope responsively with the threats and dangers now presupposed as endemic. The discursive construction of the neoliberal subject involves an implicit, and often an explicit, critique of the political habits, tendencies, and capacities of peoples and the replacing of them with adaptive ones.

The human subject is constructed within neoliberal discourse as having to accept that it is not possible to resist or secure him or herself from difficulties encountered (both individually and collectively) but instead learn how to adapt to their enabling conditions via the embrace of insecurity and unknowability (Beck 1992; Giddens 1994). Within this framing, the only role for government is that of facilitation and enablement of more adaptive and capable individual choices—a system of techniques and practices of so-called 'good governance', held to enable the better and more efficient use of markets and market-based forms of choice-making as a necessary requirement for the instauring of adaptive capacities socially (North 2005; North, Wallis, and Weingast 2009). Understanding how neoliberalism is able to legitimate itself thus requires grasping how it reflects and reproduces the problematic that minimizes or dismisses the importance of human beings thinking and acting agentially or politically in relation to their environments.

In fact, the area of the individual's transformative activity is essentially reduced to a disciplining of the inner self, while it is the task of government to facilitate and capacity-build the individual in order for the individual to undertake this transformative work. As the Royal Society for the Arts (RSA) document *Changing the Subject*, informed by recent developments in neuropsychology, notes, 'new knowledge about brains and behaviour can help adults exercise more control over their behaviour both collectively and as individuals . . . awareness and application of such knowledge might empower them to be creatively involved in changing their own behaviour' (Grist 2009: 79). The psychic or inner life of the subject, and the social milieus through which it is seen to be constructed and influenced, become the sphere of transformation in order to develop the faculties of resilience and adaptive efficiency held to be necessary to respond to external environments more securely. In this way, neoliberal frameworks reduce the cognitive and psychic life of the subject to a domain of insecurity. In effect, human subjectivity itself, the ideational, cognitive, and practical contexts of its reproduction and the psychic life of the subject especially, become problematized as dangerous.

We argue that challenging neoliberalism requires recognizing these elements of its approach to issues of human subjectivity. This critique is one that does not easily sit with dominant understandings of neoliberalism within the traditional political framework of left and right (Foucault 2008). While it is correct that neoliberalism developed through the critique of classical liberal assumptions in response to the criticisms of the left that capitalism was a barrier to progress and emancipation, ironically, the popularization of neoliberal framings owes as much to the post-Marxist and post-structuralist left. In fact, many of today's radical critiques of neoliberalism appear to merely replay neoliberalism's own understandings of the limits of human subjectivity. The deconstructions of concepts of sovereignty, security, and subjectivity that legitimize and normalize neoliberal discourses are, in fact, more likely to stem from self-declared radical critics of the system than from advocates of the status quo.

We both consider ourselves to be from the left and have long-standing concerns with questions of human emancipation. Nevertheless, it seems to us that neoliberalism cannot be overcome if we continue to rely on existing ways of understanding it as well as existing and discursively powerful, but ultimately wrongheaded, ways of theorizing its resistance. To go to war with neoliberalism, to reinvest in an open-ended and transformative account of political subjectivity and the specifically human powers and ways of being such subjectivity involves, it seems to us, necessarily involves demarcating new lines of political battle.

In building this original analytic of liberalism and neoliberalism, this book will draw significantly from the late works of Michel Foucault. Foucault's works have had a massive influence on critical literatures, particularly in international relations, in recent years, and we both have made significant, different, and conflicting contributions to that influence. But we both agree that while Foucault's thought has been inspirational for interrogation of the growth of liberal arts of government, his works have too often failed to inspire studies of political subjectivity. Instead they have been used to stoke the neoliberal myth of the inevitability of the decline of collective political subjects, describing an increasingly limited horizon of political possibilities, and provoking disenchantment with the political itself.

We are also, therefore, writing this book to work against the grain of current Foucauldian scholarship. We want to excavate the importance of Foucault's work for our capacities to recognise how this degraded understanding of political subjectivity came about. Rather than following the many interpretations of Foucault that use his work to trash the concept of the human—interpretations which have become so influential in international relations and the wider social sciences—we will explore how we can use his ideas to recover the vital capacity to think and act politically in a time when fundamentally human capacities to think, imagine, know, create, and act purposively in the world are being pathologized as expressions of humanity's hubris.

THE STRUCTURE OF THE BOOK

As we have said, we share a diagnosis of the problem with neoliberalism. But we also depart and differ from one another on some fundamental issues concerning the origins of that problem. Differences that entail us each possessing different understandings of the very nature of liberalism itself, its relations with the modern, and indeed the very nature of the modern, its promises, and its dangers. Rather than paper over the cracks and attempt to conceal those differences through sleight of hand or a banalization of our positions in order to fabricate a united front, this book is structured as a discussion between two friends who are also rivals. Friendship and rivalry have gone, of course, rather well together, ever since the Greeks, for whom it was 'the rivalry of free men, a generalized athleticism: the agon' (Deleuze and Guattari 1999: 4). We want to get to the truth of neoliberalism, in belief that there is such a truth to be had, but we are also rivals in the struggle for that truth. One of us may have a better handle on it than the other. And that is for the reader to decide. So, over the course of the next six chapters we will each take three chapters to thrash out our different understandings of the neoliberal subject. That said we both agree that the neoliberal subject can be defined as possessive of three essential attributes: resilience, adaptivity, and vulnerability. Thus we will each in our individual chapters explain our different understandings of how and why the neoliberal subject is and must be resilient, adaptive, and vulnerable. And the book is accordingly divided into three sections on these themes. The final chapter of the book, rather than offering a conventional conclusion, is an interview with the two of us given to another friend, Gideon Baker, where we attempt to address the questions our different analyses of the neoliberal subject have opened up. The remaining two chapters of this introductory section gives a brief indication of our different understandings of the neoliberal subject, its origins, and futures.

Chapter One

Debating Neoliberalism

The Exhaustion of the Liberal Problematic

David Chandler

Neoliberalism became hegemonic in the late 1970s as part of a project of social contestation involving the curbing of trade union power and the rolling back of the state, pushing responsibility for social welfare onto society rather than the state. As many theorists and commentators have powerfully described, neoliberalism's shift of emphasis from the state to society has taken a variety of forms in different national and international contexts, but all have appealed to calls for human freedom, dignity, and independence and all have been hostile to big government provision of services and of top-down interventionist policy-provision (see, for example, Harvey 2005). In exploring the shift of policy emphasis from state to society, analysts of neoliberalism often emphasize the agency of neoliberal policy-making, the needs of capitalism and big business, and neglect the ways in which the neoliberal subject—the subject at the heart of the shift to the social or the societal understanding of the modern world—is constructed and interpellated.

For many Marx-inspired theorists, such as David Harvey, neoliberalism is mainly seen as an economic phenomenon, driven by the needs of capital accumulation. In which case, the shift to societal understandings, of social or individualized security, is a straightforward one, depending on the traditional or classical liberal understanding of the subject as universally rational and autonomous. In fact, these assumptions are the source of Harvey's critique: that precisely because of the false subject of liberalism, the freedoms of the market clash with the demands of social justice (and that the left has failed to critique neoliberalism on these grounds):

> Asymmetric power relations tend . . . to increase rather than diminish over time unless the state steps in to counteract them. The neoliberal presupposition of perfect information and a level playing field for competition appears as either innocently utopian or a deliberate obfuscation of processes that will lead to the concentration of wealth and, therefore, the restoration of class power. (Harvey 2005: 68)

Harvey's left critique of neoliberalism is therefore based upon the clash between the subject as interpellated in and through neoliberal discourses as rational and autonomous and the real, sociological, socially embedded subject, which lacks the capacities and capabilities and rationalities required to compete under capitalism as if it was a 'level playing field'. Once neoliberal discourse is recognised as a 'failed utopian rhetoric masking a successful project for the restoration of ruling-class power' then 'mass movements voicing egalitarian political demands and seeking economic justice, fair trade, and greater economic security' can reemerge (Harvey 2005: 203–4). Here, the subject being interpellated through neoliberal discourses is the classical liberal subject and it is through the critique of this 'utopian' subject that neoliberal discourse can be exposed as the ideological expression of ruling-class hegemony.

Other theorists, often taking their inspiration from Michel Foucault, rather than Karl Marx, have also staked out highly influential interpretations of the neoliberal subject at the heart of the shift from state to societal provision of security. For these commentators, neoliberalism is not understood to be driven primarily by economic needs but by the crisis of liberal authority in a complex and globalizing world where traditional forms of authority can no longer operate with fixed understandings of state, nation, and community. These framings understand state-society relations as being transformed not by the withdrawal or the rolling back of the state but through its very different framework of intervention, which reconstructs state-society relations in ways which dissolve classical liberal understandings of this discursive divide.

The neoliberal problematic is then understood not so much through the economic determinants required for the restoration of capitalist social power but as a framework in which the state can restore its authority over society through new mechanisms of intervention and regulation. In this framing, the subject is interpellated differently: without the assumptions of universality, rationality, and autonomy presumed in the discourses of classical liberalism. Rather than the autonomous free play of the market under conditions of universal rationality, state intervention is understood as the precondition for both the construction of the market and the liberal political subject. As Foucault-inspired writers, such as Graham Burchell (1991; 1996), Mitchell Dean (2010), Colin Gordon (1991), Peter Miller and Nikolas Rose (2008), Pat

O'Malley (2004; 2010) have noted, the neoliberal shift from emphasis on the centrality of the state to the importance of society has involved the hands-on project of the active making of the liberal subject through societal intervention, rather than the classical liberal 'utopian' assumption of the 'naturalness' of the liberal subject.

Miller and Rose articulate the neoliberal problematic, with regard to the 'new specification of the subject of government' (2008: 213), thus:

> Within this new regime of the actively responsible self, individuals are to fulfil their national obligations not through their relations of dependency and obligation to one another, but through seeking to fulfil themselves within a variety of micro-moral domains or 'communities'—families, workplaces, schools, leisure associations, neighbourhoods. Hence the problem is to find the means by which individuals may be made responsible through their individual choices for themselves and those to whom they owe allegiance, through the shaping of a lifestyle according to grammars of living that are widely disseminated, yet do not depend upon political calculations and strategies for their rationales or for their techniques. (2008: 214)

Governing authority no longer becomes exercised in the old way, as intervention and regulation from above society, in the form of liberal government on behalf of, or over, the social whole. Rather, new forms of neoliberal governance appear as ways of 'empowering', 'capability-building', or 'freeing' the citizen, enabling neoliberal subjects to take societal responsibility upon themselves and their communities. Miller and Rose are surely correct in noting that this 'ethical a priori of active citizens in an active society is perhaps the most fundamental, and most generalizable, characteristic of these new rationalities of government' (2008: 215). Dean concurs that the task of neoliberal government lies precisely in the management and regulation of, or inculcation of, the agency of the governed. The solution to problems of societal security, whether in the form of welfare, crime, or conflict becomes that of the development of societal agency:

> Victims of crime, smokers, abused children, gay men, intravenous drug users, the unemployed, indigenous people and so on are all subject to these technologies of agency, the object being to transform their status, to make them active citizens capable, as individuals and communities, of managing their own risk. (Dean 2010: 196–97)

The neoliberal state does not withdraw from society and leave rational and autonomous subjects to bear responsibility for securing themselves, rather it is an active and interventionist state, which assumes that societal insecurity is the result of the incapacity of the subject. The neoliberal subject is therefore one which is problematized and it is this problematization that is at the heart of neoliberal interventions within the social sphere. As Dean states, once problematized: 'individuals are required to agree to a range of normalizing, therapeutic and training measures designed to empower them, enhance their self-esteem, optimize their skills and entrepreneurship and so on' (2010: 197).

In my contributions to this book on the neoliberal subject, I seek to develop and expand upon the direction taken by these Foucault-inspired theorists. I particularly wish to focus upon the shifts and transformations in our understanding of the liberal subject and how these are articulated within the broader discursive shift from the emphasis on the state as the key agent within liberal modernity to the emphasis on societal agency in discourses of neoliberalism. Where I seek to differ in emphasis, vis-à-vis the theorists briefly referred to above, is that I plan to sketch out the broader cultural and societal sensibilities and understandings underpinning the construction or interpellation of the neoliberal subject, rather than narrowly understanding neoliberalism as a set of instrumental governing technologies. Following the work of Alison Howell and Andrew Neal (2012) and others (Larner 2000), I suggest a much looser understanding of the dispositif of neoliberalism, highlighting cultural sensibilities rather than governmental or instrumental uses in terms of techniques and practices.

In fact, I will go further to argue that neoliberalism is less a programme for governing society for specific goals or ends, than the systematic retreat from such a programme. While it is clear that neoliberal sensibilities lack the view that the state should just withdraw from society and 'let freedom reign', it seems equally clear that discourses of actively creating citizens, of empowering and capacity-building individuals and communities, are more concerned with the limits to societal change than with social transformation. Neoliberalism, in fact, marks an historic withdrawal from the project of 'rule', which, thus far, has been captured neither by the Marxist focus on capitalist accumulation nor by the Foucauldian governmentality theorists.

Liberalism articulated a very clear project of rule, of social direction through a clear separation between the state and society—between the legal and political realm and the social and economic realm—and was therefore a suitable subject for governmentality analysis, reflecting upon the self-understanding of the processes, mechanisms, and limits to rule. The project of constructing or interpellating the neoliberal subject is less a concrete programme of rule and regulation than a declaration of the impossibility or attenuation of governmental agency in the current age. The problematization of the classical rights- and interests-bearing liberal subject serves to shift governing responsibility to society rather than the state. As the state is increasingly submerged within society and within social processes, it loses its rule in terms of any clear demarcation or separation of government from governed. In effect, politics becomes reduced to the administration of societal processes. Neoliberalism, in this sense, offers no positive programme for governing. In its continual effacing of the separation between state and society and reduction of politics to administration it resembles the Marxist or socialist project (which sought similarly to do away with the rule of government) rather than the liberal project which was focused on precisely the problematic of limiting and thereby reproducing state power through its suspension and distinctness vis-à-vis economic and social processes.

I will argue that the neoliberal project is more accurately understood as the exhaustion of the liberal project of modernity or the exhaustion of the progressive impulse within liberalism. Rather than understanding neoliberalism as implicit within liberal understandings or somehow a natural or organic extension of liberalism, I wish to argue that neoliberalism—as we consider it in this book and as I analyse these trends under the term 'postliberalism' elsewhere (Chandler 2010)—is parasitical on the demise of liberalism. This parasitical nature is clear in its dynamic, which challenges and dismantles classical liberal political categories and conceptual binaries: in international relations, the focus is on the inside or the internal management of the state; in normative political theory, the focus is upon the 'inside' of the social sphere and the embedded and differentiated nature of the subject rather than the formal realm of legal and political equality; in the understanding of the individual subject, the focus is on the private cognitive realm of the thought processes—the realm of psychology—rather than action in the public sphere. I will be arguing that the internalization of the liberal problematic signifies the end of liberalism as a potentially progressive outlook, capable of framing a left-right contestation over the future direction of society.

Neoliberal understandings, which operate in ways that dismantle or bypass the classical liberal conceptual categories, upon which the formal politics of representation and government depend, and reduce politics to the governance or management of social processes, are reflected in the shift in international relations theorizing from formal concerns of international politics to the informal intersubjective processes of global sociology. Increasingly, attention is drawn to the social processes constructed and reproduced through self-organizing, emergent, and complex processes of societal and networked interactions. Such a 'globalized' world of complex and overlapping social processes appears as a product of human agency but not one which is amenable to conscious political or institutional regulation and control through the mediation of the political, the construction of sovereign political institutions. As will be discussed in my chapters which follow, the globalized world of human agency appears to be one in which we have little control over the results of our own agency: without the fixity of communities and structures and traditional or established frameworks of political meaning, human agency seems to be leading to a constant flux of unexpected change and potential catastrophe.

no control over results of own agency

Neoliberalism thus operates with the problematic of change rather than the liberal teleology of progress. Whereas the discourses of progress presupposed a knowable external world open to human exploration and understanding, and to control and direction by governments, the discourse of change involves no future-orientated goals on behalf of the human subject. Change is not something that occurs under the control or direction of human agency and implies no telos of progress or increase in the bounds of human freedom. Change is something that happens independently of human planning or direction, but is understood to be an emergent product of human interaction and agential choices and behaviour. In a neoliberal world, change is something that governments and communities can only adapt to. In a world, understood as one of complex, globalized, and interconnected social processes, we are confronted with a world of our creation but not one in which we can ever live as human subjects.

In constructing our social world in these ways, neoliberal discourse interpellates the human subject as one increasingly divested of the powers and capacities through which, from the Enlightenment onward, human collectivities sought to demarcate a sphere of human freedom and progress. In this way, the subject is responsible for the world in which it lives, but this responsibility is not articulated in terms of capacities for self-determination, freedom, or political autonomy. The sphere in which liberal subjectivity was expressed, through the reasoning and contestation of the political process and struggle to determine or control the goals and direction of society is increasingly seen to be of little consequence once policy concerns shift to societal processes, practices and behavioural choices. Neoliberal discourse operates not at the level of rights and representation but at the level of societal processes in the private and informal sphere, the practices and cognitive frameworks through which we relate to others and to the external environment.

In the chapters that follow, I will draw out further the relationships between the understanding of change as the product of emergent, self-organising, or path-dependent social processes and interactions, without a telos or direction, and the shift from classical liberal understandings of the rational and transformative subject to neoliberal frames of understanding, which reduce politics to work on the construction of the subject itself. I particularly wish to do this through the analytical exposition of the three concepts flagged in the subtitle of this book: resilience, adaptation, and vulnerability.

Resilience is a key concept within neoliberal discourse, denoting a positive internal attribute of being able to positively adapt to change. The resilient subject (at both individual and collective levels) is not passive in the face of change and does not seek to resist change, but rather is active, understanding change as a necessary facilitator of self-knowledge, self-growth, and self-transformation. I will argue that resilience is used here as a normative concept, or an ideal type. There is no such thing as a fully resilient subject:

resilience is the product of a process that is ongoing and has no end as such. Resilience has to be continually produced and can only be measured or calculated as a comparative or relative quality. Some individuals or communities may be understood to be capable of adapting to change more than others but none can be understood to be fully resilient. While we are aware that our fixed understandings, derived from the past, are a barrier to resilience we are also aware that our thought-processes and cultural and social values continue to bind or limit our openness to change. We can only ever be somewhere along the continuum of resilience and therefore ultimately all are in need of enabling to become more resilient.

For neoliberal understandings, adaptive capacity is seen to be the measure of resilience. The more adaptive capacity is enhanced the more resilient we are as both individuals and communities. The inculcation or development of resilience can therefore be done through the increase in our adaptive capabilities and capacities. The more resilient we are the more fully developed we are as neoliberal subjects. In the chapter on adaptation, I will draw out how the neoliberal conception of freedom differs radically from our understanding of freedom in the framings of liberal modernity. In liberal modernity, freedom is the presupposition for the subject's autonomy and rights ownership; however, in the continuum of resilience, adaptive capacities are always under development: in this sense the neoliberal subject is never interpellated as 'free' but always in the process of enlarging or developing its freedom, understood in terms of adaptive capacity.

Vulnerabilities are thus understood in terms of the barriers or limits to becoming a resilient subject. In this sense vulnerabilities constitute our 'unfreedoms' or the restrictions, both material and ideological, that prevent us from adapting to change. The barriers to adaptation constitute vulnerabilities and subjects who lack the capacities and capabilities necessary to become resilient are therefore interpellated as vulnerable. This interpellation as vulnerable can be applied to individuals—the 'at risk', 'socially excluded' or the 'marginal'—as well as to communities—the 'poor', 'indigenous' or the 'environmentally threatened'—as much as to states themselves—the 'failing', 'failed', 'fragile', 'low income under stress' or badly governed. In the chapter on vulnerability, I will consider the interventionist discourses of the international sphere which seek to overcome the vulnerabilities of postcolonial and postconflict states and communities through the inculcation of resilience through behaviour-shaping interventions.

In all three chapters, the key theme that will be drawn out is that the discourses of neoliberalism and the concomitant focus on the agency and empowerment of vulnerable subjects is less a project of government regulation and control (whether in the cause of capitalist accumulation or liberal governmentalism) than a rejection of the liberal conception of government as standing above society. The neoliberal subject is thus a subject at home in a world in which externally orientated projects of transformation are no longer imaginable. A subject for who work on the self is understood to be liberating and emancipatory; who welcomes governance discourses of empowerment and capacity-building in the knowledge that we are all producers of our world and all share responsibility for its reproduction. In this world, with no outside, there is nothing beyond the technical or administrative management of the status quo through societal 'steering'. Politics, as a contestation over societal goals, could have no meaning in such a world.

The neoliberal framework of understanding lacks its own positive dynamic, in terms of reflecting a coherent worldview or collective project of clearly defined classes or particular interests. In fact, I think it would be an exaggeration to call it a 'project' in any sense of the word. This is not to say that there are not clear tendencies or laws at play in its development and appropriation of previous liberal understandings of security, development, and what it might mean to govern well. However, as Hannah Arendt presciently warns (2005: 190), the seemingly natural and uncontested removal of the external world as an object of political contestation has its own laws of consequence, ones very different to the laws of political action. The potentially devastating effects of this shift to the internal world of the subject will be drawn out here: in the chapter on resilience—focusing on the shift of discourses of security responsibility from the state to society; the second chapter on adaptation, considering the shift of discourses of development to considerations of community and individual capacity; and the third chapter on vulnerability, analysing how social practices and interactions are held to constitute barriers to the spread of liberal values.

Chapter Two

Debating Neoliberalism

The Horizons of the Biopolitical

Julian Reid

Liberalism, as I have explored extensively elsewhere, is a security project (see especially Reid 2006a). From its outset it has been concerned with seeking answers to the problem of how to secure itself as a regime of governance through the provision of security to the life of populations subject to it (Foucault 1981; 2007). It will always be an incomplete project because its foundations are flawed; life is not securable. It is a multiplicity of antagonisms, and, for some life to be made to live, some other life has to be made to die. That is a fundamental law of life biologically understood. This is the deep paradox that undercuts the entire liberal project, while also inciting it to govern ever more and ever better, seeking to become more inclusive and more assiduous at the provision of security to life, while all the while learning how better to take life and make die that which falls outside and threatens the boundaries of its territories (Dillon and Reid 2009). In essence liberal regimes thrive on the problematic of the insecurity of the life that their capacity to provide security to is the source of their legitimacy, becoming ever more adept at the taking of life, which the provision of security to life requires. It is not an accident that the most advanced liberal democracy in the world today, the United States of America, is also the most heavily armed state in the world. And not just the most heavily armed state today but the most heavily armed in human history.

Liberal regimes do not and cannot accept the realities of this paradox, which is why, far from being exhausted, the liberal project remains and has to be, in order for it to be true to its mission, distinctly transformative; of the world in general and hence its endless resorts to war and violence to weed out those unruly lives that are the source of insecurity to the life that is the font of its security. But also, and yet more fundamentally, of the human subject itself; for this is a paradox which plays out, not just territorially, socially, or between individuals, but within the diffuse domain of human subjectivity itself. The liberal subject itself is divided and has to be in order to fulfil its mission; critically astute at discerning the distinctions within its own life between that which accords with the demands made of it in order to accord with liberal ways of living and those which don't. Being divided means the liberal subject will always be incomplete, needing work, critical and suspicious of itself. The liberal subject is a project; one that renders life itself a project, subject to an endless task of critique and self-becoming, from cradle to grave.

Sadly many still find the concept of life to sound appealing and even utopian. We are taught to think, according to Renton's law, that we ought to choose life over emptiness or negation (Welsh 1996). In fact it is the source of the world's greatest nihilisms. Liberalism too is and has always been a nihilism. Perhaps it is the greatest of all nihilisms. In giving us over to life it gives us no ends to live for but the endless work on the self that contemporarily permeates our ways of living. This is not to say that liberalism and liberals do not have belief. They do. They believe that in order to 'make life live' whatever opposes life or does not live in accordance with the needs of life has to be destroyed or at least rendered a problem solved. Chief object among which, tragically, is the human itself. Obviously human beings live in the biological sense of the term, and have needs and interests in their biological life being sustained. Liberalism would have no hold over the human if this were not the case. But the peculiarity of human beings is our profound capacities for the transcendence of our merely biological life. Within the psychic domain of experience we are continually seeking and finding that experience, in the quotidian phenomena of dreams and reverie, for example (Bachelard 2005). The exercise of the imagination, which, for all of us, is more or less incessant, removes us, puts us at a distance from the biological domain of biological needs and wants. Humans are dreamers and schemers by dint of their mere existence.

Liberalism too, of course, has its imagination. It imagines and dreams the possibility of its security globally, through the mastery of the very antagonisms it encounters in its gaze on life and the world. Life itself, liberalism dreams, can give it the answers to the problem of how to assure its security; for it imagines that in life itself is to be found the very secret of security. But in reality what we see being imagined here is a world depopulated of properly human subjects. For the subject to secure itself it must divest itself of, or at the very least wage an ongoing war on, the psychic powers that populate its otherwise biologically defined body. What does a human body become once it is waged war upon thus? As I will explore in subsequent chapters of this book such wars are aimed at the reduction of human life to the properties and capacities that define nonhuman bodies, nonhuman living species and systems; resilience, adaptivity, and vulnerability. Worse, subjects that, in their humanity, refuse to give up their psychic life, do not become resilient, cannot adapt, or don't recognize their vulnerability, are constructed as threats to liberal peace, security, and 'good governance'. That is the tragedy of liberal modernity.

To emphasize the point, this is not the result of some recent shift or change within liberalism from its classical to its neomoorings. Of course liberalism is not a static tradition; it changes. And as we will see the contemporary flourishing of new discourses of resilience, adaptivity, and vulnerability are expressions of its motility. But the declaration of war on the human was fundamental to liberalism from its outset. And the exposure of that nihilism which permeates it is fundamental to Michel Foucault's insights, from his earliest works right through to the late lectures which took liberalism as their target. Others too have enjoined in the task of excavating that nihilism. In a brilliant book, Dominic Colas has shown how the liberal war on humanity's psychic powers of imagination has effectively entailed the will to pathologize all political utilizations of the imagination as fanatical and mad (Colas 1997). The ways in which the very existence not to say exercise of the imagination incites in liberalism the fear of the fanatic.

My hypothesis, the argument that structures the analysis I will extend in this book, is that there is a fundamental antinomy between both human and political subjectivity, and the form of biohuman subjectivity that neoliberalism is committed to producing out of human material. In essence, I assume, because I believe, that to be human is to be capable of being political by definition. One is human only insofar as one is capable of transcending merely biological existence, and exercising one's powers of imaginative action. Imaginative action does not entail human beings resiliently suffering their vulnerability to environments that are hostile to them, or enable them to adapt to their environments a la the biohuman subject of liberal modernity. In contrast imaginative action is what enables human beings to forsake the current courses of their worlds in constitution of new ones through, not the transformation of themselves, but the exercise of agency on their worlds, through the rendering of the image upon it. The world thus conceived must conform to the image the subject desires of it and not the other way around. My critics will say that Foucault was not explicitly committed to such a sourcing of imaginative action, and that I should follow him with greater fidelity, but through his explorations of what he called 'political spirituality' I will show how he can provide us with integral insights into how to go about it.

Going to war with neoliberalism requires therefore that we invest in another account of political subjectivity and the specifically human powers and ways of being such subjectivity involves. It requires that we necessarily demarcate new lines of political battle between essentially two different and radically opposed subjects; the biohuman subject of liberal modernity and what I call the psychopolitical subject. As a political project the force of neoliberalism depends not on its capacities to secure the biohuman, because no such subject of security in actuality, I will argue, exists. We always remain human in spite of ourselves. It depends in contrast on its capacities to govern us as subjects who fail to conceive of our life potentials in anything more than merely biologized terms. It requires making us believe, in other words, in the impossibility of being anything more than biohuman subjects. For liberalism to legitimate itself the horizons that determine our ways of living must be successfully biologized; which is why the political discourses of global politics are so replete today with values deriving from biological sources. The contemporary valorization of capacities for resilience, adaptive capacity, and the recognition of our vulnerabilities are expressions of this. The psychopolitical subject, in contrast, is defined by a form of experience that can only posit itself in hostility to liberal modernity and its biohuman subject; a form of experience that liberalism itself can only comprehend as threatening and fearful to its biopolitical project. Psychopolitical subjects do not merely live in order to fit in with and adapt to existing times, or desire the sustainability of the conditions for their living the lives they do. In contrast they resist those conditions, and where successful, overcome them, trans- forming them in ways that conform with the transformative work their imagi- nation demands of them; new worlds in succession of old and destroyed worlds. The task is to affirm the imaginative action of the subject, which entails not its experience of vulnerability to injury and fear of death, but the hubristic trust in itself and others with whom it decides what it wants, asserts what it possesses, and celebrates what it is able to do, in accordance with truths that transcend its existence as a merely living entity.

   'Psychic life' has of course had a life in mainstream political theoretical discourse at least ever since the publication of Judith Butler's *The Psychic Life of Power*. Her account takes the psyche as the source of subjection and more specifically the 'peculiar turning of a subject against itself' through which we are said to come to desire the terms of our own subjection (1997: 18–19). Accordingly, and perversely, vulnerability is the core property that Butler assigns to the psychic life of the subject on account of its being dependent on that which by necessity exploits it (1997: 20). In irresolvable opposition to Butler and her liberal cronies, I insist that the powers of imagi- nation through which we are able to escape power are more fundamental than vulnerability to the psychic life of the subject. The form of psychopolitics I believe in is closer to William Blake, than it is Judith Butler, therefore, in its assumption that 'the imagination is not a state: it is the human existence itself' (quoted in Bachelard 2005: 19).

Foucault's life was cut short, not least because he acted out many of his fantasies with such sovereign freedom, before he could fully explore what he meant by 'political spirituality'. In seeking to resource that concept here to theorize the psychopolitical subject of struggle against neoliberalism I will draw also on others whose works it seems to me are promising for this purpose. The work of Peter Sloterdijk, I will argue, is one of the richest theoretical resources that we have today to make use of for this task. In reading him, we also reencounter the riches of the legacy of another French thinker, somewhat marginalized in comparison with Foucault, Gaston Bachelard. One of the questions which both Bachelard and Sloterdijk's work pursues, is that of the importance of the imaginary to psychopolitical subjectivity, and explanation for its relative degradation in an era of biopolitical modernity. What is the imaginary? What is imagination? And what is it to engage in imaginative action? In political discourse and theory we speak often enough of the importance of imaginaries. I myself have written often of the power and importance of both liberal and biopolitical imaginaries in shaping modern political horizons and sensibilities (Dillon and Reid 2009; Reid 2006a. We speak likewise of the need to develop alternative imaginaries; the need to imagine the world differently, in order to struggle for such alternatives. In other words we presuppose the existence of dominant imaginaries, we demand alternative imaginaries, but rarely do we think closely about the political nature of the imagination as such; even though, obviously the imagination is the very source of the imaginaries we have available to us.

'The imagination' is quite literally, as Bachelard tells us, 'a psychological world beyond' (2005: 23). It is not only that power within the human psyche for the projection of being beyond, but that element within the human psyche which is always *already* a world beyond. The human, fundamentally, in exercising imaginative action is that which is always, already existing beyond, bound to and bound for a world beyond. How does this peculiar capacity of the human psyche for beyondness relate to the political problem today of struggles for a postliberal world? It would seem obvious to me that imaginative action is the absolute precondition for the struggle for a world beyond liberalism and that the power of the imagination is of all the attributes of the human psyche that which is most fundamental. The imagination, if we follow Bachelard, is not only the promise of a world beyond, conditional upon the adoption of a particular dispositif in the present, but the actual existence of the beyond in the psychic life of the subject. It is the enactment of the beyond now. It is not the promise of a security to come, but the enactment of a security in the present. As Bachelard himself puts it, 'the most revolutionary manifestos are always new literary constitutions. They make us change universes, but they always shelter us in an imaginary one' (2005: 27).

Within the history of liberal modernity there have been many different struggles. But the struggle to stifle the imagination, font of the psychopolitical subject would seem to me to be absolutely essential, organizing each of them. But is there a danger that in theorizing psychopolitical subjectivity we get pulled into a valorization of the imaginary in neglect of the real? I think the reverse. What would the histories of political struggles be without the immensity of the imaginaries that fuelled them? Take away the imagination and you stultify the subject of resistance. Invigorate the material of struggle with an inner imaginary and you intensify the reality of struggle tenfold. Questions I will pose here therefore include that of how to navigate the relation between the imaginary and the real? A politics of resistance to liberalism, today, requires more than ever a psychopolitical subject capable of transcending the biopolitical horizons of liberal modernity; one that will free us from its biologisms, and enable us to dream and imagine in ways that are proper to the human psyche. But in order for an imaginary to continue with enough persistence such that it produces a revolutionary manifesto with a new literary constitution, for it to be more than the vacuous pastime of poets, the imaginary must find its matter, its reality. A material element must give the imaginary its own substance. Note it is not the question of which material precedes the imaginary, but how the imaginary finds its material, such that it is able to realize itself. The political theorization of resistance to liberalism, if it is to advance, has to proceed onto these terrains and in doing so lose its idle fascination with biological properties and capacities.

Rather, then, than read Foucault with a view to ossifying already essentialized post-structuralist (and effectively liberal) positions with regards to demands to move 'beyond subjectivity', dismantle security, or deconstruct humanity, I will pursue the question of how the human subject might be reinvented—so that it can contest the limits and conditions of liberal imaginaries on some of the terrains which liberalism holds most dear: life, humanity, security, and autonomy. We get nowhere politically by simply attempting to condemn concepts. The doubly political and philosophical problem is how to reinvent them, by breathing new life into them (Deleuze and Guattari 1999: 1534). The question of how to reinvent the subject is, when opened up to inquiry via what I will argue to be a more properly Foucauldian methodology, a question not of how to refuse the care for life via which biopolitical regimes facilitate subjection, but to rethink the relations of the subject to its life differently, with a view to being able to reconstitute practices of freedom and security; so that it might recover a more fundamentally human capacity for autonomy. Once we recognize the contingency of the debasement of practices of freedom and security that follow from the biologization of the human on which the liberal project proceeds, based on the demand to constitute the human as 'biohuman', so we create for ourselves the capacity to recover human powers of autonomy; a power otherwise denied to us on the basis of the dangers that autonomy supposedly poses for us, individually and collectively. As I will explore in my chapters, this is not merely a theoretical problematique. The age of the neoliberal subject, that of resilience, adaptivity, and vulnerability, is one in which when the very practice of security, that is to say aspiring to and achieving freedom from danger, is increasingly pathologized by liberal regimes of governance, and in which the governability of subjects, collectively and individually, is said to depend, in contrast, on their exposure to danger. Contesting the global injunction to give up on aspirations for security and rethink freedom as exposure to danger requires a subject capable of imagining itself as something more than merely biological material. A subject whose humanity resides in its freedom to secure itself from the dangers that it encounters both in living and in being so secured. Foucault's works poses this problem to us, starkly. They do not solve them for us. In context of which it is necessary that we turn from the mere analysis of biopolitics to the hitherto underresourced subject of psychopolitics.

I

Resilience

Chapter Three

Resilience

The Societalization of Security

David Chandler

In neoliberal discourses of resilience there is a clear assumption that governments need to assume a more proactive engagement with society. There is probably no clearer illustration of the shift from traditional liberal framings of the role of the state in relation to society than in the area of security discourses. Here, the shift from the social contract understanding of the state standing above society and acting to secure its citizenry is fundamentally challenged by neoliberal approaches, which seek to transform and reposition the state, not as above society but as working through the choices and behavioural agency of society itself. This proactive engagement is understood to be preventative, not in the sense of a controlling state, tasked with preventing future disaster or catastrophe but in the sense of an empowered citizenry capable of making their own choices which can prevent the disruptive or destabilizing effects of any such event. In this sense, the key to security programmes of resilience is the coping capacities of citizens, the ability of citizens to respond to or adapt to potential security crises.

The subject or agent of security thereby shifts from the state to society and to the individuals constitutive of it. In many ways, this shift away from a sovereign-based understanding to a social or societal understanding of security, under the guidance or goal of resilience, could be understood as a de-liberalizing discourse, one which divests security responsibilities from the level of the state down to the level of the citizen. This chapter seeks to consider some of the genealogical aspects of discourses of resilience as a societal or agent-based understanding of security (particularly focusing on the work of Frederick von Hayek and Anthony Giddens) in order to work

through some of the consequences of the state's divestment of security responsibilities for traditional liberal framings of state-society relations.

In elucidating on the societalization of security, neoliberal approaches to
security that seek to work 'from the bottom-up' rather than 'from the top-
down', are examined. This is a fundamental shift in how security is conceptualized and illustrates well how the neoliberal subject emerges in relation to
the transformation of traditional liberal assumptions of the ordering of state-
society relations. It is not that self-organizing capacities are transferred from
the state to society, merely shifting the boundary between the public and the
private and thus extending the logic of the market. The understanding the
modern subject as autonomous and self-securing is itself problematized.
Problems themselves, from conflict to underdevelopment or environmental
degradation and global warming, are constructed from the bottom-up; as
problems of the subject's inability to govern itself on the basis of the consequences of its choices and actions. This is a far cry from unleashing the
collective ordering power of market logics based on the self-interest of the
'citizen-as-consumer'.

SOCIETAL SECURITY

Today, there is little doubting the centrality of discourses of resilience to
academic and policy-framings of international security, covering practically
the entire spectrum of threats—from terrorist attack to financial crisis, climate change, and state failure. Critical engagements with security discourses
of resilience often couch this concept within examinations of the liberal drive
to secure life, based on the foundational 'liberal commitment to making life
live' (Dillon and Reid 2009: 11; see also Dillon 2007a; 2007b; Duffield
2007; 2011a; Evans 2013; Zebrowski 2009).[1] In this framing, life—as understood by the biological and information sciences—is to be best secured
through its 'capacities for adaptation, emergence, learning, information flows
and resilience' (Reid 2010: 397). For Dillon and Reid, this biopoliticized
understanding of security reduces 'the human to the biohuman, based on an
understanding and promotion of its powers of adaptation, learning, co-evolu-
tion and information-sharing' (2009: 146). This chapter seeks to engage further with the understanding of resilience as driven by the bio- and life-
sciences and imbricated within biopolitical discourses of securing life.

In doing so, I wish to highlight the importance of the societal rather than
the sometimes abstract and essentializing conception of 'securing life' driven
by some neo-Foucauldian understandings of the biopolitical. In this sense, I
think that rather than understanding current resilience discourses as extending liberal rule through the securing of life itself, it is more useful to consider
the erosion of traditional liberal understandings of state-society relations

through a focus on how security has become societalized. I wish to argue that the societalization of security removes the liberal political content of security practices—the articulation of political communities of action shaped around a clash of competing interests (see Walker 1997), in effect, reducing the problematic of security to the generic or 'everyday' problems of individual behaviour and practices and the institutional milieu (cultural and social values, identities, power asymmetries, and information flows) which shapes these.

It is important to note that the neoliberal understanding of governance in terms of resilience, empowerment, and capacity-building is very different from classical liberal attempts to 'alter behaviour, to train or correct individuals', for example, through Jeremy Bentham's panopticon methods of disciplinary surveillance over rational subjects (Foucault 1991: 203). As Michel Foucault indicates, this shift away from sovereign and disciplinary power constitutes 'the population as a political problem' and, within this, focuses on the real lives or the everyday of individuals and communities 'and their environment, the milieu in which they live . . . to the extent that it is not a natural environment, that it has been created by the population and therefore has effects on that population' (2003: 245). It is this 'milieu' which accounts 'for action at a distance of one body on another' and thereby 'appears as a field of intervention' (Foucault 2007: 20–21). In this framework, governance operates indirectly, through work on the informal level of societal life itself, rather than through the formal framework of public law in relation to individuals as citizens: 'action is brought to bear on the rules of the game rather than on the players' as Foucault states in *The Birth of Biopolitics* (2008: 260).

In focusing on the deliberalizing of security—in its reduction to everyday behaviour and practices through the societalization of security—I wish to develop some of the themes touched upon in work highlighting the links between discourses of resilience and the shift from a state-based to a society-based understanding of security practices (Briggs 2010; Bulley 2011; Duffield 2011b; C. Edwards 2009). These works implicitly question whether security can be analytically distinguished from other spheres of policy-making once resilience policies and practices shift the focus of security from state interests and capacities to the capacities for reasoned behavioural choices of the citizenry. Fillipa Lentzos and Nikolas Rose, for example, highlight, in their critique of understandings that security discourses seem to be leading to the securitization of life, that we are witnessing 'perhaps the opposite of a "Big Brother State"' (Lentzos and Rose 2009: 243). Discourses of resilience do not centrally focus upon material attributes (military equipment, technology, welfare provisions, and such) that can be provided through government as a way of protecting populations or responding after an event. Resilience concerns attributes of the population, particularly at the level of self-knowledge and responsiveness, both at the level of individuals and as communities,

which cannot be directly provided by state authorities. For this reason, discourses of resilience do not fit well with traditional liberal framings of security practices as state-centric, national, or territorial forms of mobilization,
protection, or regulation.

As James Brassett and Nick Vaughan-Williams note in their study of UK
civil contingencies and trauma resilience training (2011), the focus of resilience practices is less upon the specific threat or 'event' (which can be
prepared for or reacted to) and more the effects of a crisis or disaster at the
level of the individual and community. Here, the discussion of trauma is
particularly useful as the resilience discourse encourages a shift from post-
hoc programmes of trauma counselling to the inculcation of mental or subjective capacities to respond to crises without becoming traumatised (see
also, Furedi 2007; O'Malley 2010). In this context, the problematic of the
inculcation of societal resilience of the subjective capabilities and capacities
needed to anticipate, respond, and adapt to crises has become a growing
focus of governmental concern (see, for example, Coaffee, Wood, and Rogers 2009; UK Cabinet Office 2011a; 2011b; Walker and Cooper 2011).

It appears that resilience practices are transforming security discourses
from concerns with external threats to fears over the domestic or internal
coping and adaptive capacities of individuals and their communities.[2] Coping and adaptive capacities are inner qualities possessed by individuals,
which are held to enable them to autonomously anticipate and respond to
complex or unexpected problems or circumstances. This shift from a focus
on the activity and provision of government to the capacity of citizens to
effectively respond and adapt to crises or problems—and increasingly to take
responsibility for 'self-government'—is of vital importance to our understanding of resilience as a set of discursive practices of governing through
societal security (O'Malley 2010: 505; for example, Dean 2009; Foucault
2010: 25–40; 2008; Miller and Rose 2008;Rose 1999a; 1999b). This chapter
seeks to draw out further this link between 'late', 'advanced' or 'post-liberal'
governmental rationalities and the security discourse of resilience (see further, for example, Chandler 2010; Dillon and Reid 2009). Following on from
the work of Pat O'Malley, it suggests that the problematic of resilience and
the discourses of societal security are: 'not specific to the governance of
particular threats, or indeed even to threats per se. It is a technology that is
imagined to equip the subject to deal with uncertainty in general' (Chandler
2010: 505).

The resilience problematic of how the population, or society in general,
proactively engages with and adapts to uncertainty has been at the heart of
recent UK policy discussions on how to empower citizens to be more capable
of governing themselves through making better life choices in the face of risk
and complexity. This broader discussion locates the threat to societal security
not in any particular or specific externally generated 'event' or 'threat' but in

the capacity or capability of citizens to proactively take responsibility both for their own security and for those around them (Dean 2011). The discussion of how society could become more self-governing and how government practices could inculcate resilience has been highlighted by the 2008 publication of *Nudge* by Richard Thaler and Cass Sunstein and the recent policy attention given to the importance of individual choice-making by the UK Cabinet Office, UK Prime Minister David Cameron's Behavioural Insight Team (the 'nudge unit') and the RSA's Social Brain project. For these authors and policy groups, the problems of societal security can be both analysed and addressed through capability-building at the level of the decision-making individual through intervention in the societal milieu or environment. This discourse illustrates how the resilience paradigm's focus on individual and community capabilities, reinscribes the security problematic within the 'everyday' of policy problems of the social and economic sphere.

The starting point for *Nudge* is that people lack the capacity or capability to adapt efficiently to their circumstances and to choose what is best for them; that the modern liberal conception of 'economic man' or *homo œconomicus* may work well in economic textbooks but that in the real world real human beings are not very good at making the right choices. It is suggested here that one useful starting point for an understanding of resilience as a discourse of societal security can be found in the distinction made by Thaler and Sunstein between economic man and real human beings—as they state, between 'Econs' and 'Humans'. While economic man can be assumed to always make the right or rational choice, the human often fails and this failure can have destructive consequences at both the individual and the societal levels. The UK Cabinet Office has taken up these concerns to suggest that governance should focus on how the 'choice environment' is shaped as citizen's appear to lack the rational capacities to make the right choices themselves without external 'nudging', 'steering' and 'priming' (IfG 2010). While it could be argued that the UK Cameron/Clegg government's Behavioural Insight Team or 'nudge unit' has had limited effects on government policy-making (Curtis 2011; Day 2011) there is little doubt that the problematization of citizens as rational choice-making actors has been placed at the centre of the discourse of resilience and security, positing the task of government in terms of governance: improving the choice-making capacity of its citizens.

The work of *Nudge* has helped to cohere the understanding of the subject as lacking in rational capacities to deal with the unexpected events and complexities of our insecure world. Relying heavily on this schema, Charlie Edwards's Demos publication *Resilience Nation* (2009) argues that:

> Thinking about choice architecture is an incredibly useful way of framing how central and local government, emergency planning officers and the emergency

services can influence an individual or community's behaviour, especially on
issues like risk . . . a fundamentally important task in making society more
resilient. Nudges also help . . . [by] shifting some of the responsibility of
resilience planning and management to communities and individuals. (C. Edwards 2009: 42–45)

In the United Kingdom, Thaler and Sunstein have been challenged, not
for their degraded understanding of individual capacities for choice-making
but rather for their underestimation of the problem of choice-shaping (Chakrabortty 2010; Day 2011). The UK RSA's Social Brain project suggests that
the problem of societal security is too large for the government to solve on its
own, through 'nudging' citizens to make better choices (Grist 2009: 9). Inter-
estingly, the RSA's Social Brain project takes up many of the central conceptions outlined in Anthony Giddens's work on *Beyond Left and Right* (1994)
and in *The Third Way* (1998) to argue that governance requires a reorienta-
tion around the politics of individual choice to create or construct citizens
who are able to respond to the problems of risk autonomously and respon-
sibly:

life politics is the politics of choice in a deep existential sense—a politics
where one is aware of what it is like to live reflexively in a post-traditional and
globalised world. . . . Whether we like it or not, in late modernity citizens need
to be able to reflexively chart their way through the choppy waters of a globalised economy. And whether we like it or not, they need to find ways of
changing the way they live if they are to counteract problems like entrenched
inequality and environmental degradation. . . . The kind of person enabled by
politics to face up to the challenges of late modernity Giddens calls an 'autotelic' self . . . an autotelic self is really just an autonomous and responsible
citizen. (Grist 2009: 16)

The RSA proposes an active programme of governance on the basis of the
need to empower modern citizens as individuated decision-makers in order to
inculcate resilience through overcoming their lack of rational decision-making capacities:

wholly rational individuals do not need the support of publicly-engaged institutions and associative groups to aid their decision-making about the issues of
life politics. They simply need to be fed information and, given their rationality, correct responses will inexorably follow. Yet people are not isolated and
wholly self-interested. . . . And neither are they wholly rational—left to their
individual devices they may make bad decisions that economists would consider 'irrational'. (Grist 2009: 29)

The project of governing for social resilience is asserted to depend upon
'the limits of personal choice' and the development of knowledge of 'how
autonomy and responsibility are produced' (Grist 2009: 29). For the Social

Brain project, the key to this new knowledge is that of 'neurological reflexivity': a greater understanding of the working and limits of the human brain (Grist 2009: 33). Through a greater use of emotional and cognitive self-awareness, the RSA suggests that 'people might gain more power over themselves by using knowledge from behavioural science to improve their decision-making, and to guide their own behaviours in ways that enrich their lives' (Grist 2010: 4).

The framework of governance and the focus on the ways in which government can influence the 'choice architecture' or the 'choice environment' in which individuals make choices and decisions fundamentally challenges the traditional liberal assumptions on which the division of the public and private spheres—the sphere of government policy-making and the sphere of individual freedom—were constructed. Once the human subject is understood as lacking in the capacity to make 'free choices', the private sphere of freedom and autonomy becomes problematized and 'life' becomes the subject of governance.[3] As Mark Duffield has highlighted, this discourse of resilience increasingly shifts the emphasis of security discourses from specific or particular problems or threats of the external world to the problematization of the inner world, and the inner capacities and capabilities of citizens (Duffield 2011).

This chapter embarks on a genealogical analysis of the ways in which this 'internalised' understanding of the limits to societal security has developed, mainly through focusing upon the new institutionalist economic literature, and tracing how these ideas have become cogently presented as the basis of a programme of governing for societal resilience in the work of Anthony Giddens (a leading British sociologist and founder of the 'third way' political approach, former advisor to Labour Prime Minister Tony Blair and Director of the London School of Economics) and increasingly materialized in discourses of the quantified self and Big Data. In the following section, I draw attention to how the work of new institutionalist economics has been a key sphere of social theorizing through which the articulation of discourses of societal resilience can be traced. In particular, I highlight the importance of the work of Friedrich von Hayek (one of the most influential free market economists of the twentieth century and pioneering exponent of the limits of human knowledge) in privileging the inner world of the subject over the external environment. The next section draws out the connection between the work of Hayek and that of Giddens, suggesting that the logical consequence of the internalizing project is that the resilient or 'autotelic' subject becomes the goal of policies of societal security and data enablement. The final section draws out the consequences of discourses of security as societal resilience for traditional liberal understandings of subject autonomy.

David Chandler

BRINGING IN THE INNER WORLD: FRIEDRICH VON HAYEK AND THE PSYCHOLOGY OF THE BRAIN

For classical liberal framings of *homo œconomicus*, the inside of the human head was as out of bounds as the inside of the sovereign state in international relations theory. Liberal frameworks of thought have always been vulnerable to critical deconstruction through the transgression of the disciplinary boundaries keeping apart the interior and the exterior worlds of the liberal subject. Many of the most radical of these critiques have come from within the sphere of economic theorizing, particularly the new institutionalist economic challenge to classical liberal assumptions of the smooth or natural operation of market rationality. These authors were keen to explain the problematic nature of market relations in terms of the cultural or ideational contexts in which the human mind operated. The critique of the rationalist assumptions of classical liberalism enabled a new programmatic of governance and societal resilience to emerge in response to the unknowability and unpredictability of the external world. In this framing of the human subject, both individually and collectively, the problematic becomes one of adaptation and resilience: how individuals and societies respond to a shifting external environment is prioritized over and against conceptions of the state as capable of planning, directing or controlling socioeconomic affairs (see Hayek 1960; Foucault 2008: 171–74).

As John R. Commons described new institutional economics back in 1936, it is based on understanding the importance of cultural and ideational contexts of choice-making—'man's relationship to man'—ignored in classical liberal economic theory 'based on man's relation to nature' (1936: 242). For Commons, the intangibles, such as good will, conceptions of rights, duties, and such, all influenced the 'reasonable' price that the buyer was willing to pay. These intangibles were understood to be shaped by collective institutions and collective norms and controls, which meant that the classic liberal assumptions of perfect competition did not exist. Commons suggested that there was a 'nationalistic theory of value': that these national collective institutions meant that it was fiction to think of the market as universalist in its operation; as much of a fiction as the belief in the universal individual subject of classical liberal political and economic theory:

> Even the individual of economic theory is not the natural individual of biology and psychology: he is that artificial bundle of institutes known as a legal person, or citizen. He is made such by sovereignty which grants to him the rights and liberties to buy and sell, borrow and lend, hire and hire out, work and not work, on his own free will. Merely as an individual of classical and hedonistic theory he is a factor of production and consumption like a cow or slave. Economic theory should make him a citizen, or member of the institution under whose rule he acts. (Commons 1936: 247–48)

This paragraph sums up the essence of societal resilience, which frees the individual from the strictures of classic liberal assumptions, allowing autonomy of choices but only once the individual is understood as a product of an institutional framework, a subject of their 'choice environment'. Commons therefore stressed that rather than treating humans as automatic pursuers of fixed interests, real life behaviour had to be understood as shaped by institutional forms, especially those of custom and social norms (Forest and Mehier 2001). The individual will was an act of volition and conscious choice but also a product of historical and social embeddedness, shaped and constructed on the basis of existing or habitual norms and values (Forest and Mehier 2001: 593).

The work of Commons and other new institutionalist economists was developed further by Herbert Simon, who directly challenged the assumptions of the rational decision-making capacity of the classical liberal subject, dethroning the autonomous rational subject—*homo œconomicus*—from economic rational choice theory. In his argument, there was no such thing as perfect information or perfect rationality, merely 'bounded rationality' where not all the facts could be known or all the possible options considered. The decisions made with 'bounded rationality' were still autonomous, that is, made on the basis of a freely willed conscious choice but they were no longer necessarily rational: resulting in furthering the collective good or in optimal outcomes. This critique of the rationality of the liberal subject forms a crucial component of the governance programme of societal resilience, which recognizes and simultaneously problematizes the decision-making autonomy of the subject.

For the advocates of societal resilience, the work of Herbert Simon, particularly the articulation of 'bounded rationality' allows the critique of the liberal subject to operate without appearing to be overtly elitist or undemocratic. As Charlie Edwards suggests, this is not an overt critique of democratic assumptions of the rational subject per se but of the late-modern subject's capacity to deal with new, unexpected, exceptional or complex events. *Resilience Nation* argues that people who seem to be rational in everyday life 'may revert to irrational behaviour, especially in response to a specific risk' (C. Edwards 2009: 41). The problematic of 'bounded rationality' suggests that societal resilience will fail if it focuses on specific and unlikely risks, which people will have little understanding of or relationship to. The inculcation of resilience, in fact, depends on the dematerializing or abstraction from specific risks or insecurities, to become a mode of life, a way of social being: 'Risk communication cannot be detached from our everyday lives. It has to be hotwired into our decision-making processes and behaviours' (C. Edwards 2009: 43). In making resilience a matter of the 'everyday', the exceptional event becomes essential to our understanding of and construction of new norms of decision-making and state-society relations.

The crucial facet of new institutionalist economics was that differences in responses to external shocks or unusual events could be understood as conscious, subjective choices, rather than as structurally imposed outcomes. The important research focus was then the individual making the decisions or choices and the subjectively created institutional frameworks (formal and informal) determining or structuring these choices. This is a social perspective that starts from the individual as a decision-maker and then works outward to understand why 'wrong' or problematic responses to events occur. In this perspective, the individual subject is understood in isolation from their structuring social and economic context. Wrong choices are understood in terms of ideational blockages at the level of culture, custom, or ideology and in terms of the formal institutional blockages—the 'choice architecture' or the incentives and opportunities available to enable other choices. This problematization of the individual shares much with therapeutic approaches, which also work at the level of the resilience of the individual (attempting to remove psychological blockages to making better choices) rather than at the level of social or economic relations (see, for example, Neenan 2009; Clarke and Nicholson 2010; Reivich and Shatte 2003) and, of course, it is from psychology that, as will be examined later, Giddens takes the conception of the 'autotelic self' (see Nakamura and Csikszentmihalyi 2009).

The leading theorist of the inversion of state-society relations and responsibilities was Austrian economist Friedrich von Hayek, whose ideas have become central to current understandings of societal security and resilience (see, for example, Walker and Cooper 2011). Writing in the 1950s, Hayek was concerned that liberal universalist teleologies of socioeconomic progress would lead to the dominance of socialist or communist frameworks of government. In order to combat this, Hayek sought to reintroduce difference as ontologically prior to universality and to flag up the internal limits to subjective reasoning. Perhaps the most insightful work in this area is his *The Sensory Order: An Inquiry into the Foundations of Theoretical Psychology* (1952). As the title indicates, for Hayek, the key area in which limits were to be located was in the psychological make-up of the subject.

For Marx, the key attribute of the human was the ability to imagine an end or goal before carrying it out—the capacity, through reason, to subordinate the self to an external object of transformation—to consciously transform the world through a self-directed aim (Marx 1954: 174).[4] Hayek, on the other hand, was interested in the hold of the past and the incapacity of the subject to cope with the external world because reasoning could only be based on the way that individual ways of thinking are predicated upon past experiences. Our minds build models and expectations based on previous experiences, which means that our behavioural responses depend less on the 'reality' we are confronted with than with the psychological preconditioning of our minds. Our consciousness, in fact, prevents us from engaging with the world in a reasoned and rational way (Hayek 1952: 25). For Hayek:

> Like many of the traditional schools of psychology, behaviouralism thus treated the problem of mind as if it were a problem of the responses of the individual to an independently or objectively given phenomenal world; while in fact it is the existence of a phenomenal world which is different from the physical world which constitutes the main problem. (1952: 28)

Hayek's focus on the mind of the subject enabled him to remove the external world as an object of universalist understanding: in effect, he argued that the external world was merely a subjective phenomenological product. The materiality of the external world as a meaningful external object was thereby removed. It therefore followed that it was not the external world of social relations which produced and reproduced difference and hierarchy but the internal differences of the human brain. The problem was not that we are not rational or 'enlightened' enough to understand the external world, but that the external world only appears through the phenomenological constructions of our minds. These phenomenologies are the products of 'interpretations' based upon inherited and learned experiences which mediate between the experience and the response: 'we cannot hope to account for observed behaviour without reconstructing the "intervening processes in the brain"' (Hayek 1952: 44). It is our brains which make us respond differently to our external environments and can help explain different developmental outcomes which reproduce the same experiences and response mechanisms. Internal differentiations therefore are reproduced and exaggerate our differential responses to events or crises, particularly those we are unfamiliar with or lack previous experience of.

In Hayek's work, we not only see how psychological explanations begin to play a larger role in understanding the importance of practices of societal resilience but also how responses to security risks or threats can be reinterpreted in terms of the internal workings of the brain. Brains are complex, integrated networks but they are also malleable and capable of adaptive change, depending upon the extent to which 'phylogenetic', inherited patterns and connections, and 'ontogenetic' aspects, acquired by the individual during the course of their lifetime, interact (Hayek 1952: 80–81). Where Marx sharply distinguished the human from the natural world, Hayek's focus on the psychology of the brain focuses on how human responses are shaped through resilience and adaption in ways which are little different to any other living organism:

> The continued existence of those complex structures which we call organisms is made possible by their capacity of responding to certain external influences

by such changes in their structure or activity as are required to maintain or
restore the balance necessary for their persistence. (Hayek 1952: 82)

Individuals, especially more complex organisms like humans, will respond
differently to external stimuli in ways which enable them to discriminate
differently between different stimuli and to react differently. Often these
differences will not be intentional but arbitrary or accidental. The key point
for Hayek is that differential experiences and reactions necessarily result
from the innate historical experiential differences of individuals and their
different internal (rather than external) environments: 'one of the most important parts of the "environment" from which the central nervous system
will receive signals producing linkages, will be the *milieu intérieur*, the internal environment or the rest of the organism in which the central nervous
system exists' (Hayek 1952: 109).

Hayek inverses the liberal framework of the autonomous and rational
subject capable of transforming the external world through asserting that
liberal frameworks and institutions are necessary precisely because the liberal subject is not capable of knowing or transforming or controlling the external world. The progressive impulse of liberalism appears exhausted in this
defence of liberal modernity on the basis that democracy and markets work
best because this enables us to adapt and to cope with problems without the
possibility of knowledge or control. In effect, this reduces human collectivities to the ontological status of biological organisms, merely capable of
adaptation through evolutionary chance rather than through conscious decision-making. Of course, it is here, in the defence of liberalism on the basis of
the inability of the subject to shape or control an external world that the
discursive practices of societal resilience become a necessity rather than an
option.

In terms of genealogical framings, it is important to emphasize that what
is key in the work of early new institutional economics and developed to its
full extent in the ideas of Hayek is a conceptual framework of critique of
classical liberal assumptions. This critique was based upon the dethroning or
decentring of the human subject as a rational agent, capable of securing itself
through knowing and shaping its external environment. Many of the aspects
of today's discourses of community resilience are present in this construction
of the subject in relation to the problematic of adaptation to external events.
However, the context in which these concerns were articulated was one very
different to our own. The chief concern was that of a defence of liberal
frameworks of rule against the backdrop of socioeconomic crisis and the
challenge of socialist or communist alternatives which stressed the potential
of human agency to shape and control events through abolishing or restrict-
ing market relations. It took the defeat of the radical, class-based challenge to
liberalism before the articulation of societal resilience could be represented

as a progressive, even radical, framework of social empowerment. The next section considers how the exhaustion of liberalism and the hollowing out of the liberal subject has been articulated anew as a dominant sensibility in our 'globalized', insecure and 'post-political' world.

REMOVING THE OUTER WORLD: ANTHONY GIDDENS AND MANUFACTURED UNCERTAINTY

In order to contextualize and situate the inner logic of discourses of societal resilience, some guidelines of resilience have been traced genealogically through the economic theories which have stressed the internal world of the decision-making subject as constituting the key barrier to societal security. The discursive importance of the internal world of the subject, however, was doomed to a marginal existence as long as mainstream liberal social theorizing was capable of providing a programmatic framework of government. It was only in the post–Cold War era that discourses of security, both broadly and narrowly defined, shifted to societal rather than state-based approaches. Today, it is clear in discourses of societal resilience that what was once a marginal preoccupation has now become central to understanding the world we live in and the role of the state in relation to society. As Foucault highlighted in his work on the birth of biopolitics (focusing on the exceptional circumstances of the postwar West German state) the governing of the social involves a shift from a focus on the state provision of the means of security to the internal capacities of individuals in civil society, understood to be potentially problematic decision-making subjects (2008). It could be argued that Foucault's work in this area was highly prescient, to the extent that today it appears that the shift to divesting security responsibility to society, and with this the shift to concern over the internal world of the individual, means that the external world could be said to no longer exist in a meaningful way for us.[5]

Anthony Giddens has made one of the most widely discussed attempts to articulate this shift from the external to the internal world in terms of an activist and proactive programme of governance in the wake of the collapse of left/right framings of liberal modernity in the post–Cold War period. In his 1990s work *Beyond Left and Right* (1994) and on *The Third Way* (1998; see also 2000) he clearly articulated the shift from the liberal modernist belief that developments in science and technology might enable the extension of humanity's control over the external world: that 'human beings can become not just authors but the masters of their own destiny' (Giddens 1994: 3). He argued that today we have become aware that the aspiration of controlling and shaping our external world was a product of human hubris and misunderstanding. Today's globalized world is a dislocated, uncertain, insecure, 'run-away world'. What is more:

> disturbingly, what was supposed to create greater and greater certainty—the advance of human knowledge and 'controlled intervention' into society and nature—is actually deeply involved with this unpredictability. . . . The uncertainties thus created I shall refer to generically as *manufactured uncertainty*. (Giddens 1994: 3–4)

These uncertainties and insecurities, because they are conceived of as human products (or by-products) cannot be dealt with through Enlightenment prescriptions of 'more knowledge, more control' (Giddens 1994: 4), but rather through coming to terms with the need to limit and rethink our understanding of humanity's relationship with the external world. The problem, for Giddens, is the indirect nature of our relationship to our environment. For him, globalization can best be described as 'action at a distance' (1994: 4): globalization—the complexity and interconnectedness of our world—means that our actions have effects at a distance from their intended effects and that similarly we are affected by the actions of others, despite their intentions. In other words, what we do has global effects upon our own security although we cannot see or predict what these may be.

For Giddens, societal resilience becomes the sphere of intelligibility for both the problems and insecurities faced by collective humanity and for the development of frameworks for governing this uncertainty. The compulsion toward resilience-based framings of the world stems from the clear and articulate juxtapositioning between these and the Enlightenment project: the cosy meanings and understandings which liberal modernity is now seen to have imposed on the world at the alleged cost of the agency and freedom of the human subject:

> Today we must break with providentialism, in whatever guise it might present itself. Not for us the idea that capitalism is pregnant with socialism. Not for us the idea that there is a historical agent—whether proletariat or any other—that will more or less automatically come to our rescue. Not for us the idea that 'history' has any necessary direction at all. We must accept risk as risk, up to and including the most potentially cataclysmic of high-consequence risks; we must accept that there can be no way back to external risk from manufactured risk. (Giddens 1994: 249)

The key point to grasp from Giddens's framework is that our decisions or our choices have much broader and more powerful consequences than we can imagine. The logical consequence is that our world becomes seen and understood as a product of our individual choices. For Giddens, there is no outside to humanity conceived of as choice-making individuals. There is no external world of structures and social relations or of natural laws open to discovery (already prefigured in his earlier work on structuration theory, see Giddens 1984; for its relation to social constructivism see Berger and Luckmann 1991). We have globalized our world, consigning the world of the Enlightenment or of liberal modernity to the history books. The liberal world presupposed a rational and law-bound external world open to our understanding and therefore to our manipulation and control. There can be no Cartesian subject without an outside and no Cartesian teleology of progress. Giddens describes the disappearance of the external world in terms of the 'disappearance of nature, where "nature" refers to environments and events given independently of human action' (1994: 6). Nothing exists outside our actions and consequently our actions are everything. If there is a problem to be addressed the only sphere of engagement can be with the sphere of human action, understood as the decisional choices of individuals.

As Giddens states: 'Manufactured uncertainty intrudes into all the arenas of life thus opened up to decision-making' (1994: 6). The world is reduced to individual decision-making and at the same time individual decision-making becomes the sphere of engagement and intervention for policy-making declarations of commitment to social progress. The reason for this is that we discover that there are major problems with the individual decision-makers: human beings. We are not equipped to exist in a world that is dependent on our decision-making capacities. Where the fixed structures and certainties no longer operate we are forced to pay particular attention to how we make decisions, as we increasingly shape our own lives, we deploy 'social reflexivity' and are in danger of increasing the problems which we ourselves are confronted with. 'The growth of social reflexivity is a major factor introducing a dislocation between knowledge and control—a prime source of manufactured uncertainty' (Giddens 1994: 7).

For Giddens, the problem is that at a time when we have to make more decisions than ever before and the consequences of our individual decision-making are of global consequence, we come up against a major barrier. This barrier is an internal one—the way in which our brains work. We are not well equipped to deal with complexity and so we need external assistance. This is where the work of Giddens develops and expands upon the work of the new institutionalist economists considered above, transforming this conceptual defence of liberalism into a programme of governance through a sensitivity of internal limits (see also, for example, North 1990; 2005). The development of governance 'choice-shaping' to assist us in our autonomous choice-making, Giddens calls 'generative politics'. The state can no longer do things for us in a directive and controlling way and so must confront the urgent and complex task of empowering the subject to make better life choices:

> Generative politics is a politics which seeks to allow individuals and groups to
> make things happen, rather than have things happen to them, in the context of
> overall social concerns and goals . . . it does not situate itself in the old
> opposition between state and market. It works through providing material
> conditions, and organisational frameworks, for the life-political decisions tak-
> en by individuals and groups in the wider social order. (Giddens 1994: 15)

This focus on the inner life of the subject rather than on the state as a
director of society, as Giddens himself notes, owes much to the work of
Friedrich Hayek, who similarly critiqued the 'cybernetic model' of a controlling and knowing state (Giddens 1994: 66–68). In fact, it is the impossibility
of knowledge in a complex and globalized world that necessitates the focus
on the individual rather than the state. For Giddens, this shift takes on full
force only in late modernity with the complexity of society. While top-down
decision-making might work for early modernizing states, in a world of
globalization and high-reflexivity only bottom-up decision-making enables
the high level of reflexivity and adaptability required for societal security.
The focus on the inner life of the individual highlights the conceptual core of
societal resilience's rejection of liberal frameworks of social order and its
drive to divest securing power. As Edwards states:

> Community resilience requires an altogether more nuanced and subtle ap-
> proach that is premised on institutions and organisations letting go, creating
> the necessary framework for action, rather than developing specific plans and
> allowing community resilience to emerge and develop in local areas over time.
> No single plan exists, never should and hopefully never will. The role of
> central government in community resilience will always be limited. It will not
> be the main protagonist, a supporting actor or an extra—rather its role will be
> played out behind the scenes by a supporting cast of players who ensure the
> system is operating to the best of its ability. Adopting this invisible role will
> not be easy for central government. (C. Edwards 2009: 80)

In this framework of societal resilience, the external world has disap-
peared in two interconnected ways. First, it is unknowable, it is globalized:
the relations of cause and effect no longer appear to operate clearly because
we seem to have lost control over the consequences of our actions. The
unintended effects overwhelm the intended ones because the world is much
more complicated and interconnected than we imagined in liberal teleologies
of progress and control. Second, the external world disappears because we
can no longer distinguish ourselves from the world. In the words of Giddens,
there is no longer any external 'nature'—our external world has been shaped
by human actions and choices; but not conscious ones. Not only is the world
unknowable, it is unknowable because it is a human world.

While it is a human world, it is not thereby a liberal world as we know it:
the external world has been closed off to us and with it there can be no

universal framing bringing us together on the basis of human beings as transforming subjects. Work on the transformation of the internal world of the neoliberal subject can only understand the subject as increasingly differentiated in its choice-making vulnerability, rather than as a potential collectivity. In this respect, the universalizing discourse of neoliberalism, which is inclusive in its emphasis on our shared nature as vulnerable subjects, is one which can only operate within and upon discourses of societal resilience, continually 'learning' that the most vulnerable are those most in need of empowering in order to cope with uncertainty and risk.

There is still a discourse of transformation but it is not about the transformation of the external world but the ongoing process of transforming the inner world of individuals. As the UK Cabinet Office's *Strategic National Framework on Community Resilience* suggests: 'This programme is part of the Government's "Big Society" commitment to reduce the barriers which prevent people from being able to help themselves and to become more resilient to shocks' (2011b: 3). Societal security is understood to depend on the social empowerment of individuals whose securing agency is held back by the wrong institutional 'choice-shaping' or cultural and ideational frameworks:

> The Government contribution to community resilience is not to dictate or measure what is being or should be done locally. Instead, the role is to support and enable local activity by making existing good practice available to others who are interested, and removing the barriers and debunking the myths which prevent communities from taking local action. (UK Cabinet Office 2011b: 7)

Giddens clearly articulates the project of societal empowerment as the development of the autonomy of the individual. The internalized nature of the project is clear in the emphasis upon the modern subject's need for 'self-help' and 'self-construction':

> The advance of social reflexivity means that individuals have no choice but to make choices; and these choices define who they are. People have to 'construct their own biographies' in order to sustain a coherent sense of self-identity. (Giddens 1994: 126)

Humans may not be able to 'master their own destiny' but, for Giddens, they need to 'construct their own biographies'. Giddens's work is very important for understanding and drawing out the consequences of an internalized conception of security within discourses of resilience and its relationship to our understanding of the human subject. One way in which he illustrates the shift is in our understanding of the threats to societal security. In the preliberal age, or pre-Enlightenment era, the main conceptual framework was that of fate or nature or God—catastrophic events could not be prevented merely accepted. In the liberal era, the dominant framework of understanding was that of 'risk' or 'accident', something that highlighted the borders of control and could be calculated, minimized, or insured against. The point being that accidents or risks were conceptualized as external factors, outside control. Giddens argues that today there is no outside, no external area, no external risk. Once the problem is understood in terms of manufactured risk, setbacks and damage are a consequence of the decisions we take ourselves and work on the self is the only area through which these problems can be addressed.

A good example Giddens gives to demonstrate the difference between an external risk and an internal one is the changing nature of health security, shifting from intervention to prevention. In the liberal world, we understood that there was a risk of getting cancer or other ailments in old age and the attempt to address the problem was in the development of medicine and forms of diagnosis and interventionist treatment. In the late-liberal world, Giddens advocates a different approach of prevention based on the inculcation of resilience, of work on the self, changing attitudes and social norms to empower individuals to make better life-choices and adopt better lifestyle habits. Societal security through resilience is understood as empowering, freeing, or as liberating the agency of the individual. Another example is Giddens's view of old age: 'Aging is treated as "external," as something that happens to one, not as a phenomenon actively constructed and negotiated' (1994: 170). Giddens seeks to argue that old age is a matter of individual choice, even aging: 'many of the physical difficulties of old age are not to do with aging at all, but rather with lifestyle practices' (1994: 170). Rather than understanding cancer as an externality, which should be provided for by government health and welfare services, the approach of societal resilience increasingly understands health problems as the production of the individual subject itself. The increasing scientific dominance of this approach is highlighted by the scientific support for the recent Cancer UK research report which asserts that over 40 percent of cancers are caused by lifestyle choices, including choices regarding smoking, drinking alcohol, salt intake, the consumption of red meat, body weight, regular exercise, and exposure to sun and sunbeds (Parkin 2011; also Roberts 2011). Where the Enlightenment philosophers, such as Condorcet, imagined that the external-orientated growth of science and technology could lead to expansions of the human life span well beyond one hundred years (Condorcet 2009), experts in societal resilience assert that the same can be achieved through internal growth and care of the self.

The key point made by advocates of resilience approaches is that societal security has to be addressed at the level of the inner life or the inner reflective capacities of the individual rather than the material level. This transformation occurs through welcoming insecurity and establishing a proactive relationship to potentially destabilizing security risks:

Schemes of positive welfare, orientated to manufactured rather than external risk, would be directed to fostering the *autotelic self*. The autotelic self is one with an inner confidence which comes from self-respect, and one where a sense of ontological security, originating in basic trust, allows for a positive appreciation of social difference. It refers to a person able to translate potential threats into rewarding challenges, someone who is able to turn entropy into a consistent flow of experience. The autotelic self does not seek to neutralize risk or to suppose that 'someone else will take care of the problem'; *risk is confronted as the active challenge which generates self-actualization.* (Giddens 1994: 192, emphasis added)

Giddens, in effect, reflects and coheres a sensibility toward societal resilience on the basis of the unknowability and the contingency of the external world. This programme is a transformative one, but the object of transformation is the inner life of the individual: the project to 'foster the autotelic self'. The autotelic self is understood as an individual capable of self-government in a world of contingency and radical uncertainty. The autotelic self turns insecurity into self-actualization: into growth. The subject being interpellated—the 'autotelic self'—is very different from the universalized subject of liberal modernity. Whereas the modern liberal subject was assumed to have the will and capacity to act on and to transform, to secure and to know its external world, the transformative activity of the autotelic self is focused upon the internal realm.

This shift can be highlighted in considering the rise of popularity of self-tracking and the quantified self-movement. The use of advances in technology allows the neoliberal aspiration of 'fostering the autotelic self' to be seen as an increasingly viable reality, through the capacity of everyday objects and wearables to generate personalized data. The major application of self-quantification has been in relation to individual health resilience—through self-knowledge of exercise, sleep patterns and dietary intake and correlations with bodily life indicators—and also to improve personal and professional productivity—through monitoring the time spent on different tasks. The quantified self-movement, initiated by *Wired* editors Kevin Kelly and Gary Wolf in 2007, has grown exponentially as the project of 'self knowledge through numbers' (Wolf 2009).

Just as new technology has assisted in fostering self-knowledge and responsiveness at the individual level, similar advances in technology and data collection are held to be able to enable communities to self-track and thereby become self-aware through the development of 'Big Data'. New access to data is held to potentially empower communities and contribute to the building of resilience by making communities aware of the risks and hazards they may encounter so that they can mobilize to protect themselves (Coyle and Meier 2009: 17). Disasters, conflicts, and other problems thus easily become reinterpreted as problems of knowledge and of knowledge/communication breakdowns within communities, with policy-makers arguing that at-risk communities need information as much as water, food, medicine, and shelter, and thereby that 'disaster is first of all seen as a crisis in communicating within a community—that is, as a difficulty for someone to get informed and to inform others' (Ahrens and Rudolph 2006: 217).

Thus, it is increasingly argued that Big Data should not merely be used by communities in response to disasters, but could play a more preventive role. Rather than starting with theories or generalizations about the external world, Big Data is self-generated knowledge: context dependent on local knowledge and correlations or factual information generated in real time. Thus the auto-telic or resilient community is imagined as knowing and managing its own security, through new distributed forms of knowledge collection, such as crowdsourcing. International agencies are increasingly promoting a 'proac-tive stance towards the use of crowdsourcing, noting that crowdsourcing could be used extensively as a way to reduce the likelihoods of disasters taking place' (Narvaez 2012: 47). An international survey of these initiatives thus concludes that its advocates see Big Data not just as reflecting reality but as transforming it through enabling community self-awareness: 'building the capacity of vulnerable groups to be resilient by making themselves aware or inform themselves of the various surrounding risks and hazards, and in so doing be able to organize the proper formal and informal interventions' (Nar-vaez 2012: 52).

CHOICE AND THE HUMAN SUBJECT

The exclusion of the external world, in the discourses of resilience and soci-etal security, both results in and reflects the removal of a whole raft of social, economic, and political concerns from public political contestation. Hannah Arendt acutely warned of just such a shift to the private or social realm, where the emphasis is on the transformation of behaviour rather than a focus on the active transformation of the external world. She argued that this per-spective would abolish the world of political struggle and reduce the state and government purely to administration (Arendt 1998: 45). Perhaps more importantly, Arendt powerfully challenged the ideological implication of choice-based theorisation, that, in the words of Giddens, we can 'be authors of our own biographies':

> Although everybody started his life by inserting himself into the human world through action and speech, nobody is the author or producer of his own life story. In other words, the stories, the results of action and speech, reveal an agent, but this agent is not an author or producer. Somebody began it and is its subject in the twofold sense of the word, namely, its actor and sufferer, but nobody is its author. (Arendt 1998: 184)

In the transition away from the external to the inner world, what humanity has in common is no longer the external world (which we can individually and collectively subordinate to our conscious will) but the inner world, the structure of our minds (Arendt 1998: 283). For Arendt, the essence of institutionalist or societal approaches to resilience is their reduction of the public or social world to the inner world of psychological processes. The social, collective, plural mediation of the world (as human artefact) no longer acts as a 'table', relating and separating us, enabling us to constitute the human as a collective, plural, active and transformative subject (Arendt 1998: 52–53).

The key point, for those of us concerned with developing an understanding and critique of neoliberal discourses and practices of societal resilience and work on the inner self, is that 'freedom' and 'choice' are entirely degraded once the world is reduced to the inner life of the individual. In making choice- and decision-making the moment of understanding and of policy-intervention, that moment—the moment of decision—is abnegated. When the UK Cabinet Office, Giddens or new institutionalist economists talk of 'choices' they are degrading the concept of choice along with the formal rights of the liberal subject. Here choice is reduced to responsibility—only irresponsible individuals and communities would choose not to become more self-aware and self-reflective and therefore make more informed lifestyle choices. Here, in the world of self-quantification and Big Data, there is no genuine choice-making, merely the allocation of blame. On the basis that as we are responsible for our decisions and choices, our inner lives are thereby open to external judgement and intervention. This discourse is universal; enabling us to understand the 'poor choice-making', or the lack of societal resilience, of our fellow citizens and neighbours, if they happen to be unemployed, to smoke, to be teenage mothers, eat fatty food, drop litter, fail to take up higher education opportunities, or to properly handle their emotions. The reduction of social, economic, political, and environmental questions to ones of individual choice-making capacities is so pervasive we often do not give the broader discourses of resilience a second thought.

The telos of tracing authorship of the world to individual choice-making removes the freedom to make choices: every point of choice-making becomes a point of potential judgement, a point of explanation and a potential point of governance intervention. What, for Arendt, made the human creative and transformative: the fact that our actions are unbounded as other autonomous humans react to them and others to their acts, becomes an argument for limitations; an argument to explain and rationalize societal insecurities and to justify the imposition of regulatory control. For Althusser, as for Arendt:

> That human, i.e. social individuals are active in history—as agents . . .—that is a fact. But, considered as agents, human individuals are not 'free' and 'constitutive' subjects in the philosophical sense of these terms. They work in and

through the determinations of the forms of historical existence of the social relations of production and reproduction (labour process, division and organization of labour, process of production and reproduction, class struggle, etc.). (Althusser 2008: 134)

The discourses of societal resilience insist that our intentionality be expanded beyond legal frameworks of regulation, insisting that 'lifestyle choices' can be securitized and thus open to regulative intervention and 'choice-shaping'.

CONCLUSION

In essence, discourses of societal resilience seek to extend the responsibility of individuals to the future consequences of their unbounded actions, to the social relations in which they act and decide. Discourses of resilience interpellate the neoliberal subject as the autotelic self, asserting that the barriers to safe and secure 'reflexive' decision-making need to be removed by government 'choice shaping' and data enabling, designed to free us as securing and self-governing subjects through the development of our inner capacities and capabilities. The programme of societal resilience is based on the transformation of the inner life of the subject to facilitate better choice-making, concomitant with this is the denial of the reasoned moral autonomy of the subject.

Our freedom to autonomously decide is taken away at the same time as the constraints of our social relations become essentialized as the internal barriers of the mind. Capitalism is naturalized and normalized at the same time as human rationality is degraded and denied. The problem for societal resilience is always the human rather than the social relations in which humans are embedded. The governance practices aimed at societal resilience and the construction of resilient communities can only be opposed on the basis of challenging the discursive collapsing of the external world into the interior of the human head.

NOTES

1. This understanding of liberal security discourses as securing life rather than territory derives from Michel Foucault's juxtaposition of sovereign power vis-à-vis biopower in *The History of Sexuality, Volume 1* (1981: 135–45; see also Foucault 2003: 239–63), though work on the biopolitical shift away from sovereign-based, territorial framings of security to societal understandings and the concern with life itself has also been informed through the work of Giorgio Agamben and Hannah Arendt (see, for example, Doucet and de Larrinaga 2011; Owens 2011).

2. The Demos Resilient Nation Advisory Group defines resilience as: 'The capacity of an individual, community or system to adapt in order to sustain an acceptable level of function, structure, and identity' (C. Edwards 2009: 18).

3. The contradiction between the asserted aim of 'reducing the state' and the consequences of nonlegislative state interference in the private sphere is well drawn out in the written evidence to the UK government Public Administration Select Committee (Richards and Smith 2011).

4. 'A spider conducts operations that resemble those of a weaver, and a bee puts to shame many an architect in the construction of her cells. But what distinguishes the worst architect from the best of bees is this, that the architect raises his structure in imagination before he erects it in reality. . . . He not only effects a change of form in the material on which he works, but he also realizes a purpose of his own that gives the law to his modus operandi, and to which he must subordinate his will' (Marx 1954: 174).

5. The dominant framings of modern social theory, from social constructivism to new institutionalism (in all its normative, historical, empirical, rational choice, sociological, and international hues) depend on the asserted overcoming of the structure/agency divide (the fundamental Cartesian divide between the inner and outer worlds) (see, for example, Berger and Luckmann 1991; Mahoney and Thelen 2010; Peters 2005; Scott 2008; Steinmo, Thelen, and Longstreth 1992).

Chapter Four

Resilience

The Biopolitics of Security

Julian Reid

Over the course of its modernity the ways in which the Western philosophical imagination understands the human has undergone dramatic shifts. From its Cartesian investment in an understanding of the human as that divinely endowed animal that, with the exercise of its unique capacity for reason, could one day achieve security from nature, to the contemporary diagnosis of the sickness of reason, the 'illusion' of security, and the vulnerability of the human to the catastrophic capacities of the biosphere on which it depends, the philosophical imaginary of Western modernity has changed significantly. Liberalism has not been an exception to or victim of this shift. In actuality it has been constitutive of it. Liberal modernity originated as a kind of challenge to the Cartesian modern by foregrounding the biological life of the human subject. As Michel Foucault explained in numerous analyses, the birth and development of liberalism was inseparable from the birth and development of the age of biopolitics, enabled as the latter was by the birth and development of biology and its allied life sciences. Tasked with the problem of how to rule in accordance with the needs and interests of the human defined in terms of its species existence, so it was not liberal political theory, political science, or international relations that has contributed most to teaching liberal regimes how to rule biopolitically. It is instead the life sciences themselves, broadly conceived, that have taught liberalism most about how to deal with the problem of human governance. It is in the emergence of the life sciences, most especially the life science of biology, that the search to understand the conditions for species development and security was most earnestly conducted from the late seventeenth century to the late twentieth century. In turn it was in these sciences that the possibility arose of being

51

able to distinguish between forms of life productive of life and those inimical to life; process and organisms that threatened life, rendered life vulnerable and insecure, warring against life and the realization of its potential. Here liberalism would learn how to pursue and realize the full emancipatory possibilities of species existence, and the material prospering of species life. The impact of these same life sciences can, for example, be traced directly in the thinking of liberal philosophers throughout the eighteenth and nineteenth centuries as much as to the twentieth century (Dillon and Reid 2009).

The trouble with life, biologically understood, of course, is that it can never actually be secured. By definition biological life is a phenomenon of vulnerability, because to live is to be a thing that can and must die—a thing that can only ever struggle to survive in competition with other living systems for the finite time of which it is capable of lasting. At best, prospering resiliently, amid its vulnerabilities to decay, by adapting innovatively to the environmental conditions it is exposed to and simultaneously dependent on. Conceiving the human this way has meant that liberalism has always been committed, unwittingly at least, to divesting the human of any belief in its abilities to transcend its mere biology and achieve security. This is precisely the point that Foucault makes concerning the origins of the liberal subject historically (2008). The liberal subject 'is a subject who is not so much defined by his freedom, or by the opposition of soul and body, or by the presence of a source or core of concupiscence marked to a greater or lesser degree by the Fall or sin' (2008: 271–72) but by an irreducible and nontransferable choice-making capacity not referring 'to any judgement, reasoning, or calculation' (2008: 272) but grounded irreducibly in the subject's preference for whatever brings it pleasure in denial of pain and the potential for suffering (2008: 271–73). That which is irreducible to the liberal subject is its preference for security from whatever may be found to threaten or reduce its capacity to live out its life in a condition of relative security from pain and suffering.

My purpose in this chapter, however, is not to excavate the biopolitical origins of the liberal subject, for that I have already done (Dillon and Reid 2009; Reid 2006a. Here I am interested in how this biologized notion of the subject is shaping the practices of liberalism contemporarily, and how that is being played out in contemporary power relations and strategies of liberal governance. For, when we examine the effects of the growth in influence of liberalism over the post–Cold War period, what we see are precisely theories and practices of governance that have been shaped around the perceived needs to develop an ever wider range of biologically determined capacities in and among the subjects of governance. In this chapter, and in chapter 6, I am interested particularly in the ways in which discourses of resilience and adaptation have arisen in response to an also growing recognition of the human's supposed vulnerability to the world in which it lives and depends on. That such ways of thinking about what it is to be human have become so popular and hegemonically propounded is not incidental to the story of liberalism's ascendancy in the post–Cold War world.

Indeed, as this chapter will show, the contemporary concern of global governmental policies and practices with the promotion of resilience is very much an expression of liberalism's growing influence. Rather than enabling the development of peoples and individuals so that they can aspire to secure themselves from whatever they find threatening and dangerous in worldly living, the liberal discourse of resilience functions to convince peoples and individuals of the risks and dangers of the belief in the possibility of security. This, also, is a classical trope of liberal thinking, reaching back to the origins of liberal tradition, which we will examine subsequently. To be resilient the subject must disavow any belief in the possibility to secure itself and accept instead an understanding of life as a permanent process of continual adaptation to threats and dangers that are said to be outside its control. As such the resilient subject is a subject that must permanently struggle to accommodate itself to the world: not a subject that can conceive of changing the world, its structure, and conditions of possibility, but a subject that accepts the danger-ousness of the world it lives in as a condition for partaking of that world and accepts the necessity of the injunction to change itself in correspondence with threats now presupposed as endemic. Thus is it that building resilient subjects involves the deliberate disabling of the political habits, tendencies, and capacities of peoples and replacing them with adaptive ones. Resilient subjects are subjects that have accepted the imperative not to resist or secure themselves from the difficulties they are faced with, but instead adapt to their enabling conditions via the embrace of neoliberalism. Resisting neoliberal-ism in the present thus requires a reinvestment in an account of political subjectivity and a rearticulation of a vernacular concept of security will be essential for such a purpose.

In drawing out the theoretical assumptions behind the promotion of resil-ience and its implications for issues of political subjectivity, this chapter will thus help us establish a biopolitical framework of analysis through which discourses of resilience, adaptation, and vulnerability can be denaturalized and challenged. In contestation of this discursive framing of the human I argue for a reconstituted understanding of the human as a fundamentally political subject; one empowered by its hubristic belief in an ability to secure itself from those elements of the world it encounters as hostile to its world, rather than being cast in a permanent condition of resilient adaptation to a biologized understanding of the nature of the world as such. Understanding how the hubris of the human has been weeded out by liberal governance requires examining the biopolitics of the neoliberal framing of the subject: the reduction of the human to its biological properties and capacities it shares with all other forms of species life and consequent constitution of a form of biohuman subjectivity. Nowhere is this trend more prevalent than in the domain of development discourse and practice itself. And as we will see the paradigm shift from development to sustainable development has been of fundamental importance to the growth of resilience discourse and neoliberal strategies for the depoliticization of the human.

When Michel Foucault originally unearthed and examined the phenomenon of the biopolitics of liberalism he was looking at regimes of power that thrived on their abilities to secure the life of human populations from whatever was found to be threatening and dangerous to it. The entrenchment of liberalism in rationalities claiming to protect life itself has only become deeper over the course of liberal modernity, and the pathologization of subjects and dispositions defined by their supposed antipathy to life itself has only become more vicious. But when we examine specifically neoliberal regimes of power we see that the terms of their legitimacy have changed in accordance with a much altered account of the life that is said to be at stake. The legitimacy of neoliberal regimes, in contrast with the classical forms of liberal regimes that Foucault examined historically, depends on claims as to their abilities to protect the life not of human populations as such, but of the biosphere. Neoliberalism, it seems to me, has broken from earlier liberalisms in that it correlates claims for its legitimacy not simply with practices for the development of the species life of humanity, as Foucault directed us to recognize, but with what I call 'biospheric life'. These correlations of governance, development, and biospheric life in and among neoliberal regimes of practice and representation increasingly comprise the foundation of its biopolitics. I have argued time and again in previous works that we cannot understand how liberalism functions, most especially how it has gained the global hegemony that it has, without addressing how systematically the category of life has organized the correlation of its various practices of governance. But this contemporary and ongoing shift in the very locus of the life that is at stake for liberal governance, from the human to the nonhuman, seems to me profoundly important for anyone concerned with resistance to liberalism. Looking at how this shift is impacting the life of peoples worldwide, this chapter will show that it is 'the poor' who are being systematically targeted, on account of there being said to be the greatest threat to the security of biospheric life. Alleviating threats to the biosphere requires targeting the poor because it is precisely the poor that are said to be the most 'ecologically ignorant' and, thus, most prone to live in nonsustainable ways. Thus, protecting the life of the biosphere require targeting the poor and relieving them of their ecological ignorance. The means to that removal is argued to reside not only in building neoliberal frameworks of economy, governance, but building neoliberal forms of subjectivity, and within the poor it is most often women who are the principal target population for such strategies of subjectification.

What I will do, therefore, in the rest of this chapter, is to chart how the discourse of resilience has been articulated, first through the emergence of the doctrine of sustainable development, and the allied rise in influence of ecology, which can itself be attributed partly to the success of the environmental movement in reshaping the agenda of liberal governance, by shifting the locus of concern from the issue of the security of merely human life to that of the biosphere, but which must also be understood as an aspect of the ways in which neoliberalism, as distinct from classical liberalism, is grounded in a posthuman understanding of the nature of life itself. Whereas resilience was originally conceived by proponents of sustainable development as a property that distinguishes the extra-economic 'life-support systems' that humans require to live well, gradually it has become reconceived as a property that humanity intrinsically possesses just like all other living systems. But as a property of human populations its growth is said to be dependent on their interpellation within markets, their diversity as economic subjects, and their subjection to systems of governance able to ensure that they continue to use natural resources in sustainable ways. Thus, as we will see, did a doctrine that started out as a critique of neoliberal policy prescriptions for development transform into a doctrine which legitimates a neoliberal model of development based upon the constitution of markets and the interpellation of subjects within markets.

CHOOSING LIFE OVER ECONOMY?

Sustainable development is proclaimed by its proponents to offer a more progressive way of framing the development problematic to that propagated historically by Western governments and international organizations. In contestation of the crudely economic rationalities that shaped the development policies of the West during much of the Cold War, and especially in protest at the implications of the reification of the economic development of societies for their environments, sustainable development seeks to secure the life-support systems that people otherwise require in order to live well and prosper (Barbier and Markandya 1990; Folke and Kautsky 1989; Gladwin et al. 1995; Khagram, Clark, Raad 2003). By privileging the security of the biosphere over and against the imperative to secure economies, 'life' is thus offered as an obstacle to 'economy' by the doctrine of sustainable development. But, as we will see, sustainable development was always likely to be reappropriated by the economic rationalities of Western governments, because of the interface between its 'alternative' rationality of security and that of specifically neoliberal doctrines of economy. While sustainable development deploys ecological reason to argue for the need to secure the life of the biosphere, neoliberalism prescribes economy as the very means of that security. Economic reason is conceived within neoliberalism as a servant of eco-logical reason, claiming paradoxically to secure life from economy through a promotion of the capacities of life for economy. This is the paradoxical foundation on which neoliberalism has constructed its appropriation of sus-tainable development. Sustainable development and neoliberalism are not the same, nor is the former simply a proxy of the latter, but they do come into contact powerfully on the terrains of their rationalities of security. This sur-face of contact ought to make for a tense and political field of contestation, but has instead made largely for a strategically manipulable relation between the two doctrines (Reid 2012).

In recent years we can see, at the very least, how vulnerable the ecologi-cal reasoning that underpins sustainable development has been to the eco-nomic reasoning of neoliberalism. Indeed, I argue that the ongoing disarticu-lation of the concept of security in the development doctrine and the correlate emergence of the concept of resilience is an expression of this. Neoliberalism is able to appropriate the doctrine of sustainable development on account of its claims not to the 'security' but to the 'resilience' of specifically neoliberal institutions (significantly markets), systems of governance, and, most impor-tantly for this chapter, conditions of subjectivity. Resilience is defined by the United Nations as 'the capacity of a system, community or society potential-ly exposed to hazard, to adapt by resisting or changing in order to reach and maintain an acceptable level of functioning and structure' (United Nations 2004: Ch.1, S.1,17). Academics concerned with correlating the promotion of 'sustainable development' with that of resilience define it as 'the capacity to buffer change, learn and develop—as a framework for understanding how to sustain and enhance adaptive capacity in a complex world of rapid transfor-mations' (Folke et al. 2002: 437). The concept of resilience arose not as a direct product of neoliberal doctrines but as an element of the critique of neoliberalism, which sustainable development itself pertained to be at its origin. This shouldn't surprise us. Neoliberalism is not a homogeneous doc-trine, nor is its particular forms of dogmatism homeostatic. Its powers of persuasion and discursive prosperity depend on its own capacity to adapt to the hazards of critique. It is, you might well say, a paragon of the resilience that sustainable development demands of its subjects. The current prosperity of the doctrine of sustainable development is also a vexed expression of the resilience of neoliberalism. It is on account of this power to absorb and align itself with the very sources of its critique that what I call the 'sustainable-development-resilience nexus' is becoming to twenty-first-century liberal governance what the development-security nexus was to its earlier post–Cold War forms. If security functioned during the first two decades of post–Cold War international relations as a rationality for the subjection of development to Western states, their governance practices, institutions, and conditions for subjectivity, then the rationality which governs that subjection is increasingly going to be resilience. Voices from within international relations calling for the dismantling of the sign of security because it is 'the supreme concept of bourgeois society and the fundamental thematic of liberalism' (Neocleous 2008: 186) miss the point. Calling for a new politics to take us 'beyond security' does little to solve the problem; indeed it obfuscates the very nature of the problem, which is that liberalism itself is outgrowing its long-standing correlation with security, and locating new discursive foundations: principally that of resilience.

But beyond showing how the discourse of resilience legitimates neoliberal systems of governance and institutions, it is as necessary to attend to the forms of subjectivity it attempts to bring into being. The account of the world envisaged and constituted by development agencies concerned with building resilient subjects is one that presupposes the disastrousness of the world, and likewise one which interpellates a subject that is permanently called upon to bear the disaster. A subject for whom bearing the disaster is a required practice without which he or she cannot grow and prosper in the world. This is what I believe to be most at stake in the discourse of resilience. The resilient subject is a subject that must permanently struggle to accommodate itself to the world, not a subject that can conceive of changing the world, its structure and conditions of possibility, but a subject that accepts the disastrousness of the world it lives in as a condition for partaking of that world and which accepts the necessity of the injunction to change itself in correspondence with the threats and dangers now presupposed as endemic. Building resilient subjects involves the deliberate disabling of the political habits, tendencies, and capacities of peoples and replacing them with adaptive ones. Resilient subjects are subjects that have accepted the imperative not to resist or secure themselves from the difficulties they are faced with, but instead adapt to its enabling conditions via the embrace of neoliberalism. Resisting neoliberalism in the present thus requires rejecting the seductive claims to 'alternative futures' offered by seemingly contrary doctrines of sustainable development and their political promises of resilience. A reinvestment in an account of political subjectivity is needed, and a rearticulation of a vernacular concept of security is essential for such a purpose.

THE POLITICAL GENEALOGY OF SUSTAINABLE DEVELOPMENT

The ideas that shaped the doctrine of 'sustainable development' became influential in the 1970s, but they only took concrete form with the 1987 publication of the Bruntland Commission report *Our Common Future* (WCED 1987). On the surface of things, sustainable development appeared to operate as the foundation for a powerful indictment of hitherto dominant theories and practices of development. Development policies were classically aimed at increasing the production, consumption, and wealth of societies. What 'sustainable development' did was to pose the problem of the implications of such economy-centred policies for the life support systems on which societies otherwise depend for their welfare (Khagram, Clark, and Raad 2003: 296–97). The doctrine of sustainable development that emerged from *Our Common Future* and which culminated in the 2002 World Summit on Sustainable Development in Johannesburg was based upon the seemingly contrary axiom that economic development had to be suborned to the need to ensure the sustainable use of natural resources, healthy environments, ecosystems, and biodiversity. Here, the utility and value of life in all of its complexities was offered by the doctrine of sustainable development as an obstacle to economy. Committed to securing life from the dangers posed at it by unfettered economic reason, the doctrine of sustainable development appeared to emerge in direct conflict with the governmental doctrine of neoliberalism, which, during the 1980s, had become increasingly hegemonic, and which would have the opportunity to go global with the end of the Cold War in 1989. The kinds of 'pure liberalism' championed by Thatcherites and Reaganites, said to reify the economy at all costs as both means and ends of development, was subject to an apparently new line of questioning, not on account of its equally questionable implications for the economic welfare of peoples, but on account of the threats it posed to something outside of the order of economy: life. Proponents of sustainable development did not claim to question the value of economic development in and of itself, but they did aspire to offer a framework for the reregulation of the economy in alignment with the needs and interests of the biosphere. And indeed its effects were palpable during the 1990s, a decade in which a Senior Vice President of the World Bank, Joseph Stiglitz, was to be heard making savage indictments of the implications of liberal policy prescriptions, and in which the advice of environmentalists was increasingly taken into account by governments and international economic institutions (O'Brien, Goetz, Scholte, and Williams 2000: 109–58).

But the relationship between the emergence of sustainable development and the crisis in liberal reason that began to trouble governments in the 1980s and 1990s is highly complex. Mark Duffield has shown how the shift from strategies of development preaching modernization to sustainable development owed much to a specifically neoliberal framing of the problematic of development (Duffield 2008: 67–70). As Duffield argues, sustainable development emerged as part of a neoliberal countercritique of modernization strategies of development, which, rather than undermining the authority of liberal reason, gave it a new and even more powerful footing. While recognizing the function of ecological reason in shaping the doctrine of sustainable development and its critique of modernization strategies, Duffield draws attention to the neoliberal rationalities which have nevertheless defined it. For one the strength of its challenge to traditional models of development owed much to its alignment with the neoliberal critique of the state (Duffield 2008: 67). Preaching that sustainable development would only follow once people gave up on state-led modernization strategies and learned to practice the virtue of 'community-based self-reliance', so sustainable development reflected a neoliberal political agenda that shifts the burden of security from states to people (Duffield 2008: 69). Sustainable development functions in extensions of neoliberal principles of economy, Duffield argues, by disciplining poor and underdeveloped peoples to give up on states as sources for the protection and improvement of their well-being, and instead practice the virtue of securing themselves. Thus does sustainable development engage in the active promotion of a neoliberal model of society and subjectivity in which everyone is demanded to 'prove themselves by bettering their individual and collective self reliance' (Duffield 2008: 69). In African states such as Mozambique, for example, it has provided 'a virtually free social security system offering the possibilities of adaptation and strengthening in order to manage the risks of market integration' (Duffield 2008: 93).

Revealing the convergences between sustainable development and the neoliberal critique of the state, the model of society and subjectivity it proposes as solutions to the problem of the state, and the economic payoffs that follow, Duffield offers a powerful riposte to those narrative accounts of sustainable development arising simply from the empowerment of ecological over economic reason. But how then should we understand the nature of the relation between sustainable development and neoliberalism? Is ecological reason just a proxy of the neoliberal rationalities that Duffield argues has shaped the agenda of sustainable development? If we understand sustainable development as a servant of neoliberalism then what should we make of those voices arising from environmental movements, and the many other ways in which ecological reason has been mobilized, to critique economy-based strategies of development in the interests of sustaining life? Answering these questions requires grappling further with the fundamental and complex correlations of economy, politics, and security with life in neoliberal doctrine; what Duffield rightly names its biopolitics (2008: 4–8). Neoliberalism is widely understood as a 'theory of political economic practices proposing that human well-being can best be advanced by the maximization of entrepreneurial freedoms within an institutional framework characterized by private property rights, individual liberty, unencumbered markets, and free trade' (Harvey 2007: 22). Less understood, however, is how its claims to be able to increase wealth and freedom are correlated with ways to increase the prosperity and security of life itself. Its capacities to correlate practices for the increase of economic profit and prosperity with those dedicated to increasing the profitability and prosperity of the biosphere are precisely why the doctrine of sustainable development is so compatible with it.

In the first instance this is a problem of the neglect of the complexities of economic doctrines per se. If we examine the origins of economics we find that it was from its earliest usage conceptualized as a domain of knowledge concerned with the prosperity not just of human communities, families, and subjects, but a knowledge that was meant to increase that prosperity in alignment with the needs of nature in its entirety. For Aristotle, economics, it was said, 'must conform to nature . . . in as much as nature has already distributed roles and duties within the species themselves' (Mondzain 2005: 19). 'Implicit', therefore, 'within the economy is the notion of an organic objective and functional harmony . . . a providential and natural order to be respected while acting in the service of the greatest cohesion of utility and well-being' (Mondzain 2005: 19). Moreover, and as Giorgio Agamben has demonstrated in his account of the theological origins of the concept, economy evokes the idea of an administrative praxis not only of the natural course of things, but which is itself, as praxis, 'adapting at each turn, in its salvific intent, to the nature of the concrete situation against which it has to measure itself' (2011: 50). In other words economy pertains not merely to a mode of governance of nature but was itself conceived from its very beginnings as a praxis of governance that functions naturally by adapting to the nature of the object of governance.

Agamben has taken Foucault to task for not pursuing the theological genealogy of economy, but that was not Foucault's project (2011: xi). What Foucault's historical analyses show us is that with the birth of the modern discipline of political economy so 'nature' lost its status as the major correlate of economy and thus did life began to play that role (Foucault 1997). For political economists of the modern age, however, the life which economy had to respect was specifically that of the human species; the question of the prosperity and security of human populations became conceived as limiting conditions for the exercise of economic reason and practices. Neoliberalism breaks from earlier liberalisms and traditions of political economy insofar as its legitimacy rests on its capacities to correlate practices for the increase of economic profitability and prosperity not just with practices for the securing of the human species, but with the life of the biosphere. These correlations of economy, well-being, freedom, security, and biospheric life in and among neoliberal regimes of practice and representation comprise some of the foundations of what have been named its biopolitics (Cooper 2008; Dillon and Reid 2009; Duffield 2008; Reid 2006a). And if there is anything 'fundamental' to liberalism then it is this; one cannot understand how liberalism functions, most especially how it has gained the global hegemony that it has, without addressing how systematically the category of life has organized the correlation of its various practices of governance, as well as how important the shift in the very understanding of life, from the human to the biospheric, has been for changes in those practices.

Examining neoliberalism biopolitically means we can understand better how it is that ecological reasoning has enabled the growth of strategies for the promotion of market-based entrepreneurial capitalism in and among developing societies. Of particular importance here are the ways in which the very account of security deployed by neoliberal states and their development agencies has begun to change through its correlation with ecological reason. Crucial to this story is the relatively recent emergence of the discourse of resilience. When neoliberals preach the necessity of peoples becoming resilient they are, as I will show, arguing in effect for the entrepreneurial practices of self and subjectivity which Duffield calls 'self-reliance'. Resilient peoples do not look to states or other entities to secure and improve their well-being because they have been disciplined into believing in the necessity to secure and improve it for themselves. Indeed so convinced are they of the worth of such capabilities that they proclaim it to be a fundamental 'freedom' (UNEP 2004). But the emergence of this discourse of resilience within the doctrine of neoliberalism owes massively, I argue, to the power of ecological reason in shaping the very rationality of security which otherwise defines it. In other words comprehending how a neoliberal rationality of security functions in shaping the agenda of sustainable development requires us to examine the constitutive function of ecological reason in shaping both. Far from being a proxy of the neoliberal rationalities shaping sustainable development, ecological reason has been formative of them.

FROM SECURITY TO RESILIENCE

The strategic function of sustainable development in the global expansion of neoliberalism has been to naturalize neoliberal frameworks of governance; the institutions, practices, and forms of subjectivity that it demands are brought into being on account of the desire for increase of the economic profitability and prosperity of human communities. But how is it that neoliberal ways of governing came to be conceived as an answer to the problem of sustainability? Some of the answer to this question can be given, I believe, by looking closely at the emergence and discursive expansion of the concept of resilience, because that is the concept against which all such institutions, practices and subjectivities are increasingly legitimized. It is no accident that the concept of resilience derives directly from ecology, referring to the 'buffer capacities' of living systems; their ability to 'absorb perturbations' or the 'magnitude of disturbance that can be absorbed before a living system changes its structure by changing the variables and processes that control behaviour' (Adger 2000: 349). Living systems are said by ecologists to develop not on account of their ability to secure themselves prophylactically from threats, but through their adaptation to them. Exposure to threats is a constitutive process in the development of living systems, and thus the problem for them is never simply how to secure themselves but how to adapt to them. Such capacities for adaptation to threats are precisely what ecologists argue determines the resilience of any living system. Sustainable development started out by preaching that the economic development of societies must be regulated so that it contributes not just to the security of states and their human populations, but so that it increases the resilience of all living systems; shifting the object of concern from that of human life to that of the biosphere, incorporating every known species, as well as habitats of all kinds, vulnerable to the destructions wrought by economic development. Life not economy, it said, must provide the rationalities according to which peoples are entitled to increasing their prosperity. The emergence of such a doctrine had to have significant implications for the ways in which not only the problem but the very nature of security was conceived in developmental circles. Once the referent object of development became the life of the biosphere, rather than simply states and their human populations, the account of security to which development is allied was required to transform. Security, with its connotations of state and governmental reason, territoriality, military capacities, economic prosperity, human resources, and population assets became less fashionable and gradually gave way to the new concept and value of resilience. Resilience is a useful concept, the proponents of sustainable development argue, precisely because it is not a capacity of states, nor merely of human populations and their various political, social, and economic practices, but a capacity of life itself. Thus did resilience emerge within the doctrine of sustainable development as a way of positing a different kind of policy problematic to those formulated in the security doctrines of neoliberal states and their more conventional development agencies; one that would privilege the life of the biosphere in all its dimensions over and against the human focus that shaped the 'development-security nexus'. If one aspect of the subordination of rationalities of economy to rationalities of life in developmental discourse has been the shift from doctrines of economic development to sustainable development then a correlate shift has been that from security to resilience.

Allied to this shift, then, the doctrine of sustainable development brought into being a new guiding axiom, one which created a surface of friction with the rationalities of economic development pursued by Western states and development agencies up until the 1980s. And this in turn, during the 1990s, gradually brought into being a 'sustainable development-resilience nexus' to rival the development-security nexus woven by previous regimes. By the time of the 2002 World Summit on Sustainable Development in Johannesburg, however, a summit that is widely recognized as the coming-of-age party of 'sustainable development', new ways of thinking about resilience were coming into view. A major report prepared on behalf of the Environmental Advisory Council to the Swedish Government as input to the process of the World Summit described how resilience is a property associated not just with the diversity 'of species', but also 'of human opportunity', and especially 'of economic options—that maintain and encourage both adaptation and learning' among human populations (Folkes et al. 2002: 438). In an adroit reformulation of the problematic, neoliberal economic development, in which the function of markets as generators of economic diversity is basic, became itself a core constituent of the resilience which sustainable development had to be aimed at increasing. Thus was it that, post-Johannesburg, the correlation of sustainable development with resilience started to produce explicitly neoliberal prescriptions for institutional reform. 'Ecological ignorance' began to be conceptualized as a threat, not just to the resilience of the biosphere, but to humanity (Folkes et al. 2002: 438). Resilience began to be conceived not simply as an inherent property of the biosphere, in need of protection from the economic development of humanity, but a property within human populations that now needed promoting through the increase of their 'economic options'. As remarkably, the biosphere itself began to be conceived not as an extra-economic domain, distinct from and vulnerable to the economic practices of human populations, but an economy of 'services' which 'humanity receives' (Folkes et al. 2002: 437).

There is a double and correlated shift at work here, then, in the elaboration of the sustainable-development-resilience nexus post-Johannesburg. In one move resilience has shifted from being a property of the biosphere to being a property of humanity, while in a second move service has shifted from being an element of economy to being a capacity of the biosphere. Crucified on the cross that this double shift carves are 'the poor'. For they are the segment of population of which resilience is now demanded and simultaneously the population said to threaten the degradation of 'ecosystem services'. Increasing the resiliency of the poor has become a defining goal, for example, of the United Nations Environment Programme (UNEP) in the post-Johannesburg years (UNEP 2004: 39). Alleviating threats to the biosphere requires improving the resilience of the poor, especially, because it is precisely the poor that are most ecologically ignorant and thus most prone to using ecosystem services in nonsustainable ways. Thus does ensuring the resilience of the biosphere require making the poor into more resilient kinds of subjects, and making the poor into more resilient subjects requires relieving them of their ecological ignorance, and the means to that removal is argued to reside in building neoliberal frameworks of economy, governance, and subjectivity. Developing the resilience of the poor is said to require, for example, a social context of 'flexible and open institutions and multi-level governance systems' (Folke et al. 2002: 439). 'The absence of markets and price signals' in ecological services is a major threat to resilience, UNEP argues, because it means that 'changes in their conditions have gone unnoticed' (UNEP 2004: 13). Property rights regimes have to be extended so that they incorporate ecosystem services and so that markets can function in them (UNEP 2004: 15). 'Markets' it is argued 'have proven to be among the most resilient institutions, being able to recover quickly and to function in the absence of government' (Pingali, Alinovi, and Sutton 2005: S18). When and where the market fails to recover, development policies for increasing resilience have to be aimed at 'ensuring access to markets' (Pingali, Alinovi, and Sutton 2005: S18). Ensuring the resilience of the poor also requires the building of neoliberal systems of governance which will monitor their use of ecological services to ensure they are sustainably managed (UNEP 2004: 39). The poor, in order to be the agents of their own change, have to be subjectivized so that they are 'able to make sustainable management decisions that respect natural resources and enable the achievement of a sustainable income stream' (UNEP 2004: 5). 'Over-harvesting, over-use, misuse or excessive conversion of ecosystems into human or artificial systems damages the regulation service which in turn reduces the flow of the provisioning service provided by ecosystems' (UNEP 2004: 20). Within the poor itself women are the principal target population. 'I will transform my lifestyle in the way I farm and think' has become the mantra that poor women farmers in the Caribbean region are demanded, for example, to repeat like Orwellian farm animals in order to receive European Union funding (Tandon 2007: 12–14).

This double shift is integral, I argue, to the strategy by which neoliberalism has absorbed the critique of sustainable development. Whereas resilience was originally conceived by proponents of sustainable development as a property that distinguishes the extra-economic life-support systems which humans require to live well, it has become reconceived post-Johannesburg as a property which humanity intrinsically possesses, is capable of developing further, and which it can never have too much of. As a property of human populations it is dependent moreover on their interpellation within markets, their diversity as economic subjects, and their subjection to systems of governance able to ensure that they continue to use natural resources in sustainable ways. Thus did a doctrine which started out as a critique of neoliberal policy prescriptions for development transform into a doctrine which legitimates a neoliberal model of development based upon the constitution of markets and the interpellation of subjects within markets.

Traditionally, development has been understood to serve the aspirations of the poor to improve themselves economically. Today, in the context of sustainable development, 'poverty reduction' means altogether something else. As poverty is now said by the UNEP to be caused by the poor's dependence on and mal-use of ecosystem services so the aims of poverty reduction have shifted from providing them with economic security to improving their so-called ecological security (UNEP 2004). In effect these UNEP policies for the provision of so-called ecological security aim at 'making poor people's livelihoods more productive through an 'ecosystem approach' (UNEP 2004), while keeping them economically poor. In other words they aim at improving the immaterial well-being of the poor while ignoring their material disadvantage. Rhetorically the emphasis of these UNEP policies may be 'on empowering individuals to become agents of change rather than victims requiring aid'. But what does that mean in practice? 'Empowerment' in such contexts means divesting the poor of the forms of access to aid through which they might otherwise develop to become economically more equal to the wealthier populations of their own societies. Of course there is nothing wrong or disadvantageous in policies that work to improve the ecological security of poor peoples. We all need access to clean water and air in order to live well. The point, however, is that such UNEP policies, aimed as they are at developing the ecological security of the poor, are functioning to displace the very issue and problem of economic inequality. Ecological security is being substituted for economic security in a crudely binary form of blackmail. 'The focus', it is argued, 'must not be on improving human well-being in terms of material wealth' (UNEP 2004).

Such policies elide the material gaps in wealth between rich and poor, by reconceptualizing the well-being of the poor in nonmaterial terms. In effect they assume that it is fine for the poor to remain materially poor so long as they are immaterially 'well'. The poor must be given the instruments of economic living—inclusion in markets, access to small amounts of credit, and participation in work, but not the material benefits that comes with economic well-being. Life, not wealth, becomes the measure of well-being for the poor, while the rich are allowed to remain both wealthy and well. As such the UNEP's ecoystem approach to poverty is functioning to destroy the desire for economic development of the poor, while increasing their productivity, health, and participation. It is an approach which extends the reach of the market to include the poor while naturalizing the inequalities between poor and rich within the market. The argument of the UN indeed is that this is what the poor want—that clean water and air is their priority (UNPEP 2008). Indeed they have validated their ecosystemic approach to poverty through the polling of the poor who supposedly answer that their interests are immaterial and not economic:

> A better life for me is to be healthy, peaceful and live in love without hunger.
> Love is more than anything. Money has no value in the absence of love.
>   —a poor older woman in Ethiopia (UNPEP 2008)

THE DISASTROUS AND POLITICALLY DEBASED SUBJECT OF RESILIENCE

Having established how sustainable development, via its propagation of the concept of resilience, naturalizes neoliberal systems of governance and institutions, I want to consider how it functions to constitute subjects amenable to neoliberal governance. Every regime of governance invokes its own particular subject of governance. Producing subjects the liberal way has long since been a game of producing self-securing subjects. Subjects that are capable of securing themselves are less of a threat to themselves and, in being so, are not a threat to the governance capacities of their states nor to the governance of the global order either. In this sense the correlation of development with security feeds upon the political imaginary of liberalism predicated as it became upon the belief that a global order of self-securing subjects would in turn deliver a more secure form of world order (Rosenau 2008; Rosenau 2002; Rosenau 1992). What, then, does the shift in the correlation of development with security to resilience tell us about the nature of the subject that development is now aimed at producing? What differences are entailed in being a resilient subject as opposed to a merely secure subject? Is the emergence of this new object of development just an extension of the liberal rationalities of governance that feed upon what is otherwise described as the development-security nexus?

There is, in fact, a considerable shift here. The major condition of possibility for the subject of sustainable development is that it sacrifices its capacity and desire for security. Security, here, is less than which liberalism demands of its subjects than what it forbids them. The resilient subject of sustainable development is, by definition, not a secure but an adaptive subject; adaptive insofar as it is capable of making those adjustments to itself that enable it to survive the hazards encountered in its exposure to the world. In this sense the resilient subject is a subject that must permanently struggle to accommodate itself to the world. Not a political subject that can conceive of changing the world, its structure and conditions of possibility, with a view to securing itself from the world. But a subject that accepts the disastrousness of the world it lives in as a condition for partaking of that world and which accepts the necessity of the injunction to change itself in correspondence with the threats and dangers now presupposed as endemic. One can see readily how this plays out in relation to debates, for example, over climate change. One enthusiast for resilience as an answer to the problem writes:

> What is vital to understand is not the degree of climate change that we should
> expect, nor necessarily the impact that we might anticipate on water resource
> management, coastal defence, food security, species survival, etc. What is

important to grasp is that we do have the abilities to adapt and adjust to the
changes that climate change will bring. (Tandon 2007: 12)

Sustainable development is no longer conceived, thus, as a state of being on
account of which a human is capable of securing itself from the world, and
via which he or she becomes a subject in the world. Once development is
said to follow ecological laws of change and transformation, and thus once
exposure to hazard becomes a condition of possibility for development, so
the question which sustainable development poses for the communities and
individuals subject to it is; can you survive in the world without securing
yourself from the world?

This is precisely why resilience has become so intimately tied in the
policy, practice, and theory of sustainable development, not just to neoliberalism but to disaster management. Indeed the latter is also crucial in legiti-
mating the former. The ability to manage exposure to hazard in and among
developing societies is dependent, the UN says, on their maintenance of a
healthy and diverse ecological system that is productive and life sustaining,
but it also demands a healthy and diverse economy that adapts to change and
recognizes social and ecological limits (UN 2004: Ch. 1, S. 2, 18). It requires
'capturing opportunities for social change during the "window of opportunity" following disasters, for example by utilizing the skills of women and
men equally during reconstruction' (UN 2004: Ch. 1, S. 2, 20). As fundamentally it requires making societies 'aware of the importance of disaster
reduction for their own well-being' (UN 2004: Ch. 3, S. 4, 1), because 'it is
crucial for people to understand that they have a responsibility towards their
own survival and not simply wait for governments to find and provide solutions' (UN 2004: Ch. 3, S. 4, 20). Disasters, thus construed, are not threats to
the development of human beings from which they might aspire to secure
themselves; they are events of profound 'opportunity' for societies to transform themselves economically and politically. Disasters are events which do
not merely expose communities to dangers from which they must be saved in
order that they might be set back onto the path of development. But, rather,
where communities, in their exposure, are able to undergo novel processes of
developmental change in reconstitution of themselves as neoliberal societies.
Exposure to disaster, in this context, is conceptualized in positive terms as
constitutive of the possibility for the development of neoliberal systems of
governance. But the working of this rationality depends on a subject that will
submit to it. Sustainable development requires subjects, the UN report insists
in a remarkable passage, to understand the 'nature' of hazards. The passage
of societies to such knowledge must in turn involve, it states

a consideration of almost every physical phenomenon on the planet. The slow
movements in the earth's mantle—the convection cells that drive the move-

ment of continents and the manufacture of ocean floors—are the starting and
also the sticking point. They lift mountains and shape landscapes. They also
build volcanoes and trigger potentially catastrophic earthquakes. Like those
other invisible movements that take place on a vast scale through the atmos-
pheric medium—the carbon cycle and the water cycle and the nitrogen cycle—
volcanoes and earthquakes, along with technological advancements, provide
the bedrock of strong nations, rich industries and great cities. They do, of
course, also have the potential to destroy them. (2004: Ch. 2, S. 1, 4)

The account of the world envisaged and constituted by development
agencies concerned with building resilient societies is one that presupposes
the disastrousness of the world, and likewise one which interpellates a subject that is permanently called upon to bear the disaster. A subject for whom
bearing the disaster is a required practice without which he or she cannot
grow and prosper in the world. This is precisely what is at stake in the
discourse of resilience. The resilient subject is a subject that must permanently struggle to accommodate itself to the world, not a subject that can conceive of changing the world, its structure and conditions of possibility, but a
subject that accepts the disastrousness of the world it lives in as a condition
for partaking of that world, which will not question the reasons why he or she
suffers, but which accepts the necessity of the injunction to change itself in
correspondence with the suffering now presupposed as endemic.

The human here is conceived as resilient insofar as it adapts to rather than
resists the conditions of its suffering in the world. To be resilient is to forego
the very power of resistance. Two ideologues of sustainable development,
Handmer and Dovers, claim, 'The imperative of adaptation rather than resistance to change will increase inexorably' (Handmer and Dovers 1996). In
their enthusiasm for the 'inexorable increase' of this 'imperative' theorists of
sustainable development engage in some vivid discursive representations of
the human. 'As a species, humanity is immensely adaptable—a weed species. We are also capable of considerable adaptability as individuals, and also
as households (variously defined)—the latter being the perennial and universal human social unit' (Handmer and Dovers 1996). The combination of the
imperative of humanity to adapt with the representation of humanity as a
'weed species' recalls the discursive currency of similar combinations within
the concentration camps of Nazi Germany during World War II. Those
camps were, as Barrington Moore has demonstrated in a brilliant and wide-
ranging historical study, sites for the constitution of precisely such resilient
subjects and the honing of precisely such adaptive capacities. The inhabitants
of such extreme spaces of suffering often failed to exhibit any sign of resistance, seeking to survive through the development of complex and ultimately
failed strategies of 'adaptation' to the conditions of their suffering (Moore
1978: 66). The 'conquest' of the perception of inevitability and necessity of
circumstances is 'essential', Moore argues on the other hand, 'to the develop-

ment of politically effective moral outrage' (1978: 459). The making of resilient subjects and societies fit for neoliberalism by agencies of sustainable development is based upon a degradation of the political capacities of human beings far more subtle than that achieved in Auschwitz and Buchenwald. But the enthusiasm with which ideologues of sustainable development are turning resilience into an 'imperative' is nevertheless comparable with that of the SS guards who also aimed 'to speed up the processes of adaptive learning' among those Jews and other populations in their charge by convincing them of the futility of resistance (Moore 1978: 66).

DEVELOPMENT CONTRA NEOLIBERALISM?

Can the doctrine of sustainable development be retrieved from the grip that neoliberalism seems to have achieved on it? The purpose of this chapter has not been to argue against claims as to the necessity of concern for the state of the biosphere, but to raise the problem of the surface of contact between such an ecological mode of reasoning and a mode of economic reason complicit with the degradation of the biosphere as well as a mode of political reason which degrades the fundamentally political capacities of human beings. While sustainable development deploys ecological reason to argue for the need to secure the life of the biosphere, neoliberalism prescribes economy as the very means of that security, while pathologizing political subjectivity as the very source of the problem of environmental degradation. Economic reason is conceived within neoliberalism as a servant of ecological reason, claiming paradoxically to secure life from economy through a promotion of the capacities of life for economy while diagnosing politics as that tendency of the human most inimical to the needs of life as such. If, then, sustainable development is to escape its appropriation it would seem imperative that it contest the nexus of relations on which claims as to the necessity of neoliberal frameworks for the sustainability of life are based. For a start this has to mean rethinking the ways in which it engages with the concept of resilience. The problem here is less the demands to improve the resilience of ecosystems which distinguished the agenda of sustainable development in its early years than it is the post-Johannesburg shift to propagating resilience as a fundamental property and capacity of the human. The ecological imaginary is colonizing the social and political imaginaries of theorists and practitioners of development in ways that are providing fertile ground for the application of neoliberalism as a solution to the problem of sustainability. Understanding how that is possible requires understanding the biopolitics of neoliberalism, how its claims to be able to increase wealth and freedom are correlated with ways to increase the prosperity and security of life itself. For its capacities to correlate practices for the increase of economic profit and prosperity with those dedicated to increasing the profitability and prosperity of the biosphere are precisely why the doctrine of sustainable development is so compatible with it.

What is needed is a policy and practice of sustainable development reflexive enough to provide space for a 'speaking back' to the forms of neoliberalism that are currently being pushed by Western states and international organizations as answers to the problem of sustainability. A policy and practice that will cut the poor and underdeveloped some slack when it comes to issues of environmental degradation, climate change, and struggles for and over natural resources. A policy and practice that will, while taking into account the grave nature of these problems, take seriously the degradations of capacities for the development of political subjectivity that occur when adaptation rather than resistance to the conditions of worldly suffering becomes a governing imperative. We have enough voices, now, calling within the chorus of development for the saving of the planet. But where are the voices that will call for the saving of the political? For sustainable development to reinvent itself it needs to master the ecological reason from which it emerged and forge newly political paradigms of thought and practice. Why is it that the conception of ecology at work in sustainable development is so limited that it permits neoliberalism to proliferate, like a poison species, taking over entire states and societies in the wake of their disasters, utilizing their suffering as conditions for its spread, installing markets, commodifying anything it can lay its hands on, monetizing the value of everything, driving peoples from countryside into cities, generating displacement, homelessness, and deprivation? Isn't this an ecological problematique? Why is this death and suffering producing machine tolerated in the name of sustainability? It is not only living species and habitats that are today threatened with extinction, and for which we ought to mobilize our care, but the words and gestures of human solidarity on which resistance to such biopolitical regimes of governance depends (Guattari 1995). A sense of responsibility for the survival of the life of the biosphere is not a sufficient condition for the development of a political subject capable of speaking back to neoliberalism, nor is it a sense of responsibility for the life of humanity. What is required is a subject responsible for securing incorporeal species, chiefly that of the political, currently threatened with extinction, on account of the overwrought fascination with life that has colonized the developmental as well as every other biopoliticized imaginary of the modern age.

But building such a subject requires a first step of refusing the stories we are told about the subject by the liberal tradition. Political subjects do not merely depend on their milieus, or desire the sustainability of the conditions for their living the lives they do; rather, they resist those conditions, and where successful, overcome them and transform them into that which they were not, in the process establishing new conditions by which to live differently. Hubris, I argue, and we will go on to explore in a later chapter, is the constitutive power through which political subjects come into existence, the fantasy of the possibility of another life, another existence. Liberalism is what is finite. It will die. The question is how and when. And the political confidence of peoples, while challenged by liberal modernity, remains the well from which we have to draw. The renewal of such a political confidence—that these regimes of governance will be destroyed and replaced by new and better ones—remains the singular precondition for human resistance and revolt in the world. And as we will go on to see, Foucault's analytic of the outside to liberalism can help us in the development of that task. First, however, we must go deeper into the analysis of neoliberal thinking and practice to examine how it is operating in ways that not only deny the subject its capacity to think politics as a task of security and transformation, but robs the subject of its belief in the possibility for autonomy. When liberals engage in the discourse of resilience today they do so in terms that aim at preventing humans from conceiving their capacities to determine their own ways of life in freedom from others as a state to strive for and, in contrast, as a potential risk unto themselves. Autonomy, it is said, equals a diminished capacity to connect with others, and so to be autonomous has become conceived less as a condition to strive for, and more as a source of danger to oneself and others. Exposed to the dangers on which its life is said to thrive, the neoliberal subject is nevertheless called upon to fend off the formation of anything like an autonomously determined way of life, on account of the risks posed by autonomy to the sanctity of its life. These are the paradoxical stakes of the contemporary and ongoing war over the subject.

II

Adaptation

Chapter Five

Development as Adaptation

David Chandler

As argued in chapter 3, which introduced the discourse of resilience, the neoliberal subject is understood both empirically and normatively through the discursive construction of governance as the enablement of the adaptive capacities necessary for resilience. This chapter on adaptation thus concerns the development of the neoliberal understanding of how to govern for resilience: how to enable and develop adaptive capacities in individuals and populations. Just as security no longer refers to governing 'from above', in terms of the provision of protection, but increasingly to the inculcation of the subject's own adaptive capacities, so development discourses similarly shift from the measurement of state-level gross domestic product (GDP) or the state-led development projects of modernity to focus more on 'development from below'. The neoliberal subject thus becomes both the means and the ends of development, understood as a process of building and maintaining adaptive capacities.

This discourse transforms the problematic of governance from 'development' understood as transforming the external world to work on neoliberal forms of development understood as the transformation of the adaptive capacities of the subject. In these discourses, new information technology is increasingly seen as essential to the transformation of adaptive choice-making:

> More diverse, integrated, timely and trustworthy information can lead to better decision-making and real-time citizen feedback. This in turn enables individuals, public and private institutions, and companies to make choices that are good for them and for the world they live in. (United Nations 2014: 2)

Problematic and poorly adaptive decision-making by individuals and institutions is increasingly seen as the key area through which governance interventions need to operate in neoliberal discourses of capacity development. The United Nations has called for 'a data revolution for sustainable development' arguing that 'improving data is a development agenda in its own right' (United Nations 2014: 3) and that the divides between rich and poor can be mitigated through the provision of more data enabling better, more effective, choice-making at all levels of society.

High level international collaborative initiatives—like the UN Global Pulse, established by the UN Secretary-General to research and coordinate the use of Big Data for development,[1] the World Bank's Open Data for Resilience Initiative (OpenDRI), seeking to capacity build to reduce vulnerability to natural hazards and the impacts of climate change,[2] and the Pop-Tech and Rockefeller Foundation initiatives on Big Data and community resilience,[3] highlight that data-led understandings of development and adaptive capacities for choice-making are clearly at the heart of contemporary neoliberal constructions of resilience, adaptation, and vulnerability.

In neoliberal discourse, societal intervention with the goal of transforming the subject is articulated in terms of the development, 'freeing' or 'empowerment' of the subject. It is of fundamental importance that this neoliberal discourse of development, freedom or empowerment is not confused with traditional or classical liberal understandings of the 'liberation' of the subject or with modernist understandings of development as material progress. As will be analyzed in greater detail in this chapter, the neoliberal discourse of the active construction of the adaptive subject is not primarily concerned with external material preconditions or institutional frameworks for the exercise of freedom and equality (the basis of the construction of the liberal subject), but with the self-knowledge necessary to enable the adaptive capacities and capabilities of the subject. In neoliberal development economics, 'poverty is best understood as capability failure, not just as shortage of commodities or even of income and wealth' (Nussbaum 2011: 143).

The knowledge capacities and capabilities necessary for the neoliberal subject are very different from those of the traditional or classical liberal subject. The capabilities and capacities required are those that enable the subject to actively embrace and adapt to change rather than resist it. In this case, a liberal education in the arts and sciences is held to be of less value than a capacity to adapt efficiently and effectively through greater self-awareness and emotional reflectivity. What is needed is reflective and reflexive learning about the self and one's community, for example (as considered in chapter 3), in relation to one's own diet, exercise, and lifestyle choices and the effects which they have on life expectancy and the community and the environment in which one lives. The neoliberal discursive construction of the world as a product of human agency (considered earlier in terms of societal resilience) is even more starkly articulated in the understanding of development in terms of adaptive individual choice-making. In its reinscription of poverty and underdevelopment in terms of the problematic of the adaptive capacities of the poor and marginalized, neoliberalism fully reveals the exhaustion of liberalism's emancipatory ethos.

As will be considered in this chapter, the discourse of developing adaptive capabilities and capacities—of inculcating resilience—removes the traditional government policy goals previously associated with state-led development policy-making. Whereas liberal frameworks of governmentality focused upon how governments might regulate and control specific levers of the economy—inflation levels, unemployment rates, interest rates, and such—under neoliberal approaches, the governance of economic processes is displaced by the enabling of societal processes, particularly of knowledge and communication, facilitating the adaptive capacities of individuals, enabling them to make better or more efficient lifestyle choices. Recasting development in terms of societal processes and problematic individual and collective choice-making removes poverty and inequality from the macro or state-level of policy-making. Rather than liberal macroeconomic policy-making, based on government programmes and goals, development becomes a question of the efficiency of societal adaptation. The liberal programmatic of government becomes hollowed out as liberal economic policy goals are displaced by the societal goal of knowledge empowerment or 'capability-building', often presented in terms of 'human development'.

This chapter engages with these neoliberal discourses of adaptive capability- and capacity-building through reference to Michel Foucault's critical exploration of shifts and transformations in liberal frameworks of understanding the role of government. Here, Foucault's work is very insightful in highlighting how our understanding of the human subject has been transformed within neoliberal development discourses. In today's dominant conceptualization of human-centred approaches to development, individual behavioural choice—'the rationality of the governed' (Foucault 2008: 312)—is the central motif for understanding the problematic of development. Human agency has been placed at the centre and is increasingly seen to be the measure of development, in terms of individual adaptive capacities and capabilities. The individualized understanding of development takes a subjective perspective, starting with the understanding of the individual, often called an 'agent-orientated view' (Sen 1999: 11). This chapter seeks to critically engage with the view of the human and of human agency articulated within this approach.

The work of Nobel Prize-winning economist and philosopher Amartya Sen has been central in establishing the conceptual foundations of the human development discourse of adaptation which underpins the dominant understanding of development in the UN Development Programme's annual Human Development reports and formed the basis of the Human Development Index. For the advocates of human development, it is the growth of adaptive capabilities and capacities that are central: through the empowerment or freedom of the individual. In fact, as Martha Nussbaum notes, this approach is often more usefully termed the 'Capability Approach' or the 'Capabilities Approach' (Nussbaum 2011: x). Here, development is taken out of a macro socioeconomic context and seen as a question of individual inclusion and choice-making capabilities.

The first annual UN Human Development Report (1990) opens with these paragraphs:

> This Report is about people—and about how development enlarges their *choices*. It is about more than GNP growth, more than income and wealth and more than producing commodities and accumulating capital. A person's access to income may be one of the *choices*, but it is not the sum total of human endeavour.
>
> Human development is a process of enlarging people's *choices*. The most critical of these wide-ranging *choices* are to live a long and healthy life, to be educated and to have access to resources needed for a decent standard of living. Additional *choices* include political freedom, guaranteed human rights and personal self-respect.
>
> Development enables people to have these *choices*. No one can guarantee human happiness, and the *choices* people make are their own concern. But the process of development should at least create a conducive environment for people, individually and collectively, to develop their full potential and to have a reasonable chance of leading productive and creative lives in accord with their needs and interests.
>
> Human development thus concerns more than the formation of human capabilities, such as improved health or knowledge. It also concerns the use of these capabilities, be it for work, leisure or political and cultural activities. And if the scales of human development fail to balance the formation and use of human capabilities, much human potential will be frustrated. (UNDP 1990: 1, emphasis added)

The seven occasions on which the word 'choices' is used in the first three paragraphs have been italicised in order to emphasize that human development is inextricably tied to adaptive capacity-building, which is understood as the extension of choice-making capabilities. The key point to note is that these capabilities are not directly connected to the level of material social and economic development. As the third and fourth paragraphs emphasize, choice-making capability is not merely about external resources or material inputs. There is a large subjective element to the capability approach—the concern is with 'the use of these capabilities' and with the conducive information and communication 'environment' in which efficient adaptations, through good choice-making, can take place.

Sen is the leading academic exponent of adaptation as human development. There has been a lot of academic and technical discussion over the merits and applicability of Sen's approach, which has generally sought to expand Sen's subjectivist, internal, or 'agent-centred' approach but relatively little critical engagement with it (for a good summary see Clark 2005). When Sen has been the subject of criticism, this has generally focused on the need for collective political struggle to constitute development and freedom for the postcolonial subject or for paying too little attention to the structural constraints of the world market and capitalist social relations (see, for example, Chimni 2008; Harvey 2005: 184; Navarro 2000; Samaddar 2006). The human development capabilities approach has also been substantially critiqued from a traditional development perspective for the shift away from material definitions of development to a more subjective measurement (see, for example, Ben-Ami 2006; Duffield 2007; Pender 2001; Pupavac 2007). Mark Duffield's work is emblematic in this respect and he highlights the problematic of development as a technology of liberal governance in his influential book *Development, Security and Unending War* (2007):

> Sustainable development is about creating diversity and choice, enabling people to manage the risks and contingencies of their existence better and, through regulatory and disciplinary interventions, helping surplus population to maintain a homeostatic condition of self-reliance. (2007: 115)

This chapter seeks to mount a different engagement with the knowledge capabilities approach, instead taking seriously the claim of 'development as freedom' to explore Sen's rereading of development as the inculcation of adaptive capabilities and capacities. While Duffield describes well the implications of reinterpreting development in subjective rather than material terms, in shifting to self-reliance, this chapter is less concerned with critiquing human-centred development primarily from the viewpoint of it as an economically rationalized governmentality discourse of intervention, policing, regulation, and control. Rather than a consideration of adaptive capacity-building as a technology of liberal governmentality, this chapter seeks instead to consider Sen's work in a broader context of the understanding of the neoliberal subject itself; particularly as this subject is articulated at the limits of liberalism and helps to construct and shape these limits—in terms of the problematization of the adaptive capacities of the colonial and postcolonial subject.

It will be suggested that Foucault, following Karl Marx, powerfully theorizes the problematic of the shifts and transformations within liberal thought as the liberal project increasingly exhausts the emancipatory potential of the Enlightenment.[4] These shifts are incrementally reflected in the shrinking of the liberal world and in the reduction of the liberal understanding of the subject, as barriers and limits are increasingly introduced, at first as external to the liberal subject and finally, as internal (to the neoliberal subject). For Foucault, the shifting understanding of the liberal subject was of crucial importance: his work on biopolitics and the governance of the self can be read as a critical engagement with understanding the reshaping of liberal aspirations from a concern with the knowledge of and transformation of the external world to the enabling of decision-making capacities of subjects, articulated clearly in the shift from government, based upon liberal frames of representation, to neoliberal governance, the regulation of societal processes. In this shift, our understanding of what it means to be human, and of what being human means for our engagement with the world we live in, have been fundamentally altered.

Foucault deals with this problematic on several occasions, most notably in his work on *The Birth of Biopolitics* (2008), but also through analogy in his study of the decay of Greek democratic thought, especially as reflected in the work of Plato (Foucault 2010). I want to suggest that in Sen's work this shift can be seen in its fully articulated form: the conception of 'development as freedom' inverts classical or traditional framings of both these terms as Sen shifts the emphasis of both problematics to the adaptive capacities of the subject. For Sen, development is no longer a question of material transformation: development is no longer about the external world. In fact, development disappears—it has no external material measurement—it is deontologized, or rather assumes the ontology of the human subject itself. At the same time, freedom is also dissolved as a meaningful way of understanding the political or legal status of the subject: freedom also loses its materiality as it loses its external universalist moorings and instead becomes relocated to the interior life of the individual.

The bringing together of discourses of freedom and development—their removal from liberal universalist conceptions of the liberal subject (framed within sovereign states and the formal rights of citizenship and within liberal teleologies of progress as linear material development) and their reassertion in discourses of neoliberal governance—is serving the task of apologia for difference and inequality. Rather than take the route suggested by Duffield and others, of understanding development or freedom themselves as universalising, liberal or problematic concepts, which need to be avoided, maybe we should be thinking of how these liberal concepts have lost their progressive and universalist content in their reduction to the adaptive capacities of the neoliberal subject.[5]

FOUCAULT'S WORK ON THE GENEALOGY OF THE SUBJECT

In *The Birth of Biopolitics*, Foucault drew out the implications of neoliberal approaches and was very keen to highlight the limitation of the left or Marxist thinking of his day, which saw in neoliberalism merely the rolling back of the state and the expansion of market forces, with the increased emphasis on the self-reliance and the responsibilization of the subject (which critical work by both Marx- and Foucault-inspired theorists, such as David Harvey and Mark Duffield, seems to replicate) (Foucault 2008: 129–50). Foucault's focus is upon why it would be problematic to see this discourse as purely an economic discourse, which assumed that its only affects were economic ones and that its contestation could be easily understood in terms of left versus right or state versus market. He argued that the discourses of neoliberalism reflected a major shift in how politics could be understood or contested, and that this shift was entirely missed in traditional left/right polemics (2008: 116–17).

Foucault highlighted major shifts and transformations within liberal discourse, which made this transformation in the relationship between the subject and the state of fundamental importance (2008: 118). Essentially, he argued that neoliberalism shrinks the understanding of human subjectivity, removing the foundational sphere of rational autonomy. In so doing, Foucault suggested that, with neoliberal approaches, the binaries of liberal thought are dissolved: that there was no longer a conceptual distinction between the external world and the inner world, between subject and object, between public and private, between the formal sphere of politics and law and the informal sphere of social and economic relations (2008: 267–86). There was no longer the universal starting position of the Enlightenment subject—capable of knowing and transforming the external world—of the collective human project of social emancipation. There was no longer a liberal teleology of progress.

Foucault suggested that neoliberalism inverts our understanding of the human subject, at the same time making the internal life of the subject the subject of governance. Power and agency are reduced to the level of individual decision-taking. Individual decisions construct the world in which we live and shape the context for further decisions that individuals make. This world is continually being made and remade by the human subject. But the human subject is not the classical subject of the Enlightenment: there is no assumption of growth in knowledge or understanding or progress. Governance constantly needs to intervene to adapt institutions to enable better individual decisions, to work on the empowerment of the decision-making individual, or its adaptive capacities in the language of today's resilience-based theorizations. This is a continual process of preventive management of soci-

David Chandler

ety based upon the indirect shaping of the adaptive capacities and conduct of
its individual members (Foucault 2008: 159–79).

For Foucault, the subjection of the subject—precisely through its capacity
for subjective will, as a subject of individual choices, which are both irreducible and nontransferable—was crucial to an understanding of liberalism and
the Enlightenment inheritance. In *The Government of the Self and Others*,
Foucault returned to this question in a discussion of Immanuel Kant's *What
is Enlightenment*, where he suggested that despite the framework of self-
emancipation, the Kantian project had an ambiguous approach to internal
agency which facilitates and legitimizes the need for an external or outside
agency which acts to 'free' the subject, in Kant's case the Enlightened mon-
arch or, later, the French Revolution (Foucault 2010: 37–39). The call for the
self-emancipation of the subject thereby implicitly allows for the possibility
that those who have not emancipated themselves can be understood to lack
their own agential capacity for choosing freedom and to require development
through external agency to enable them to make better choices. Of most
importance for the analysis presented here is that Foucault emphasizes that,
for Kant, the external agency does not free the subject merely by removing
external barriers to freedom.

The barrier to the Enlightenment of the individual is considered to be an
internal or subjective one—the flaw of the subject is a matter of 'will' (Foucault 2010: 29). The lack of freedom is not due to external oppression or
material deprivation, but 'a sort of deficit in the relationship of autonomy to
oneself' (Foucault 2010: 33). The King of Prussia or the Revolution does not
act to free the subject in the formal terms of liberation or self-government,
but in enabling the subject to act according to reason and through enabling
reason to guide his choice-making. The fact that this is an inner problem
means that the lack of freedom is not a fixed, natural, or inevitable product,
and therefore introduces the possibility of transformation, but this framing
also insists that the subject cannot be freed merely by the action of others—
by ostensible or self-proclaimed 'liberators' (Foucault 2010: 34). Foucault is
keen to emphasize that Enlightenment as transformation/development is an
internal matter of enabling the subject to free itself—to govern itself through
reason—to use its faculties for reason in the correct way.

Therefore, for Foucault, the Enlightenment subject was always one which
was a potential subject of/for development understood as freedom in similar
terms to those articulated by neoliberal economic theorists and international
development agencies which emphasize the need to capacity- and capability-
build the individual subject today. Implicit within Enlightenment assumptions—hidden behind the autonomous subject—was a potential subject in
need of neoliberal governance: a subject which could establish the need for
societal intervention and which could set the limits to external transformation
or the resolution of societal problems through its own (lack of) develop-

ment—understood as internal capacities for self-governance, will, or adequate choice-making.[6] This framing is of vital importance to understand the discourse of 'development as freedom', and other similarly constructed neoliberal frameworks, which operate on the basis of the development of adaptive capacity, of self-realization, of empowerment, and of vulnerability and resilience from the perspective of the individual as the self-transformative actor or 'agent'.

Government is no longer conceived as wise management directing or controlling society as in the preliberal or premodern age of Machiavelli, nor is government based on developing society and calculative progress as in the age of the classical liberalism of modernity, where mass society and the nation-state meant that 'society must be defended' (see Foucault 2003; 2007). Under neoliberalism, for Foucault, the assumption is that the liberal world is reduced to work on the adaptive governance of the self. Sen's development of the capabilities approach to development fits squarely into this analysis. Sen critiques both the market-based liberal conception of the rational autonomous individual capable of assuming responsibility for its own development but also the state-based, top-down social democratic conception of the subject as passive and the object of social engineering projects of modernization. For Sen, the individual is the only agent of development, but the individual is constructed as a vulnerable subject (the focus of chapter 7 on vulnerability), needing to gain self-knowledge and self-reflexivity through being empowered by an external agency: the individual is thereby both the ends and the means of development as freedom.

DEVELOPMENT AFTER THE COLONIAL/POSTCOLONIAL PROBLEMATIC

At the centre of the shift from development as material progress to development as adaptive informational capacity is the problematization of the inner world of the subject. Rather than the assumption of *homo œconomicus*, the rational decision-maker, there is an emphasis on the importance of differentiated subjectivity: on superstition, culture, ethics, and irrationality to decision-making. As Sen argues, there is no evidence for the view that individuals engage in rational choice-making on the basis of the pursuit of rational self-interest. In his view, the liberal understanding that 'we live in a world of reasonably well-informed people acting intelligently in pursuit of their self-interests' is misplaced in a world where our intersubjective understandings and affectivities mean that it is the human subject itself which introduces difference and inequality into the analysis (Sen 1987: 17). Once there is no universal rational subject, but different rationalities, adaptive choice-making begins to open up as a sphere for understanding difference and for intervening on the basis of overcoming or ameliorating difference through capacity-building. As Sen notes:

> to attach importance to the agency aspect of each person does not entail ac-
> cepting whatever a person happens to value as being valuable. . . . Respecting
> the agency aspect points to the appropriateness of going beyond a person's
> well-being into his or her valuations, commitments, etc. but the necessity of
> assessing these valuations . . . is not eliminated. . . . [E]ven though 'the use of
> one's agency is, in an important sense, a matter for oneself to judge', the need
> for careful assessment of aims, objectives, allegiances, etc., and of the concep-
> tion of the good, may be important and exacting. (1987: 42)

The neoliberal critique of liberal rationalist economic assumptions, necessarily focuses on the internal life or inner life of the human subject. Their 'valuations, commitments, etc'. then become the object of analysis and intervention. The understanding of irrational outcomes of market competition is transferred from the study of capitalist social relations to the study of irrational (nonuniversalist) human motivations and understandings which become barriers to adaptive efficiency.

The crucial facet of this approach in economic theorizing, often called 'new-institutionalism' (see, for example, North 1990; 2005) is that differences in outcomes can be understood as products of poor information processing and thereby as subjective choices, rather than as structurally imposed outcomes (as we saw in chapter 3 on resilience). The important research focus is then the individual making the decisions or choices and the subjectively created institutional frameworks (formal and informal) determining or structuring these adaptive choices. This is a societal perspective which starts from the individual as a decision-maker and then works outward to understand why 'wrong' choices are made, rather than equipping the individual with a set of universal rational capacities and understanding the differences in outcomes as products of social and economic contexts and relationships. This perspective is much more individual-focused, but the individual subject is understood in isolation from their social and economic relations. Wrong or inefficient adaptive choices are understood first in terms of institutional blockages at the level of custom, ideology, and ideas and then in terms of the formal institutional blockages—the incentives and opportunities available to enable other choices. This problematization of the individual shares much with therapeutic approaches, which also work at the level of the individual (attempting to remove psychological blockages to making better choices) rather than at the level of social or economic relations.

As Foucault noted, the work of these neoliberal or new institutionalist theorists was not narrowly concerned with economic theory; the institutionalist approach was closely tied to psychological and sociological framings and drew on legal and historical problematics, raising 'a whole series of problems that are more historical and institutional than specifically economic, but which opened the way for very interesting research on the political-institutional framework of the development of capitalism, and from which the American neo-liberals benefited' (2008: 135). Of particular importance, for this chapter, is the impact of these ideas on United Nations development programmes and World Bank policy-making frameworks from the mid-1990s, which can be clearly traced in the influence of writers such as Douglass North and, of course, Sen.

I want to suggest that while new institutionalist approaches only became dominant after the end of the Cold War, their appearance, especially in the field of international relations, can be genealogically traced through the discourse of development as a defensive understanding of the gap between the promise of freedom and economic progress under the universalist teleological framing of liberal modernity and the limits to this telos in the lack of economic, social, and political progress and the failure to generalize liberal modes of government in the colonial and postcolonial world.

Colonialism was substantially politically challenged and put on the defensive only with World War I, which led to the rise of the discourses of universal rights of self-determination, articulated both by Vladimir Lenin, with the birth of the revolutionary Soviet Union, and by U.S. President Woodrow Wilson, with America's rise to world power and aspiration to weaken the European colonial powers. Once brought into the universalist liberal framework of understanding, the discourse of development was used to both legitimize and to negotiate the gradual withdrawal of colonial power. Given its clearest intellectual articulation in Lord Lugard's *Dual Mandate* (1923) British colonial domination was justified on the basis that the difference between the Western subject and the colonial subject was a question of culture and values—a problem of the inner subjective world—preventing economic and social development. Lugard was the first to articulate an institutionalist understanding of development, concerned as much with the inculcation of values and understanding through the export of political institutions of integration, as through economic progress itself. Development was conceived as the barrier to self-determination as much as the achievement of development was conceived as a justification for external rule, for it was through Western 'enlightened' knowledge and experience of transforming the external world that the colonial subject could be emancipated.

The discourse of development, of the *Dual Mandate*, serving both British imperial interests and the self-interest of the colonial subject, could be construed as a discourse of *Development as Freedom*, but one conceptually distinct from that articulated three-quarters of a century later by Sen. For the colonial mind, the cultural and moral incapacities of the colonial subject prevented development and therefore it was a civilizational task of transforming the subject to create the conditions for autonomy, for the emergence of the liberal subject—for freedom as self-determination. In Lugard's own words:

> As Roman imperialism laid the foundation of modern civilisation, and led the wild barbarians of these islands [Britain] along the path of progress, so in Africa today we are repaying the debt and bringing to the dark places of the earth, the abode of barbarism and cruelty, the torch of culture and progress. . . .
> If there is unrest, and a desire for independence, as in India and Egypt, it is because we have taught the values of liberty and freedom. . . . Their very discontent is a measure of their progress. (1923: 618).

As Foucault notes in his reflections upon Kant's 'What Is Enlightenment?', the Enlightenment project of civilizing those not enlightened enough to civilize themselves was seen to be the work of external agency. In order to be freed, the subject first had to be subjected—just as the civilized Romans had to subject the barbarian Britons. Of course, it was not surprising that the denial of liberal universalist understandings of the subject—explicit in colonial rule and the denial of formal liberal freedoms of self-rule and sovereign independence—should take a civilizational focus. Social and economic difference was used to justify the denial of political and legal equality and at the same time subordinated to universality through the assumption that the colonial power was capable of assisting the colonial subject in their journey toward development understood as a higher and more enlightened, 'modern' or 'liberal' existence.

The colonial discourse of development can, of course, be critically engaged with in the manner of Edward Said's, Foucault-inspired, groundbreaking framework of *Orientalism* (1995), as presupposing 'Western superiority and Oriental inferiority' (1995: 42). There can be little doubt that the birth of the Enlightenment brought with it a Eurocentric view of the world that was universalistic in its assumptions that differences would be progressively overcome through development (see also Burgess 1997; Todorova 1997; Wolff 1994). This understanding of progress or civilization as a universal teleology demarcating those states and societies which were more or less 'advanced', was based on the presupposition that the Enlightenment brought economic and social progress to the West and demonstrated a path which could be universally replicated through the enlightenment of the colonial subject through the external agency of colonial power.

However, what is missing in this framework is the distinct difference between the discourse of development under colonialism (and in much of the early postcolonial era) and the understanding of development under today's neoliberal assumptions. The colonial subject was not interpellated as a liberal subject, but a subject understood as lacking autonomy—the liberal subject had to be created in the case of the colonial 'exception', on the assumption that the subject could become a liberal and thereby an autonomous and self-governing subject. Here development was separated temporally and spatially from freedom. In the classical liberal modernist teleology, the liberal world would expand spatially as the external world progressed temporally toward freedom. There was a liberal teleology of progress, which was expressed in both spatial and temporal terms; in terms of a liberal 'inside' and a nonliberal 'outside', seen as shrinking with the progress of development. Development was the mechanism through which the world would be universalized; through which the gap between the liberal vision of the future and the realities of the present would be bridged.

The discourse of 'the West and the Rest' (Hall 2007), of the liberal and the colonial/postcolonial world, articulated the limits of liberalism as external, thereby giving an ontological content to development in terms of both spatiality and temporality. There could only be discourses of spatial and temporal differentiation with the understanding that the limits to liberal universalist frameworks of understanding were external ones. The key point to understand with regard to today's articulation of 'development as freedom' is that the bifurcation—both in spatial and temporal terms—between the West and the rest, has been obscured through a universalizing framework of adaptive capacities which internalizes rather than externalizes the limits of liberalism.

The internalizing of the understanding of limits, alleged to be a condition of our globalized and interconnected world, starts from the basis that we are all neoliberal subjects—that the world is a neoliberal world—but that differences are internally generated through our internal differentiation: through the fact that individuals make decisions and choices in complex, embedded, and often irrational ways. Rather than the lack of will—of subjective choice-making capacity—being the exception, explaining the contingent nature of spatial and temporal limits to universalizing progress, the lack or differentiated nature of adaptive capacity is the norm, explaining the necessary or inevitable existence of difference and inequality. Here we have a very different neoliberal universalism, one which universalizes the understanding of the vulnerable subject, in need of development understood in terms of adaptive capacities and capabilities. In this respect, development becomes a permanent project of self-development, of freeing the subject from their inner limitations. This project is necessarily inclusive because there is no longer any outside.

THE HUMAN-CENTRED FRAMEWORK OF ADAPTIVE CAPACITY

In Sen's 'agent-centred' world, there are no external universals and therefore there is no framework or yardstick for an external measurement of development. The transformative project of development is reduced down to that of enlarging individual agency understood as the adaptive choice-making capacity of the subject able to actively embrace change. Freedom now becomes an internal process of empowerment, one with no fixed measure of comparison and no fixed end or goal (the embrace of change presupposes no goal outside the individual). Where the colonial subject needed development for the fixed and universal goal of self-government as freedom, Sen's subject has an ongoing struggle for freedom in which the reasoning capacities of adaptation are both the means for freedom and the measure of freedom:

> Expansion of freedom is viewed, in this approach, both as the primary end and as the principal means of development. Development consists in the removal of various types of unfreedoms that leave people with little choice and little opportunity of exercising their reasoned agency. (Sen 1999: xii)

Individuals have to be freed from unfreedoms, which can take both material and immaterial or ideological forms. Where Sen goes beyond the framings of liberal modernity is that development and freedom can only be understood in relation to the inner adaptive capacities of the individual.

Development understood in terms of adaptive capacities and capabilities cannot be measured materially because these capacities are internal to the individual (or internal to the society or community which is the object of neoliberal concern). Capabilities cannot be measured in terms of surface outcomes: a society may be healthy or wealthy but still lack adaptive capabilities. This is because wealth may have stemmed from good fortune or specific characteristics, which cannot be sustained or cannot be replicated. The adaptive capabilities approach is not directly concerned with the material outcomes of development policies, nor is it directly concerned with the inputs provided to individuals. At the heart of the concern with adaptive capacity is the inner capability of individuals to choose freely what is in their own and their society's interests. It is the lifestyle choices, freely made, that count. As Nussbaum stresses: 'There is a huge moral difference between a policy that promotes health and one that promotes health capabilities—the latter not the former, honors the person's lifestyle choices' (2011: 26). The inculcation of adaptive capabilities is hostile to functionalist or utilitarian approaches, which would support paternalistic or coercive health interventions for societal ends. It is the process of individual choice-making that counts, not the social outcome. Both Sen and Nussbaum ascribe a high value to choice, and place it at the centre of their moral philosophical frameworks (see Nussbaum 2011).

The central point I wish to make here is not that development is degraded to a subjective level of the material resources which are considered necessary or desirable for the sustainability of poverty, maintaining the 'bare life' of the 'uninsured' (Duffield 2007), but that the subject and object of development—understood as adaptive capability- or capacity-building—is entirely internalized. Development is judged on the basis of the individual's use of 'reasoned agency'. Development is the project of giving the individual the choice-making capacity necessary to adapt efficiently—to become resilient—in today's globalized world. Development is the task of all stakeholders but can only be measured in the individual's inner achievement of 'resilience as freedom'. Here, freedom is a continuum, the goal of which is never reached as barriers or 'unfreedoms' to 'reasoned agency' can always reappear and can only be known post-hoc. Both development—the process of achieving freedom—and freedom itself are internal processes. This is why Sen talks of the 'expansion of freedom' never of the achievement of freedom.

The individual's 'freedom' is conceptually crucial for Sen and becomes the starting point, the means, and the end point for understanding human development in terms of adaptive capabilities:

> Societal arrangements, involving many institutions (the state, the market, the legal system, political parties, the media, public interest groups and public discussion forums, among others) are investigated in terms of their contribution to enhancing and guaranteeing the substantive freedoms of individuals, seen as active agents of change, rather than as passive recipients of dispensed benefits. (1999: xii–xiii)

If people are not exercising 'reasoned choice-making', then there is something wrong with the institutions of society and the inner world of opinions and beliefs. If choice-making is limited or unreasoned, then people lack freedom and development is necessary to act on the institutions that are blocking this process of free and reasoned choice-making. Unlike liberal framings—in which the interests of the subject are revealed through their preferences and choices, rather than problematized—choices are understood as '*adaptive*' products of individuals' lack of freedom, like the fox in the fable who calls the grapes sour after he finds that he cannot reach them (Nussbaum 2011: 54). As can be seen from discussions of data as development, governments are understood to be responsible for enabling the development of this reasoning capacity, not for the material provision of life's necessities to enable freedom as an assumed capacity for choice-making. In liberal discourse the provision of food and nutrition to the poor would be seen as a valuable step to enabling free choice-making; however, in the neoliberal discourse of adaptive capacities, the provision of food is no more an answer to famine than it is to a lack of nutrition because 'a policy that just doles out food to people rather than giving them choice in matters of nutrition is insufficiently respectful of their freedom' (Nussbaum 2011: 56).

We begin to see here that Sen's framework is doing a lot more than merely downplaying the need for material development or taking the social struggle out of the process of freeing individuals from oppression. Sen's framing of development in terms of the inculcation of individual capacities and capabilities takes the understanding of socioeconomic and political processes out of the framing of liberal modernity. There is no teleology of progress as an external measure of growth in human well-being, there is no universalist framing and there is no longer the understanding of the liberal subject—as either a rights- or an interest-bearing rational and autonomous actor.

For the capabilities approach to adaptive capacity, there is no such thing as the universal liberal subject, there are merely capacity differentials in choice-making that are constituted through the unfreedoms with which individuals are confronted. Freedom—adaptive choice-making capacity—has always to be expanded. This need for the expansion of freedom is as necessary for Western subjects as for postcolonial subjects. For Sen, there is no divide between the West and the Rest, no sphere of liberalism and sphere of the nonliberal or a-liberal. The contradictions of liberalism are not overcome externally—through the transformation of social relations—but internally through understanding material difference as a product of the adaptive (choice-making) individual—universalized precisely upon the basis of the differentiation of individuals as the irreducible choice-making agents/subjects of neoliberalism.

Sen, in his work, uses this view of the differentiated subject as irreducible agent to transform and overcome all liberal binaries based on the construction of legal or political collectivities. The starting point of the freedom of individual agency is at the centre of all his wide-ranging studies: whether it is deconstructing the idea of material equality (judged by an external measure of equal opportunities or resources or of equal outcomes) (Sen 1992); deconstructing the idea of collective identities (Sen 2006); deconstructing ideas of justice (on the basis that formal frameworks of politics and law cannot measure how individuals grow as choice-makers) (Sen 2009); or deconstructing material measures of development (Sen 1999). For Sen, there is no divide between the West and the non-West as there are no exclusive social or economic collectivities—the level of development in terms of GDP is no longer of decisive relevance, nor is the type of political regime in itself. There is no universal external yardstick available to give content to freedom in either the economic and social or the political and legal realms. The lack of freedom can exist as much in a wealthy liberal democracy as under any other society as the concern is not with an 'exclusionary' liberal modernist understanding of freedom. Any individual can become unfree if Sen's conception of 'the more inclusive idea of capability deprivation' is taken up (1999: 20).

In this conception, political freedom and market economic competition are to be valued because they help facilitate individual choice-making capacities and enable their expression, thereby enabling efficient adaption to changing circumstances. The assumption is that without development individuals will not be free, in the sense of no longer lacking the capabilities necessary for efficient adaptation. Here none of us are free from the need for development. Development is the process of altering the institutions that shape our capacities and capabilities for adaptive choices. In this understanding of freedom, there can be no assumption of originatory or universal autonomy and rationality, such as that underpinning social contract theorising: the mainstay of the political and legal subject of liberal modernity. To this '*arrangement-focused*' view, Sen counterposits a '*realization-focused* understanding of justice' (2009: 10). For Sen, justice, like development cannot be universal but only understood in terms of individual empowerment and adaptive capacity-building:

> The question to ask, then, is this, if the justice of what happens in a society depends on a combination of institutional features and actual behavioural characteristics, along with other influences that determine the social realizations, then is it possible to identify 'just' institutions for a society without making them contingent on actual behaviour[?] . . . Indeed, we have good reason for recognizing that the pursuit of *justice is partly a matter of the gradual formation of behaviour patterns*. (2009: 68, emphasis added)

Justice is not a matter of liberal institutional arrangements but about empowering or capability-building individuals; there is no abstract universalism but rather the recognition that 'realization' comes first. On the basis of injustice, or unfreedoms then justice (like development) becomes a process of realization 'aimed at guiding social choice toward social justice' (Sen 2009: 69). Justice aims at enlarging justice as freedom in the same way as development aims at enlarging development as freedom. Justice is a continuous process not a fixed and externally measurable end or goal.

ADAPTATION VS. FREEDOM OF CHOICE

For Sen, there are no external frames of reference. It is not liberal institutions or economic development that serve to gauge the problematic of the subject but the 'realization of the individual's capabilities'—this is an ongoing process not a measurement against a fixed point. Sen, in his work *The Idea of Justice*, is keen to highlight the importance of difference over universality— the embeddedness of the human subject—and in doing so he is happy quoting Gramsci:

> In acquiring one's conception of the world one always belongs to a particular grouping which is that of all the social elements which share the same mode of thinking and acting. We are all conformists of some conformism or other, always man-in-the-mass or collective man. (2009: 119)

Sen suggests that it is our social embeddedness which restricts our capacities for transition. That we need an 'anthropological way' (2009: 120, 121) of understanding the ways in which our subjectivities may constitute a barrier to the development of adaptive reasoning. He expands on how our 'local conventions of thought' (2009: 125) may limit our ability to reflect and to adapt and become resilient subjects; that individual and collective worldviews and understandings may be partial and one-sided. However, this is not just a call for more information or greater material equality. The key to Sen's perspective of development as freedom is adaptive capabilities. It is not instrumental outcomes per se, nor resource inputs, but the individual's 'capability to choose' (2009: 235).

It is vital to understand that 'capability to choose' is very different from the 'freedom to choose'. The later conception is that of classical liberalism, which assumes that freedom is all that is required for the rational autonomous subject. The former is the key to understanding Sen's neoliberal perspective. Sen disagrees with the liberal perspective, which assumes autonomy is freedom. For Sen, freedom is an ongoing process of empowering the individual; this empowerment is not measured in external outputs but internal processes of valuation and decision-making. It is not an outcome, not even a nonmaterial outcome, such as 'well-being' or 'happiness' (2009: 271). It is an internal outcome—it is a 'way of living' (2009: 273): a way of living that we conceptualise as resilience.

Sen's work, highlights how the neoliberal discourse of resilience, vulnerability, and adaptation reproduces the elitist theorizing of Plato in focusing on the inner world rather than the outer world. Sen, in a footnote, states:

> In seeing freedom in terms of the power to bring about the outcome one wants with reasoned assessment, there is, of course, the underlying question whether the person has had an adequate opportunity to reason about what she really wants. Indeed the opportunity of *reasoned assessment* cannot but be an important part of any substantive understanding of freedom. (2009: 301)

Sen is essentially seeking to measure the internal or moral life of the subject and arguing that this should be the actual object of policy-making and also the indirect means of measuring the extent of freedom. The internal capacities of individuals are revealed only in relation to the adaptive choices which they make, in their own understandings of their own needs and interests. Subjects that lack the adaptive capacities for resilience therefore are held to choose poorly, to reveal not their potential efficient adaptive capacities but merely their lack of freedom. Nussbaum stresses the distinction between this neoliberal assumption—that interests are not revealed in subject choices—vis-à-vis the liberal assumption that the subject is only a subject because they are rational choice-makers:

the Capabilities Approach is not based upon subjective preferences, although it takes preferences seriously. It argues strongly against preference-based approaches within development economics and within philosophy. It views preferences as often unreliable for political purposes. Only the most fully corrected informed-desire approaches play even a subsidiary role in political justification. (Nussbaum 2011: 80)

This very much follows the preliberal framing of Plato in *Gorgias*, when Socrates famously argued with Polus that tyrants lacked power because they lacked a true understanding of their ends, of what would do them good (Plato 1960: 35–39). In other words, the neoliberal subjects in need of development are not able to autonomously or rationally judge what is in their own interests in terms of the adaptive choices necessary for a fully resilient society. For Sen, the subject of development is one who lacks the capacity to answer the Socratic question: 'How should one live?' (Sen 1987: 2). For Sen, development—the task of good governance—is to enable individuals to answer this question correctly, in terms of the adaptive embrace of change. In fact, Sen turns back on Plato his assumption that there is no such thing as evil, merely ignorance, suggesting with regard to the parochial understanding of the Greeks, in their practice of infanticide, that even Plato suffered from a limited and narrow 'local' understanding of the world (2009: 404–7). People choosing to live badly—the limits of human reason—constitute the demand for and limit of adaptive governance, for development as freedom.

Where does this leave the human subject in Sen's thought? On one level the human subject is all that there is. The goal of policy-making is the enabling and the empowering of this subject—of enabling its adaptive capabilities and capacities. There is no goal beyond the human subject and no agent beyond the human subject and no measurement beyond the human subject. But the human subject does not set goals; the human subject has no agency and no measuring capacity itself. In adaptive capability-building the subject is denied its own capability as a subject. The human subject is the end to be achieved, through the process of development, justice, democracy, and so forth—the project of humanizing is the human. For Sen, as for Plato, the project is an internal one rather than an external one. As Foucault suggests, this focus on the inner life connects Platonic thought with Christian thought, similarly denying transformative agency (Foucault 2010: 359).

This shift to work on the inner self rather than the external world enables us to understand development as a process of freedom: as developing adaptive capacities rather than as material or political transformation. As Nussbaum argues, governments need to pay specific attention to the fluid and dynamic nature of an individual's *internal capabilities*, which can be best enhanced through education and physical and emotional health and support (2011: 21). Those who most need to be 'freed' are the poor and marginal who need 'enabling': those who lack the means to adapt; those who are vulnerable need to be empowered, capability-built, and secured through resilience (WRI 2008). Wherever there is a decision to be made, this is the nexus for interventionist/regulatory nexus of 'development' as internal adaptive capacity: how can this decision or this choice be better made? How can the institutions of governance help enable a better 'choice environment'? What capabilities do the poor and marginalized need to enable this choice? The human-centred logic of neoliberalism, so well-articulated by Sen, sets out a framework of understanding and of policy-making, which focuses on the internal life of individuals as shaped by the immediate context of family and child-rearing, especially the transition to the decision-making subject. The 2007 World Development Report, *Development and the Next Generation*, articulates the consequences:

> Decisions during the five youth transitions have the biggest long-term impacts on how human capital is kept safe, developed, and deployed: continuing to learn, starting to work, developing a family, and exercising citizenship. . . . Young people and their families make the decisions—but policies and institutions also affect the risks, the opportunities, and ultimately the outcomes. (World Bank 2006: 2)

Development as freedom means adaptive capability-building starts often with the young as a way of transforming society through reshaping their internal worlds. The report's discussion of how decision-making can be altered is quoted below:

> If death rates are the benchmark, young people are a healthy group: the average ten-year-old has a 97 percent chance to reach the age of twenty-five. Mortality is a misleading measure of youth health, however, because it does not reflect the behaviour that puts their health at risk later on. Youth is when people begin smoking, consuming alcohol and drugs, engaging in sex, and having more control over their diet and physical activity—behaviours that persist and affect their future health. . . . Because the (sometimes catastrophic) health consequences of these behaviours show up only later in life, they are much more difficult and expensive to treat than to prevent. But for many young people, the search for a stable identity, combined with short time horizons and limited information, encourages them to experiment with activities that put their health at risk. . . . Reducing risk-taking among youth requires that they have the information and the capacity to make and act on decisions. Policies can do much to help young people manage these risks, especially if they make young people more aware of the long-term consequences of their actions today. (World Bank 2006: 8)

The logic of the argument is that social and economic problems are the result of poor adaptive capacities or poor choice-making, especially by young people who lack the adaptive capacities for good choice-making. Development no longer takes the form of economic and social transformation but of capability-building: empowering the poor and marginal to make better choices and thereby to become more resilient to external threats and pressures, through 'bringing the least informed people and institutions up to the level of the most informed' (United Nations 2014: 8). Empowerment through access and use of data for more efficient and self-aware decision-making is increasingly at the top of the international development agenda. For the United Nations: 'Many people are excluded from the new world of data and information by language, poverty, lack of education, lack of technology infrastructure, remoteness or prejudice and discrimination' (United Nations 2014: 7). It is increasingly held that it is the 'data gap' (in terms of the access and use of information) that is the problem that development needs to solve to stop or reverse growing inequalities (United Nations 2014: 5).

In the deterministic approach of the neoliberal understanding, capability- and capacity-building can never start early enough, if every individual is to be fully empowered. Thus, one key focus on information as empowerment is in the role of parenting expertise to promote more positive cognitive and behavioural outcomes, as Nussbaum argues:

> Empirical studies show that early intervention is crucial, building the case for pre-school interventions and programs that partner with families . . . a great deal of human potential is being wasted by a failure to intervene early, both through programs designed to enhance future human being's health *in utero* and through programmes after birth. (2011: 194)

Once the focus upon human development is on the internal adaptive capacities of the individual, the understanding of problems of conflict or of a lack of development involves a retreat into the delicate understanding of the development not of the external world of economic and social products of human activity and labour but of the internal world of the human mind. According to Nussbaum, the development of '*basic capabilities*' is not a product of nature, not 'hardwired in the DNA', but rather is a product of human intervention and therefore for government policy-making to ensure the correct 'maternal nutrition and prenatal experience' (2011: 23). Once the problem is no longer the material circumstances, but the postcolonial subject's lack of freedom—their lack of capability to adapt efficiently to their circumstances—the neoliberal discourse of capacity-building infantalizes the postcolonial subject.

For capability theorists such as Nussbaum, this infantalization is clear in the fact that she argues that the capabilities approach can be applied to nonhuman animals as much as to humans. Once the rational capacity for choice-making is denied to the human political subject—as it necessarily is in all neoliberal approaches which argue that the political subject has to be constructed through governance interventions in societal processes—then there is no basis for liberal representative political and legal theory. Neoliberal governance practices cannot derive their legitimacy through representational theory that assumes universal rationality, such as contract theory, which assumes representational equality. Nussbaum, for example, explicitly argues that animals and other sentient beings with agency can be considered to be 'subjects of a political theory of justice, whether or not they are capable of understanding or assessing that theory' (Nussbaum 2011: 88, 157–63). The discourse of human development and of adaptive capacity- and capability-building, in assuming that the human subject is the source of problems of conflict and underdevelopment, inevitably end up in reducing the status of the subject. The internal gaze of neoliberal discourse ends up removing the subject itself not merely the importance of the material relations of its external world.

CONCLUSION

The postcolonial subject may be at the centre of the development discourse of adaptive capacities, but it is always this subject's lack of capability which is highlighted. This human-centred approach replicates that of Kant's understanding of the internal and individual nature of barriers to enlightenment. The lack of material development is read as evidence of the lack of the postcolonial subject's capabilities to efficiently adapt and to actively embrace change. In a globalized world, with access to information and resources, it appears that the postcolonial subject is exercising agency in choosing poorly and, in effect, is the object of its own subjection and lack of self-realization. The subject's difference or otherness is understood and confirmed by its world of economic and social inequalities. The fact that we accept the universal understanding of the autonomous liberal choice-making subject now becomes an apologia for difference rather than a call for its transcendence. The source of this difference is then located in the postcolonial subject itself, in the inner world of the poorly adaptive subject. The problems of development or the barriers to the eradication of difference are then searched for in terms of the difficulty of changing or transforming individual and collective decision-making processes and of enabling the transmission of self-knowledge and self-awareness through technological advances (as will be considered further in chapter 7 on vulnerability).

NOTES

1. United Nations Global Pulse Initiative Website can be found at http://www.unglobalpulse.org/.
2. The World Bank's OpenDRI Web pages can be found at https://www.gfdrr.org/opendri.

3. For information on the Data-Pop Alliance see http://www.datapopalliance.org/; and for the Rockefeller Foundation http://www.rockefellerfoundation.org/our-work/current-work/resilience.

4. For Marx, 1830 marked the turning point, from which point onward the science of political economy, which reached its highpoint with Ricardo, could only degenerate and become vulgarized:

> In France and England the bourgeoisie had conquered political power. Thenceforth, the class struggle, practically as well as theoretically, took on more and more outspoken and threatening forms. It sounded the knell of scientific bourgeois economy. It was thenceforth no longer a question, whether this theorem or that was true, but whether it was useful to capital or harmful, expedient or inexpedient, politically dangerous or not. In place of disinterested inquirers, there were hired prize-fighters; in place of genuine scientific research, the bad conscience and the evil intent of apologetic. (1954: 24–25)

5. Foucault argued that this was a practical as much as an intellectual project of constructing a 'critical ontology of ourselves, of present reality' (2010: 21): 'I shall thus characterize the philosophical ethos appropriate to the critical ontology of ourselves as a historico-practical test of the limits that we may go beyond, and thus as work carried out by ourselves upon ourselves as free beings' (1984: 8).

6. For Marx and Engels, the idealism of the Enlightenment perspective, which Foucault so correctly highlights and deploys as the basis of his critique of neoliberalism, was perceived to have been overcome through the materialist analysis of social relations and the emergence of a universal class which needed to transform these relations in order to emancipate itself: the industrial proletariat. Of course, if this collective agent of self-transformation were not to appear or if it was to suffer a historical class defeat rather than achieve its ultimate aims, then it would appear that it was the Enlightenment that both gave birth to and foretold the death of the 'human' as a self-realizing subject. The inability of humanity to give meaning to the world through the Enlightenment and therefore the shift to conceiving of itself and its meaning-creating subjectivity as the problem in need of resolution is, of course, acutely articulated by Nietzsche (see, in particular, 'Our Note of Interrogation', in *The Gay Science* 2006: 159–60).

Chapter Six

Adaptation

The War on Autonomy

Julian Reid

As we saw in chapter 4, while security has functioned historically as the major rationality for the subjection of populations to liberal governance, the rationality that governs that subjection is fast becoming that of resilience. As such the policy problematic of liberal regimes of governance is undergoing a global shift from that of how to secure the human to how to render it resilient. When policy-makers engage in the discourse of resilience they do so in terms which aim explicitly at preventing humans from conceiving danger as a phenomenon from which they might seek freedom from and even, in contrast, as that which they must now expose themselves to. This owes to the ways in which the modelling of neoliberal subjectivity reifies, as we also saw in chapter 4, its biological life as the domain of agency and governance. Life, biologically understood, is a difficult entity to secure. It has a habit of dying on you, undergoing change, eluding your grasp, and defying your will to control it. Not only is it difficult to secure, but the very attempt to secure it can, it is said, have deleterious effects on it. The more you try to secure it the worse you make it, even to the point of eventually killing it. Security is dangerous, paradoxically, because it defies the necessity of danger, preventing the necessary exposure to danger, without which the life of the neoliberal subject cannot grow and prosper. Since life, it is said, cannot be secured without destroying it, so the framing of the human in terms of its capacities for resilience functions to disqualify its capacities to claim or pursue security. Once the practice of freeing oneself from danger is rendered, as it is now a pathological disposition of humans, so the problem becomes not how to secure the human but how to enable it to outlive its proclivity for security: how to alter its disposition in relation with danger so that it construes danger not as something it might seek freedom from, but which it must live in exposure to. Resilient subjects are precisely these: subjects that have learnt the lesson of the dangers of security, in order to live out lives of permanent exposure to dangers that are not only beyond their abilities to overcome but necessary for the prosperity of their lives.

In this chapter, I want to pursue this aspect of the modelling of neoliberal subjectivity further, into the terrain of another concept and capacity, dear to the liberal tradition: that of autonomy, because an interconnected shift to that which we have already observed in the context of security applies with respect to the problem of autonomy. Traditionally, we are used to thinking about the liberal subject as the autonomous subject. By autonomous I mean a subject defined by its disconnection from other human beings, and a certain nonadaptivity or resistance to the will of others. Disconnection and non-adaptation were once understood as conditions of possibility within the liberal tradition. As Isaiah Berlin describes in his classic essay, 'Two Concepts of Liberty', the liberal wishes to be a subject, not an object; to be moved by reasons, by conscious purposes, which are his own, not by causes which affect him, as it were, from outside. He wishes to be somebody, not nobody; a doer—deciding, not being decided for, self-directed and not acted upon by external nature or by other men as if he were a thing, or an animal, or a slave incapable of playing a human role, that is, of conceiving goals and policies of his own and realizing them' (Berlin 1969: 131). In contrast with Berlin's classical vision, when liberals engage today in promoting the life of human beings, they do so in terms that aim at preventing us from conceiving our capacities to determine our own ways of life in freedom from others as a state to strive for and, in contrast, as a potential risk unto ourselves. Autonomy, it is said, equals a diminished capacity to connect with and adapt to others, and so to be autonomous has become conceived less as a condition to strive for, and more as a source of danger to oneself and the life of others. Exposed to the dangers on which its life is said to thrive, the neoliberal subject is nevertheless called upon to fend off the formation of anything like an autonomously determined way of life, on account of the risks said to be posed by autonomy to the sanctity of life. These, as we will see, are the paradoxical stakes of the contemporary and ongoing shift in discourses of governance and subjection characteristic of neoliberalism (Reid 2012b).

As with the pathologization of security under conditions of neoliberalism, so the pathologization of autonomy and subsequent valorization of adaptation has been fed by ideas and discourses deriving not just from outside of political science, but from beyond the social sciences strictly conceived. It is the life sciences that account for much of the thinking concerning the problematic nature of autonomy and importance of adaptation and connectivity as requisite capacities for the development of neoliberal subjectivity. The ongoing pathologization of autonomy began itself not in the political discourses of liberal practitioners or thinkers, but in the context of scientific studies of nonhuman living systems. To a certain extent the pathologization of autonomy follows from the pathologization of security and the shift to resilience. As we saw in chapter 4, ecology has played a powerful discursive role in enabling the rise of the latter concept. But the life science of biology has been equally important in shaping the critique of security within neoliberal discourse, as well as enabling the proliferation of ideas concerning the importance of adaptivity and correlate arguments for the diminishment of autonomy. Understanding how neoliberalism has problematized and pathologized autonomy requires contextualizing that move within the deeper scientific problematization and pathologization of security that we began to trace in the emergence of resilience as a key marker of neoliberal subjectivity in chapter 4.

CONNECTING WITH DANGER

If it is ecology that has been most vocal in pronouncing the finitude of human life, the fragility of its dependence on the biosphere, and its consequent exposure to the dangers of ecological catastrophe, then it is molecular biology that has been most powerful in expressing faith in the potential of the human to be able to go on living and thriving in a context of such finitude, vulnerability, and potential catastrophe. Indeed the very idea of life as a phenomenon of finitude, vulnerability, and exposure to danger has been valorized by molecular biology throughout its history as a condition of possibility, rather than an obstacle, for human development. To the extent that theories of economic growth have, over the last ten years, tended to merge and benefit from their intersection with theories of how life grows and develops, at the molecular level, through exposure to danger, especially (see Cooper 2008: 45–50). I am not going to recount the history of molecular biology here. There are already some excellent such histories written (Hayles 1999; Kay 2000; 1993). But significantly it was in the 1990s that influential molecular biologists such as Stuart Kaufman, for example, began to argue that living systems cannot, by definition, be secured from dangers, because their very capacity to go on living depends, fundamentally, not on their *freedom from* danger but on their *exposure to* danger. The evolutionary development of living systems, it is said, is dictated by the fundamental law of 'emergence', which requires that they engage in a continual process of exposure to danger even to the point of potential catastrophe (Kauffman 2000: 157). Without that exposure to danger, living systems cannot evolve, and those that do attempt to disconnect themselves from their dangers will lose touch with their own powers of propagation, to the extent that they will finally wither away and die. As we saw in the last chapter, the concept of resilience refers to the 'buffer capacities' of living systems, their ability to 'absorb perturbations' or the 'magnitude of disturbance that can be absorbed before a living system changes its structure by changing the variables and processes that control behaviour' (Adger 2000: 349). Living systems develop not on account of their ability to secure themselves from dangers, but through their abilities to absorb the perturbations that occur on account of their necessary exposure to them. Exposure to danger is a constitutive process in the development of living systems, and thus their problem is never how to secure themselves from it, but how to develop the resilience which enables them to absorb the perturbations, disturbances, and changes in their structure which occur in the process of their exposure to it. And so it is said, once the human is conceived in accordance with the laws that determine the life of other living systems, must it develop the selfsame capacities for resilience, enabling it to avoid the temptation to secure itself from danger, exposing itself in contrast to danger, while learning how to absorb the perturbations that occur to it in that process of exposure.

Such accounts of how life 'connects with danger' in the biological domain may well hold some validity. A political scientist is not necessarily well-positioned to question knowledge and laws deriving from the life sciences as they are applied to the study of the interface between biological species and the ecological systems with which they are said to coevolve. My concerns are for what happens when such frameworks are transferred to the human world of peoples, because the results are debasing, not least in terms of the relation of the subject to the regime that governs it. For it is on account of such an errant transfer of assumptions that the subject is denied the capacity to demand of the regime that governs it that it provide it with freedom from the dangers that it perceives as threatening it. This element of the terms of legitimation of modern regimes of political power has, of course, been fundamental historically, and yet is now in process of rapid erosion, on account of the influence of these scientific ways of thinking about life and danger within liberal discourse. The neoliberal subject is not a subject which can conceive the possibility of securing itself from its dangers, but one which believes in the necessity of life as a permanent struggle of adaptation to dangers. Indeed the neoliberal subject accepts the dangerousness of the world it lives in as a condition for partaking of that world and accepts the necessity of the injunction to change itself in correspondence with the dangers now presupposed as endemic. Building neoliberal subjects involves the deliberate disabling of the aspirations to security that peoples might otherwise nurture and replacing them with adaptive ones. Resilient subjects are subjects that have accepted the imperative not to secure themselves from the dangers they are faced with, but instead adapt repeatedly to their conditions, in the same manner that living systems, right down to weed species, adapt continually to the changing topographies of danger they encounter.

Once exposure to danger becomes a condition of possibility for the subject, so the question posed of the subject is no longer can you exercise freedom in securing yourself from the dangers that you are faced with in living, but can you construe your freedom to live in the form of exposure to danger? Can you, in other words, as Michel Foucault detailed in his *Birth of Biopolitics* lectures, accept and rise to the neoliberal injunction to 'live dangerously'? At its classical origins, however, and as Foucault detailed in those lectures, the liberal subject, while living on the basis of an understanding as to the necessity of and even stimulus of danger, nevertheless aspired to achieve a condition of 'least exposure to danger' (Foucault 2008: 66). Its exercise of freedom was problematized as a dangerous activity, one that could have dangerous effects, for itself and those affected by it, but which could nevertheless be governed in a way that enabled it to minimize the extent of its exposure. Thus was the emergence and development of liberalism as an art of governance conditioned by what Foucault described as 'strategies of security' (2008: 65). In contrast, the displacement of the very aspiration to security and shift to a discourse of resilience tells us a lot about the changing nature of liberalism, indicating as it does the extent to which danger has become that which the subject is governed to seek, rather than minimize its exposure to. It is no longer a question of how to secure freedoms for the subject in the condition of their potential to become dangerous, either to the individual or the collective, but how the subject might practice freedom so that it achieves exposure to danger on behalf of itself and that population to which it contributes, because danger is productive of life, individually and collectively.

The submission of the subject to this injunction to expose itself to danger requires, however, its prior subjection to the biological lore that, in spite of its humanism and discourses on freedom, actually underwrites liberalism. In other words its conception of relations between its own life and the dangers it encounters must conform to the demands of liberalism's biological account of life. Since biological life cannot free itself from danger without endangering its very capacities to go on living, so must the liberal subject accept the same terms and conditions for the exercise of its political freedom in determining its way of life. Its freedom to determine the way in which it lives must be circumscribed by the biological imperative to expose itself to danger. It cannot live a life premised upon achieving freedom from dangers, because to do that is to oppose the laws of life as determined by biological necessity. Recognizing the constitutive function of the biological lore of liberalism means we can only obtain a superficial grasp of how neoliberal regimes of governance achieve this dual debasement of the subject's capacities for security and autonomy by focusing on the so-called economic dimensions of the injunction to live dangerously. There has been much talk, since the publication of *The Birth of Biopolitics* lecture series, of how Foucault abandoned his prior ideas of how to approach liberalism and gave himself up to a quasi-Marxist understanding of liberalism as a regime of economy. To the contrary, Foucault's discussions of neoliberalism do not suggest 'that the security sought by biopolitics is mediated by a fundamentally economistic horizon of thought' (Kiersey 2009: 365). The incitement of the subject to 'engage in risk taking and entrepeneurialism' is only explicable in context of the biologization of the subject that liberalism is founded on, and subsequently, the shift in thinking concerning how biological life profits in the world through a continual process of exposure to danger. Even if there is not much reference to the 'biopolitics' of the liberal subject as such, in *The Birth of Biopolitics*, and in spite of the focus on the economic rationalization of liberal governance in these lectures, it is clear, to me at least, that his understanding of liberal economy remains committed to revealing its biopoliticization. In no sense can 'the inculcation of an entrepreneurial spirit' (Kiersey 2009: 381) be considered the end of biopolitical governance. To think so is to fail to grasp the depth of the concept of biopolitics. The incitement of the liberal subject to take risks is the means by which the life of that subject, it is assumed, can be saved from itself and all that threatens its prosperity. It is life, not economy abstractly understood, that mediates the horizons of liberal thought and practice, for Foucault. The concept of economy is merely one powerful and important discourse within which liberal understandings of the nature of life, as such, operates.

Of course it is true that discourses and practices of resilience are intimately tied to neoliberal economic policies, dedicated to developing and protecting neoliberal institutions, including markets and market-based forms of governance. But the legitimacy of these institutions, practices of governance, and subjectivities depend on the virtues they are said to possess vis-à-vis the welfare of the life of the liberal subject. This is precisely why, for example, and as we saw in chapter 4 to some extent, the development of neoliberal economic policies has become so vigorously correlated with strategies for disaster management.

REVALORIZING SECURITY

In an interview given toward the end of his life, titled 'Risks of Security', Foucault reflected on some of the political problems that pertain to the concept of security (2001). It has, of course, become commonplace in critical traditions of international relations (IR) to denounce the political functions that the concept of security has played in constituting the discursive conditions that modern regimes of power require in order to legitimate their governance of particular populations. Discourses of security cannot function without constituting a differentiation between an inside and outside. The offer and undertaking to secure something or someone always assumes the delineation of another that is the threat or obstacle to such security. These problems with the discourse of security are well rehearsed in IR by now (see Burke 2007). Foucauldian analytics of liberal regimes of power have contributed much through their more acute examination of how the discourse of security has functioned to dislocate liberal claims to be concerned with promoting freedom, demonstrating why liberalism is better understood as dedicated to determining the conditions for the securitization of human freedom rather than to simply enunciating the imperative to be free (see Dillon 2007). In contrast with much of the critical analysis inspired by him since his death, however, Foucault engages in this interview with both the concepts of security and freedom in a more politically creative manner. Rather than seeking to condemn the concept of security, denouncing it as a merely ideological or discursive construct, or exploring how it functions as a prop for power, Foucault asks the question of what security might yet become. How it might be reconceptualized to perform different functions to those it has done to date. As such Foucault does not see the claims of political authorities to provide security to their populations as necessarily mendacious or merely discursive. Nor does he, as has become so popular for Foucauldian theorists of security, seek to detach political imaginaries and projects from the concept of security as such by simply stripping it from our political lexicons, as if political power would automatically become something less exclusive and violent in its operations. Indeed he warns here against buying into influential 'antisecurity arguments' that perform their rejection of the concept of security 'in a somewhat simplistic manner' (2001: 366).[1] Instead Foucault asks a different kind of question in seeking to constitute a different kind of politics of security, one whereby the nexus of relations between security and freedom might be given a new affirmative twist. Specifically, he asks how we might constitute a new concept and practice of security, one which will perform a double function to 'free us from dangers *and* from situations that tend to debase or to subjugate us . . . a security that opens the way to richer, more numerous, more diverse, and more flexible relationships with ourselves and others, all the while assuring each of us real autonomy' (2001: 366).

In this sense, and right at the end of his life, Foucault was well-positioned to see into the future development of liberalism, so geared as it has become, to denying subjects the abilities to seek freedom from danger, demand it from their regimes, as well as making us suffer an ever increasing diminishment of autonomy. These arguments do not make Foucault a liberal. He was not interested in returning to some outdated model or discourse of liberalism, as if it was just a question and problem of remembering what historical texts said about a true nature of liberalism that has somehow been forgotten or lost. He understood and saw the ways in which liberal discourses on security, freedom, and autonomy could not possibly survive or legitimate themselves in context of their being underwritten by biopolitical rationalities concerned fundamentally with the collateral effects of practices of security, freedom, and autonomy for the life of the subject. Set in context of the earlier arguments Foucault had made concerning the importance of discourses and practices of security, freedom, and danger for the legitimization of liberal regimes of governance in particular (2007), and against the backdrop of how Foucauldian theorizations of security have themselves laid siege to the concept, this was, rather, a significant attempt to move beyond liberalism, in two fashions. First, it demonstrates, as we might expect of Foucault, a cognizance of the potential, and in his own period, actualized dangers, that problematizations of security have posed to the life of the subjects secured, insofar as strategies of security, in their provision of freedom from danger, can also serve to diminish the autonomy of the subjects being secured, by turning them into dependents. But second, it demonstrates an acceptance of the political potentialities of regimes of security organized around problematics of dangers and the practice of freeing subjects from them. In other words his approach to security, here, presupposes the actuality of dangers from which subjects, in spite of the degradations and subjugations that they risk in accepting it, can demand provision of 'freedom from'. Danger, here, is not assumed to be a merely discursive construct, functioning to shape the subject of security in legitimization of the regimes that govern it. Instead it is assumed to be an irreducible problematic that subjects may 'expect' their regimes to provide them with freedom from (2001: 366). Instead of simply denouncing security, Foucault is calling into question the particularity of regimes of security that in their practices of security 'impose a determined way of life that subjugates individuals' (2001: 369). The problem here, then, is not with security as such, but with the particularity of those regimes that subjugate in the process of securing. But crucially he insists on the contingency of the relation between the ways in which a given regime provides subjects with freedom from dangers and the means by which, in the very process of doing so, it risks subjugating them, diminishing their autonomy.

The question he implores us to ask, then, is not simply how to free subjects from apparatuses of security in the manner asked by 'antisecurity' forms of political critique, but how subjects can demand and receive security without conceding the conditions for their own subjugation.[2] The problematic of danger to which the concept and practice of security is ineluctably tied is, therefore, doubled here. Foucault is demanding an apparatus of security that can free subjects from the range of dangers that are posed to their biological life and well-being in combination with freedom from the dangers which that apparatus poses to the subject's capacities to determine its own 'way of life'. Indeed the more or less classical conceptual distinction drawn here by Foucault between the *biological life* of the subject and its capacity for an autonomously determined *way of life* is crucial. He considers the securitization of biological life to be depoliticizing only insofar as it encroaches upon the capacities of subjects to determine their own ways of life. The problem isn't therefore how to render contingent the relation between biological life and security, through what Sergei Prozorov simplistically calls a 'refusal of care' (2007: 59–67), but how to forge a politics via which subjects can demand that their regimes provide them with security for their biological life, without, in the process, enabling those regimes to encroach upon that terrain of subjectivity in which autonomy is exercised and through which ways of life are determined. The relationship between autonomy and security is poorly conceived, in other words, as an either/or. Indeed Foucault is clearly also posing the issue of that terrain of autonomy in terms of its security. How to enable the existence of regimes whose legitimacy depends on their capacities to secure the biological life of subjects while also rendering secure the autonomy of the selfsame subjects from those regimes? As of danger, so is the problematic of security doubled, here, then. The renovation of the political subject depends on its capacities, he argues, not to subtract itself from problematics of danger and security, nor simply to offer 'an attitude of indifference' (Prozorov 2007: 63) to biopolitical regimes, but to perform these parallel and deeply interconnected double moves, to each of which the modern political problematic, par excellence, of life, is indispensable as foundation and horizon.[3]

Foucault posed the possibility of such a different apparatus of security only in the form of a question: What would it involve, or how to go about, creating such an apparatus? He berated the absence of, while calling for, innovative thinking and practices through which to develop it. For inspiration as to the possibility of such conceptual and practical innovation, he drew on a range of historical projects that in their own times and places functioned, he argued, as sources for such 'conceptual efforts', and gave special mention to Keynes and Beveridge, whose ideas had been so influential in determining the once novel apparatuses of security that the states of Western Europe deployed in relation with their subject populations in his own time (Foucault 2001: 371). In our time, of course, the political problem of security is quite different, given the considerable changes in the practices and conceptualizations of security that have occurred. The contemporary, and increasingly global, hegemony of neoliberalism has in many ways fed off the kind of critique of the problem of dependency and valorization of autonomy that Foucault articulated in this late interview. Foucault's aims were not, of course, to advocate a neoliberal approach to the problem of security, but to avoid the blackmail of a choice between regimes that offer security to the biological life of their subjects combined with diminishment of their autonomy on the one hand, and those that withdraw security of biological life in exchange for a supposed (but, in actuality faux) increase in the autonomy of subjects, on the other. The intolerability of that choice means, he argued, that we need to conceive a subject capable of demanding both security from the dangers posed to its biological life and well-being combined with security from the danger of the loss of its autonomy. In spite of the time that has elapsed since Foucault originally posed this problem, and in spite of the changes in the problematization of security that have occurred under the duress of neoliberalism, the question remains, therefore, a very contemporary one, which is why his work remains so useful.

The problem, then, is neither security as such, nor life as such. Life, like security, is not an ontological category, but an expression of changing regimes of practices that are historical and political in formation. Life can be expressed, thought, constituted, and indeed *secured*, in many different ways. Discourses on life are subject to revision, on account of our capacities for political engagement with the problematic of life and what distinguishes it. The struggle with liberalism requires us not simply to reject but to contest its biologized account of life. Liberalism, as Foucault and other theorists of liberal biopolitics have demonstrated, understands life, fundamentally, in biological terms (Esposito 2008; Foucault 2007; 2008). Liberal governance was biopoliticized from its beginnings: its object of governance that of the biological life of human beings and its governmental practices guided by what it can know of that biology. In governing so, it has served to reduce the life of the human to its biological capacities, conceiving the human in the form of 'the biohuman' (Dillon and Reid 2009; Reid 2009; 2010). Once human life is conceived in terms of the properties and capacities it is said to possess on account of its biological existence, suborning the life of the individual to its species existence, so the human is constituted as the biohuman. As a political project the hegemony of neoliberalism depends not on its capacities to secure the biohuman, because no such subject of security in actuality exists. It depends in contrast on its capacities to govern us as subjects that fail to conceive of our life potentials in anything more than merely biologized terms. It requires making us believe, in other words, in the impossibility of being anything more than biohuman subjects. For liberalism to legitimate itself the horizons that determine our ways of living must be successfully biologized, which is why the political discourses of global politics are so replete today with values deriving from biological sources. The contemporary valorization of capacities for resilience and adaptive capacity, nationally and internationally, are symptomatic expressions of this strategy.

This is not to argue against the security of life, or to argue against the human as such. On the contrary, it is to revive the question of the human and its relation to life, and conditions of its security, anew. Can we conceive a subject that seeks and achieves security for its biological life without sacrificing its human capacity for autonomously determined ways of living? A subject the properties and capacities of which are not governed by what can be known of its species' existence. I believe this is an absolutely fundamental question for us to answer in order to tackle the problem of security as it was articulated by Foucault in the interview 'Risks of Security'. Equally, to pose the problem of the subject of security in this way is not to inaugurate yet another attempt, via a reading of Foucault and others, to 'move beyond subjectivity' as if subjectivity were merely just another problem to be solved by theoreticians (as implied, for example, by Edkins and Pin-Fat 1999: 9). This is not to subscribe to simplistic arguments against 'the subject.' Just as Foucault did not subscribe to such simplistic arguments or naïve anti-humanisms (see Han-Pile 2010). It is to pose the political problem of the hegemony of biohuman accounts of subjectivity, which, on account of the power and influence of liberal discourses and practices globally, have come to colonize contemporary political imaginaries. Likewise, it is to invest in the potential and political necessity of alternative accounts of subjectivity capable of constituting peoples in ways, collectively, that might enable them to emancipate themselves from regimes whose authority rests on the discursive power of the biohuman subject. Human subjectivity and biohuman subjectivity are not the same, and to attempt to move beyond the former is to risk suborning oneself to the latter.

Renovating the human subject in ways that can enable it to speak back to and contest the biohuman requires not, therefore, that we simply argue against the conjugation of its life with security, but develop the means to diversify our understanding of what its life comprises, recognize the conflict that exists between that life when read biologically and when read in terms of the human capacity for autonomy. Once we do so, the problematic of how to secure its life becomes that much more complicated as well as urgent. Not only because the life being secured is doubled and at conflict with itself, but because, nowadays, the life of the biohuman, regimes of liberal governance preach, is antinomous to the very practice of security. As we have seen, security in Foucault's account in 'Risks of Security', fundamentally, in spite of the many different ways in which it can be construed, presupposes *freedom from danger*. The sources of danger may change in constitution of different regimes of security but once the practice of achieving freedom from what we regard as endangering us disappears so we are no longer doing, in effect, security. And as we have also already seen, Foucault, in his reformulation of the problematic of security in this interview, doubles the problem of danger. It is not enough, he argues, to construe security in terms of the freedom of the biological life of the human from danger, we also have to account for the reformulation of the problematic of what is dangerous to the human, when the apparatuses which provide its biological life with security degrade and subjugate it, threatening its capacities for autonomously determined ways of life. But what if biological life itself cannot, by definition, be freed from the dangers that threaten it? Or what if, more accurately put, the practice of attempting to provide the biological life of the human with freedom from that which endangers it paradoxically functions to destroy it? This is precisely what is now argued by regimes of liberal governance that preach the necessity of peoples giving up on the possibility of achieving freedom from the dangers that threaten them and embrace, instead, the potential to be had in *exposing themselves to danger*. Thus security itself, in terms of the practice of freeing life from danger, is increasingly pathologized by liberal regimes of governance as that which endangers life.

Here we reach the crux of the contemporary problematic of the politics of security, a crux at which we are also faced by the limits of Foucault's approach to that problematic in 'Risks of Security' and his wider works, and on account of which we will have to modify the terms in which that problematic was posed by him. For it is not the case that, today, we can say, simply, that subjects are degraded insofar as their capacities for autonomy are diminished by regimes that subjugate them through the provision of security to their biological life, and that we therefore need to secure the terrain of autonomy on which subjectivity grows from the hold which any given security apparatus achieves over that terrain on account of its interventions upon the biological life of its subjects. Nor is it simply the case that the provision of security to the biological life of subjects has been withdrawn in return for disingenuous offers of an increase in their autonomy, and that we therefore need to renovate the capacity of subjects to demand provision of security to biological life from regimes that govern through the discourse of autonomy. Today the terms and conditions of subjection are different. For once the subject is conceived in biohuman terms—the account of the freedom of which it is capable so thoroughly determined by what can be known of its biology—the very aspiration to free oneself from danger, becomes deemed as dangerous, not because to be provided freedom from danger would risk diminishing the autonomy of the subject, but because exposure to danger is now conceived as fundamental to the potentiality of its biological life to grow and prosper. The biohuman subject must be prepared to undergo permanent exposure to danger, because it understands such an exposed relation with danger as fundamental for its capacities to profit from the world.

Likewise, while liberalism may traditionally have espoused the value of autonomy for the subject, understood in terms of its capacities to determine its own way of life free from interference by others (Berlin 1969; Geuss 2005), so we must also address the reproblematization of autonomy that is occurring on account of the biologization of the liberal subject and the consequent emergence of discourses on, and practices surrounding, the biohuman. For once the subject is conceived in biohuman terms so autonomy is construed less as a state of being that subjects may strive for and protect than as a sign of incapacity from which they must be saved. One of the most significant, if as yet still underexplored mechanisms by which liberalism has learnt to produce and govern the human as biohuman is via its cross-fertilisation of concepts and theorems concerning how biological life evolves from the life sciences (Cooper 2008; Walker and Cooper 2011). And so, the political authorization for such problematizations of autonomy derives from what the life sciences tell us about the dangers of autonomy. Living systems evolve and prosper, it is said, not on account of their capacities to achieve autonomy from other systems, but to connect and adapt to them (Kauffman 2000). Thus now, given that the power to connect and adapt is said to be fundamental to the evolutionary development of all forms of biological life, so liberalism, in the throes of its biologized account of the subject, has come to reconceptualize the freedom of the subject in terms that radically undercut its traditional espousals of the value of autonomy. Freedom, under conditions of belief in the biohuman, is construed not as *autonomy from others*, but capacity to *connect to others*. Far from preaching the value of autonomy from others, liberalism has come to espouse an account of the subject predicated on its radical interconnectivity with others. Indeed, to be regarded as autonomous is to be regarded not just as unfree, but as dangerous, for autonomous individuals and peoples are said to be risks unto themselves and to others. One can encounter this reproblematization of autonomy as dangerous occurring within IR[4] as well as every other form of science concerned with the necessary conditions for healthy subjectivity, not least among which is psychology (see, for example, Pinto 2004).

CONSTITUTING ADAPTIVITY

Consider, for example, the underside of liberal theories of IR addressing the implications of the global interconnectivity wrought by the information revolution. Social, political, and governmental transformations are presumed to have followed from the utilization of the new extents and qualities of connectivity produced by this techno-scientific revolution. From it a new kind of people is said to have emerged: the 'Connected' (Katz 1997). The Connected represent, no less, it is said, than 'the transformation of sociability' itself (Castells 2006: 11). The Connected are more social than any other historical social formation. Never has there been a people, we are told, more social, that has had more friends and contacts, or been more socially and politically active, than the Connected (Castells 2006). Facebook is its niche space of habitat. The Connected are more skilled than any other historical social formation. Never has there been a people more competent analytically, emotionally, and imaginatively (Rosenau 2002: 278). Learning is its way of life. Never has there been a people, we are also told, more informed. For the Connected are more informationally rich than any other historical social formation. Networking is its source of power. But this is not simply a sociological phenomenon demanding new mapping practices from ethnographers. The 'skills revolution' formative of the Connected has initiated what one leading liberal in IR hails as no less than 'a major transformation of the global structures that govern world affairs' (Rosenau 2002: 279). A transformation in governmental vision and practice has followed as old ideals of world government have been outmoded by new concepts of global liberal governance that aspire to generate order 'from below', through the networking practices, information sharing, and learning activities of the Connected, thus obviating the need for recourse to the institutions and practices of state sovereignty. Thus is the Connected said to constitute the social basis for a new self-organizing system of IR that is gradually transforming existing institutions and practices of state sovereignty into something more benign and beneficent to human life on a global scale.

From where does this evolutionary account of the nature and power of connectivity, and its fortunate coincidence with information technologies, derive? To understand why proponents of global liberal governance like Rosenau think about connectivity in the terms that they do, and to understand why they are thus able to accord a status of neutrality to technologies that enable connectivity, requires understanding the development of the theory of connectivity and its importance for research into learning and the discovery of the functions of information which have, since the 1940s, gradually transformed the ways in which the life sciences understand the conditions for human evolution. It would then require us to engage with the vexed and convoluted processes of epistemic transfer via which that theorization has impacted on the social sciences, including IR. I cannot recount that entire history here, or cover the multiple literatures in which connectivity has been thus theorised in IR. To simplify, since the 1940s and the scientific event that was the advent of cybernetics, it has been said that, of all known species, humans are superiorly endowed with the capacity to learn. 'The human species', the founder of cybernetics, Norbert Wiener, argued, 'is strong only insofar as it takes advantage of the innate adaptive, learning faculties that its physiological structure makes possible' (1954: 58). The interior complexity of the physiological structure of the human, the immense interconnectivity of its body, enabling an unrivaled corporeal capacity for the circulation of information, in turn is said to have constituted the conditions in which it is able to forge connections with members of its own species as well as with other species, and learn, specifically through the exchange of information with them and the environments in which they coevolve, how best to adapt in the great struggle for life that shapes existence in the biosphere. Wiener's gambit was, as is now well recorded, that if humans could create a machine distinguished with a physiological structure as connected as the one that they themselves possessed, they would in effect be able to create a machine endowed with those powers of learning which had hitherto made them superior (Hayles 1999; Galison 1994; Kay 2000). The digital machine was the first of these. A machine consisting in a 'sequence of switching devices in which the opening of a later switch depends on the action of precise combinations of earlier switches leading into it, which open at the same time' and which thus corresponded in function to the physiological 'transmission of impulses across layers of syntactic connections' through which messages of information traverse human bodies and via which the human learns (Wiener 1954: 64).

Wiener's achievement in constructing the first digital device is not in itself to be diminished. This was a new form of techno-scientific know-how, based on remarkable insights into the centrality of information and connectivity for the processes of learning through which living systems, the human chief among them, adapt and evolve biologically. It was a know-how that proved to be of significance, because of the technological spin-offs it spawned, for the military capacities of the allied powers to win the war against fascism in Europe and beyond (Galison 1994). It is a know-how that has made possible the immense further discoveries and advances in science and technology that have impacted so widely on the organization of liberal democracies in the decades since World War II, as well as empowered the liberal way of war that has enabled the global hegemony of liberal democratic states worldwide since the end of the Cold War (Dillon and Reid 2009). But it was also a know-how that entailed a dramatically revised account of what it is to be human as well as what it is to be a living thing (Hayles 1999; Kay 2000). And given, especially, the now widespread manifestation and exploitation of the ability to create machines said to display the same forms of intelligence possessed by humans as well as all other living systems, it was a knowledge which effectively collapsed conceptual distinctions between human, living, and technological systems (Haraway 1991). A posthuman knowledge which undercut modernist understandings of the specificity of the human, its claims to distinction from other species, as well as the political categories on which human specificity was previously constructed in the sciences and beyond.

It is precisely this revised and radically posthuman ontology that we encounter at work in liberal theories of IR championing the emancipatory potentials of the Connected. Rosenau's work in IR is a case in point, but while following cybernetic narratives by arguing for an understanding of the Connected as the culmination of a 'continuous process of evolution' (1998: 33), Rosenau also cautions his readership as to its nonteleological character. The emergence of the Connected, he warns,

> does not just suddenly happen. Circumstances have to be suitable, people have to be amenable to collective decisions being made, tendencies towards organization have to develop, habits of cooperation have to evolve, and a readiness

not to impede the processes of emergence and evolution has to persist. (1998: 33)

This is an important qualification. Alerting us as it does to the political dimensions of connectivity, which is to say its fundamentally nonneutral qualities. The amenability of people, the development of tendencies, the production of habits, the removal of impositions, the persistence of evolutionary processes already in train; all of these, we are told quite explicitly, are prerequisite conditions for the emergence of the Connected. What these qualifiers tell us, of course, is that the advance of the Connected does not depend, simply, on the unfolding of inherently natural processes of evolutionary improvement, but on the securing of strategic conditions in which the connected can be constituted. If the Connected exists its emergence has to be explained politically, not simply with reference to forces of nature or biological evolution.

What are those conditions and by what methods are we to suppose that they might be secured? As Foucault has taught us, the liberal project is distinguished by its faith in the ability to correlate the political development of humanity with a knowledge of its biological properties and capacities. Its success has depended, ever since its inception in the early modern era, on strategies to promote those tendencies and habits within governed populations that accord with the 'biological destiny of the species', and that has required the deployment of all manner of what Foucault called technologies of security (2007: 10–11). Since the eighteenth century, for example, the 'technologies of security' deployed by liberal regimes have been concerned with promoting biopolitical tendencies and habits for and of 'circulation' (Foucault 2007: 16–17). Today they are as concerned with promoting tendencies and habits of connectivity. Connectivity, like that of circulation, is thus a fundamentally biopolitical attribute of populations (Dillon and Reid 2009: 57–58). The information technologies that enable us to connect more and better, be they mobile phones, laptop computers, or iPods, are far from neutral. They are all complexly enfolded within technologies of security that, rather than being used by humans to increase natural propensities and desires, are deployed to constitute humans with specific tendencies and habits. As Martin Heidegger also taught us, technology is never merely an instrument that humans use; it is a way of enframing the human as a thing that both uses and can be made use of, specifically made use of as a thing that in its utilizing practices is useful for securing a technologized order of utilizing things (Heidegger 1977; see also Dillon 1996). The enframing of the connected repeats the same maneuver. For here is a subject that in order to realize its capacities for connectivity has to be taught how to be connective. As Rosenau's qualifications makes clear, the connected does not merely use information technologies; it requires technologies of security to constitute the connective habits and tendencies that will subject it to the lore of connectivity from which information technologies derive their utility. For the Connected to emerge subjects must be amenable to connectivity as such. Where they are not, or when they contest connectivity, they will require transforming, and if not transformable then removing, if necessary, with violence, force and war (Dillon and Reid 2009; Reid 2006a). Either way disconnected and autonomous peoples must be made into connected and dependent ones.

Different formations of disconnectivity demand different strategies and modes of engagement. There is the 'Disconnected' one can transform through establishing and promoting connectivity itself. Knock a hole in the wall of a slum, install a computer kiosk within it, allow the children of that slum to use it freely, and so the theory goes, you transform the Disconnected into the Connected, without recourse to physical force, law, or military violence (Mitra 2005; Mitra and Rana 2001). But there is also the Disconnected that refuses the connection and by dint of which refusal demands either violent transformation or annihilation. Thomas P. M. Barnett, adviser in the United States to the Office of the Secretary of Defence (OSD), and a leading advocate of the liberal way of war, describes how there exists today a global divide between a 'Functioning Core' of connected peoples and a 'Nonintegrating Gap' of disconnected ones (Barnett 2009: 429–31). But the disconnection that Barnett describes is not merely technological, nor can it be measured along an axis determined by analytical, emotional, or imaginational variables. For it is, he argues, peoples disconnected from the 'rules' that define the organization of life within the liberal core, that by dint of that failure, 'demand attention from U.S. military forces' (Kennelly 2003: 17). As Barnett argues, 'disconnectedness defines dangers. If you're looking for instability and threats to the functioning of the international system and the global economy, you're looking at this Nonintegrating Gap. That's where you're going to find the transnational terrorist networks. That's where their interior lines of communication are found' (Kennelly 2003: 18).

It is a fact, however, that many of the major, supposedly most dangerous and violent enemies of the so-called Functioning Core today are themselves deeply connected. The current conflict in Syria is said to be the most socially mediated war to date (Lynch, Freelon, and Aday 2014). Members of the Islamic State in Iraq and Levant (ISIS), the rebel jihadist group which has grown out of al-Qaeda's actions in Iraq, are documented as being especially connected, making widespread use, as they do, of social media platforms such as Facebook and Twitter, to connect with whoever wishes to follow or friend them (Carter, Maher, and Neumann 2014). These fighters and enemies of the Functioning Core are sharing the desire for and practice of connectivity that supposedly defines neoliberal subjectivity while going to war with neoliberal regimes, contesting their power in the name of Islam. It is a fact, of course, that ISIS has recruited heavily from the Functioning Core itself—

many of its soldiers are so-called foreign fighters (Carter, Maher, and Neumann 2014). And, in a sense, the engagement in connectivity of this group demonstrates its relative nonautonomy from the very forms of power it desires to contest. The use of social media by ISIS is already rebounding on it, undermining its own cause. Using off the shelf network-analysis software, public, private, and academic bodies are mining Facebook and Twitter for social and political information on the group that in the past would have been considered military grade intelligence. In other words the connectivity of this group feeds into the Pentagon's desire to integrate enemies with a view to suborning them.

There is a fear and anxiety that characterizes the reactions of neoliberal regimes to these politically Islamic insurgencies, born of the will to subdue them, control and striate them, governing the ways in which they will turn out, the political forms that will result, and so on, to ensure their liberalization. That is entirely predictable. But as problematic is the anxiety of the European left to make historical and political sense of these still nascent projects before they have had sufficient autonomy to develop their own imaginaries and become according to their own potentialities. That, too, is a phenomenon of liberal governance. The social mediation of these revolts has already been so heavy; they have been networked before they have been able to properly begin. How would Mao's Long March have turned out in a context of social media self-broadcasting and coverage? Such socially mediated insurgencies have little prospect of success in context of their complicity with neoliberal strategies of connectivity.

CONCLUSION

In addressing the contemporary problematic of security one is no longer, then, faced with the form of blackmail that Foucault was concerned with thinking beyond in the early 1980s. It is no longer the question of how the subject might claim security from the dangers posed at its biological life along with security from the subjugations and degradations that develop out of its reliance on the regimes that do the security provision. The problematic is how to conceive freedom from danger as a political aspiration, capacity, and potential practice in the face of the fact that we are governed by regimes that declare that our growth and prosperity in the world consists in our necessary and continuous exposure to danger. Likewise it is how to reclaim the political value and capacity of autonomy from regimes that declare connectivity and the absence of autonomy as necessary conditions for our health and governability as subjects. In other words the problematic today is not simply how to conjugate security and autonomy anew, but how to stake out a subject position from which we can reconstitute both these practices given their contemporary and dual denigration. Voices from within IR calling for the further dismantling of the sign of security because it is 'the supreme concept of bourgeois society and the fundamental thematic of liberalism' (Neocleous 2008: 186) miss the point. Calling for a new politics to take us 'beyond security' (Burke 2007) does little to solve the problem; indeed it obfuscates the very nature of the problem, which is that liberalism itself is outgrowing its traditional correlation of life with security, and locating new discursive foundations for its biopolitics. The longstanding critique of the discourse of autonomy in liberalism will also have to be rethought inter alia with this task.

Rather than read Foucault with a view to ossifying already essentialized post-structuralist positions with regard to demands to move 'beyond the subject', escape biopolitics, dismantle security, or deconstruct humanity, this chapter has sought to pursue the question of how the subject might be reinvented—so that it can contest the limits and conditions of liberal imaginaries on some of the terrains which liberalism holds most dear: life, humanity, security, freedom, and autonomy. We get nowhere politically by simply attempting to condemn concepts. The doubly political and philosophical problem is how to reinvent them, by breathing new life into them (Deleuze and Guattari 1999: 1534). The question of how to reinvent the subject is, when opened up to inquiry via a more properly Foucauldian methodology, a question not of how to refuse the care for life via which biopolitical regimes facilitate subjection, but to rethink the relations of the subject to its life differently, with a view to being able to reconstitute practices of freedom and security, so that it might recover a more fundamentally human capacity for autonomy. Once we recognize the contingency of the debasement of practices of freedom and security that follow from the biologization of the human on which the liberal project proceeds, based on the demand to constitute the human as 'biohuman', so we create for ourselves the capacity to recover human powers of autonomy, a power otherwise denied to us on the basis of the dangers that autonomy supposedly poses for us, individually and collectively. As we have sought to explore, this is not merely a theoretical problematique. We live in an age when the practice of security, that is to say aspiring to and achieving freedom from danger, is increasingly pathologized by liberal regimes of governance, and in which the governability of subjects, collectively and individually, is said to depend, in contrast, on their exposure to danger. Contesting the global injunction to give up on aspirations for security and rethink freedom as exposure to danger requires a subject capable of seeing itself as something more than merely biological material, a subject whose humanity resides in its freedom to secure itself from the dangers that it encounters both in living and in being so secured. As Foucault's late works serve to remind us, we are a long way still from achieving such a human form of subjectivity.

NOTES

1. The simplicity of 'antisecurity' arguments might be compared thus with the simplicity of 'antiwar' arguments, which likewise presuppose that war can simply be condemned. The point, especially when thinking from Foucauldian grounds, is not to condemn war, but to reconceptualize war, as well as discover the minoritorian forms that war has, can, and does still take. Foucault's own late works, as well as that of others influenced by him, entail a significant interrogation of what I have called the counterstrategic tradition (see Reid 2006a and Reid 2006b).

2. There is an important difference here, then, between the problematization of apparatuses of security as elaborated by Foucault and that pursued by Giorgio Agamben, via a very partial reading of Foucault, whose assumed task is that of freeing 'living beings' from the apparatuses in which they are, as subjects, captured (see, especially, Agamben 2009: 12–15).

3. Prozorov's argument for 'indifference' as condition of resistance to biopolitical regimes would be much better argued via Baudrillard than Foucault. See especially my account of Baudrillard's theorization of indifference as strategy of resistance to biopower (Reid 2006a: 62–81).

4. 'Eradicating disconnectedness is the defining security task of our age, as well as a supreme moral cause in the cases of those who suffer it against their will' (Barnett 2009: 429).

III

Vulnerability

Chapter Seven

The Self-Construction of Vulnerability

David Chandler

As we have seen in the chapters on resilience and adaptation, neoliberal discourse starts with the irreducible choice-making individual and then works up to reconstruct the world as one made of poor-choices and under-standings. The world is produced through our own knowledge and informa-tion capacities and vulnerabilities (or incapacities) and therefore one that we bear responsibility for. However, the pluralization of access to, and forms of, knowing and consequent behavioural choices means that there is no shared world that we can all relate to; in effect, different individuals and commu-nities create their our own multiple and differentiated worlds of risk, devel-opment, and security, which to some extent may be overlapping, depending on the question of concern and the level of analysis. We are held to assemble, construct, and contribute to the appearances of the world as individuals, bearing responsibility for our lifestyle choices, but also presumed to create our worlds as families or communities, which are often seen to have generat-ed or reinforced environmental or societal problems such as poor parenting or crime. Collectivities and societies are also held responsible for the creation of their worlds at the level of states, with problematic national cultures or state-society relations preventing access to and use of adequate information, and at the global level, where the whole of humanity faces the problems of anthropomorphic global warming or the effects of global financial crisis, understood as products of poor information handling and decision-making.

The worlds through which the neoliberal subject is interpellated are es-sentially worlds of vulnerability. Vulnerable subjects are problematic or even dangerous subjects. The ascription of vulnerability suggests that the subject lacks the rational information-processing and choice-making capacities re-quired of it. Denise Polit and Cheryl Beck, in a medical practice context, define vulnerability in terms of 'being incapable of giving informed consent' or 'at the high risk of unintended side-effects' (Polit and Beck 2004). This draws out the distinction between vulnerability as an internal attribute, in relation to the capacity to make reasoned choices, and vulnerability as a product of objective circumstances or susceptibilities (see further, Kottow 2002). The shift from understanding vulnerability as a product of objective or structural context and understanding vulnerability as a subjective question of understanding and awareness is forcefully highlighted in questions of development and disaster risk reduction that have been at the top of the international agenda since the United Nations 2005 Hyogo Framework for Action and the high level discussions preparing for the Post-2015 Framework for Disaster Risk Reduction adopted by UN Member States in Sendai, Japan, in March 2015.

Whereas traditional responses to disasters saw them as external or exogenous factors ('acts of God'), which societies and individuals took little responsibility for causing, new frameworks of disaster risk reduction increasingly understand disasters as endogenous processes—products of state and society decisions and behaviours (UNISDR 2014: xv). Different societies and communities are thus understood to bear responsibility for their levels of awareness of potential problems (both natural and man-made) and for developing the necessary multilevel capacities to plan for and cope with risks and shocks. With disaster risk reduction increasingly built into all levels of policy-making both domestically and internationally, understandings of vulnerability have grown exponentially alongside the recognition that vulnerabilities take many different forms: in terms of awareness of, access to, and use of information, and the capacities for adaptive behaviour necessitated by multiple and overlapping risks. Where resilient communities are held to be able to have the capacities to be aware of and to adapt to risks and threats, vulnerable communities are seen to lack these capacities and thereby to put lives and development possibilities at risk.

In the shift to understanding development, security, and disasters in frameworks of neoliberal vulnerability, the world is pluralized in ways which increasingly tend to blame 'vulnerable' communities for their own shortcomings in how information and knowledge is accessed and used, and that thereby seek to empower these communities through providing the self-awareness of 'vulnerability and capacity assessments' (UNISDR 2014: 59) and the 'use of knowledge, innovation and education to build a culture of safety and resilience at all levels' (UNISDR 2014: 87).

In neoliberal discourse, the focus is always upon the knowledge and understanding of the vulnerable; the importance of these choice-making and behavioural capacities, of course, vary and indeed become greater in today's world, where it is held that both ecological and technological threats and risks have magnified. In a globalized and rapidly changing world, attributes that may not have constituted vulnerabilities may become so, once the importance of efficient adaptation to new risks and threats becomes greater. In this way, the problems of the world in which we act demonstrate our vulnerabilities in terms of choice-making capacities. How individuals and communities can overcome vulnerabilities and learn to process information to become self-aware and to govern themselves more reflexively is the problematic of neoliberalism.

In the chapter on adaptation (chapter 5), I described how adaptive capacity was understood to be a subjective characteristic that could be inculcated by environmental choice-making and data enablement, making it possible for the subject to free itself from the 'unfreedoms' preventing the efficient adaptation to change. This chapter considers in more detail how the barriers to change have been reinterpreted as problems existing at the subjective and cognitive level of the processing of information, rather than at the level of the structures of our social relations. The key to the subjectivization of the limits of liberalism has been the shift to the importance of cognitive processes, clearly articulated in the sphere of IR since the end of the 1980s. It was this shift toward subjective processes of decision-making (whose consequences were considered in chapter 5) that constructed the discursive grounds upon which the problematization of the human subject could become central to neoliberal understandings from the late 1990s onward. This, it is argued, is implicit within sociological constructivist understandings that dissolve exogenous structures of social relations into endogenous intersubjective processes of the self-production of differentiated worlds.

This chapter charts the problematization of subjectivity and the construction of problems in terms of vulnerable subjects, analyzing how this shift has been reflected through three conceptually distinct and chronologically distinguishable stages[1]: the early 1990s view that liberal transformation would be universalized with the Cold War victory of liberal ideals and the spread of new global norms of good governance; the mid- to late-1990s view that barriers to the promotion of social and economic transformation could be understood as the product of state or elite self-interests; and the neoliberal perspective, dominant since, that the promotion of security and development necessarily involves much deeper and more extensive external assistance in order to enable the subject to efficiently process information, if necessary, through transforming social institutions and societal practices.

Through charting the shifts putting the vulnerable subject at the centre of social explanation, this chapter seeks to highlight the problems inherent in neoliberal discourses that emphasize the importance of subjective agency, behavioural choices, and cultural communicative and informational frameworks of understanding. However, it should be noted that this framework of starting from the presupposition of difference, problematizing the vulnerable human subject, is a universal one: the gaze of neoliberalism constructs all problems as having their 'root cause' in vulnerabilities (UN 2004: 96). Thus international questions of security and development are reinterpreted in terms of potentially dangerous vulnerable communities, just as domestic problems are constructed through the problematization of those who are interpellated as bad parents, criminals, the unemployed, the obese, smokers, and so forth.

The neoliberal interpellation of vulnerable subjects as the 'root cause' of and, in fact, constitutive of the social, economic, or environmental problems, being addressed by governance interventions to inculcate resilience, has already been touched upon in the analysis of discourses of societal resilience and development as adaptive capacity-building (addressed in chapters 1, 3, and 5). As will be seen below, the discourses of resilience and adaptation are entirely imbricated within those of vulnerability, where it is often understood that appeals to reason, through health information or public engagement, can no longer be effective if people lack the capacities and capabilities to govern themselves according to neoliberal reason.

The discursive construction of subject-centred worlds, at the heart of the neoliberal problematic, dissolves or removes the external world as an object that potentially brings us together. This construction of self-produced or subject-centred worlds of experience and understanding puts the emphasis upon the choice-making capacities of the subject (discussed in chapter 5) and seeks to explain the world from the basis of the way information is accessed and processed, rather than to explain our thoughts and understandings on the basis of our external world. Explaining and seeking to address problems from the starting point of the individual agent, or their subjective processes, produces a world that appears highly differentiated. The internalized understandings of neoliberalism then operate to frame this differentiated world as a product of different, distinct and overlapping endogenous processes, which can apparently explain the differences and inequalities in the world of appearances. This world of appearances is then reproduced as a world of differential vulnerablities. Rather than social and economic relations producing vulnerable and marginalized subjects, neoliberal discourse inverses previous understandings to posit social and economic problems as symptoms or consequences of poor informational choices by vulnerable subjects. The problematic of vulnerability thereby becomes a problem of subjectivization rather than an external problem of the world.

In this framing, the differentiated appearances of the world: the vast structural inequalities across continents, regions, states, and societies become reinscribed as evidence of the distinctiveness of the differences of subjective adaptive capacities and capabilities. However, this focus on human difference is not described in the traditional or old institutional language of race but understood in the neutral terms of data empowerment, self-reflectivity, and the role of social and cultural institutions and networks. Like resilience, vulnerability is not a fixed category of understanding but a relative one: in a world of change and difference, vulnerabilities are different and changing. In the neoliberal framing, as we produce our world and confront the problems of change, our differential vulnerabilities are revealed. In this way, globalization is held to increase differentials rather than to bring us together, as some cultures are held to be more vulnerable to change and find it harder to adapt than others (North, Wallis, and Weingast 2009: 12). The construction of a segmented and differentiated world is a far cry from earlier social constructivist assumptions of global civil society and constructions of the world as a 'global neighbourhood' in the 1990s (CGG 1995). However, by focusing on the role of sociological institutionalism or social constructivism in the understanding of agency and societal change since the early 1990s, this chapter highlights how the vulnerable subject has moved to the centre of our explanations of the problems of the international sphere.

THE CHALLENGE TO UNIVERSALISM

At the end of the Cold War, the resolution of problems of the international sphere—for example, in relation to conflict or the overcoming of international economic inequalities—become increasingly conceptualized in terms of the international diffusion of global liberal norms, of human rights, the rule of law, and good governance (for example, Carothers 2004; McFaul 2004; Thomas 2011; Youngs 2002). In the era of liberal internationalism, it was assumed that as the Cold War divisions and barriers were removed, the universal, 'natural' liberal subject would be revealed, leading to shared understandings of governance and the construction of a global community. While it was accepted that formal state and interstate institutions would take time to adapt to these changes, it was thought that global norms of understanding would constitute a framework in which this formal transition would be eased and facilitated. Norms are generally understood as shared meanings or expectations with regard to the standards of appropriate and acceptable behaviour.[2] The study of liberal global or universal norms and their diffusion entered the mainstream of international relations theory with the constructivist understanding that state interests and identities were heavily influenced through intersubjective engagement within the international sphere itself. From the early-1990s onward, it was argued that as the world became more globalized, states increasingly shared the standards of behaviour ascribed to progressive liberal norms (Finnemore 1996a).

In the academic discourses of the 1990s, theoretical work on the diffusion of liberal norms was understood to be successfully challenging and overcoming the universalist rationalist framings of the international sphere. The classical liberal, or rationalist, framework of subjects as atomized autonomous self-interested actors was dominant in the discipline of international relations during the Cold War period.[3] Constructivist agent-centred theorists inversed this understanding of the international sphere, asserting that states' understandings of their own interests and identities were socially—intersubjectively—constructed: that states coconstituted themselves and the international sphere through their collective interaction (Wendt 1992). Exogenous factors and relations were removed—the structuring of the international sphere was the product of states' own intersubjective choices and interactions. This framing freed states from the external or exogenous structural constraints of rationalism, allowing a much more agent-centred understanding, in which ideational factors, rather than material constraints, played a major role in the understanding of international change. Within this context, work on liberal norms and their diffusion became an important area of international academic and policy concern (for a good overview, see Cortell and Davis 2000).

To analyse the development of sociological subject-based theorizing in international relations it is necessary to draw out how the discourse of liberal norm promotion gradually morphed into a neoliberal, or agent-centred, understanding that makes vulnerable or less capable subjects the key to understanding the problems of the world from conflict, to underdevelopment and catastrophic disasters. This understanding of vulnerability as ineffective adaptive capacity is one which argues that incapacities lie in understanding and information-processing. A precondition for understanding vulnerability as a subjective capability was the assumption that there was no external or structural limit to agential choice-making.

The focus on the problematic agency of the vulnerable was the product of a three-stage process, outlined below, in which sociological, constructivist, agency-based approaches shifted focus from the closed framing of intersubjective engagement in the international sphere, in which actors were understood to be collectively self-constituting—freed from the structural constraints of exogenous interests—to the frameworks of knowledge reproduction within states and societies held to be resistant to neoliberal understandings of adaptive change. Thus neoliberal understandings became dominant in international relations through the development and application of endogenous agency-based approaches to the international sphere and the transfer of their application to the domestic level of the vulnerable or 'failing' state. The focus on culture, social interactions, and information access and use within postconflict or postcolonial states facilitated the problematization of these states and their populations as vulnerable. In this way, neoliberal approaches reproduced and gave new life to previously discredited endogenous frameworks of understanding, which have historically been used to explain and rationalize gross inequalities of treatment on the basis of apparently inherent cultural and societal distinctions.

In removing exogenous structural or material constraints, the constructivist or sociological institutionalist gaze understands problems of risk management, conflict, or social and economic inequality through the reproduction of ideational choices, rather than as reflecting material economic or sociopolitical structural constraints (Checkel 1998; see also, Hay 2006; Peters 2005: 107–22; Scott 2008). These choices are seen as problematic cultural and informational barriers which necessitate much more intrusive modes of assistance in order to empower and enable vulnerable populations held to lack the capacity to make adaptive choices for themselves.[4] This understanding of the barriers to the promotion of good governance and adaptive behaviours either operates as an apologia for existing social relations and inequalities or as the rationale for external projects of social engineering and behavioural change in order to 'civilize' or 'empower' societies to free them from their allegedly self-imposed ignorance and backwardness.

SOCIAL CONSTRUCTIVISM

In the wake of the unexpected and unpredicted collapse of the Soviet Union, agency-based, subjective ideational approaches were advanced as a counter to earlier rationalist and structural materialist perspectives, which were now held to be unable to theorize transformational change (see, for example, Barnett 2008; Jackson and Sorensen 2010: 159–80; Reus-Smit 2001). The sociological perspective (see Wendt 1992; 1999) both built on and challenged Cold War understandings of the extension of democratic norms and rights protections as a reflection of shared, preformed, rational economic interests (Katzenstein 1996b: 528). Where international relations theorists analysed shared normative understandings or the role of institutions in shaping behaviour, they tended to treat agreements on shared democratic norms (such as those emerging from the Helsinki process of the Organisation for Security and Co-operation, the Council of Europe, or the European Commission) merely as external constraints to action (for example, Keohane 1989; Krasner 1983).

Constructivist approaches built upon this earlier work through challenging its underlying rationalist approach, and so freed the operation and development of agential choice from its material ties (Katzenstein 1996a; Kowert and Legro 1996). Social constructivism, by contrast, sought to emphasize the social environment in which states interacted and through which they constructed their self-identities and their perceptions of policy and governance needs (Katzenstein 1996a: 4). The emphasis on the international social context rather than exogenous social and political relations imposed a different understanding of the choices states as agents made in terms of liberal norms: one that emphasized the importance of global or international 'norms, identity and culture'.

Through working backward, by process-tracing, theorists sought to establish how norms had both 'constitutive effects' in the intersubjective construction of actor understandings and behaviour as well as 'regulative' effects describing 'collective expectations for proper behaviour', including domestic behaviour (Katzenstein 1996a: 5; see also Giddens 1984; Berger and Luck-mann 1991). This framework emphasized the importance of transformative agency and ideas at the international level: reflecting upon 'how structures of constructed meaning, embodied in norms or identities, affect what states do' (Finnemore 1996b: 157; Jepperson, Wendt and Katzenstein 1996: 66).

The two crucial grounding assumptions for this 'first generation' of social constructivist theorizing were: first, that there was an increasingly global social environment influencing states' attitudes toward democratic norms; and, second, that it was through analyzing intersubjective interaction and engagement within this environment that the diffusion of governance prac-tices could be understood (Katzenstein 1996a: 26). Attention was thereby drawn to the ease of accessing, communicating, and processing knowledge as a way of explaining liberalizing shifts toward shared global norms that ap-peared not to fit traditional power- or interest-based understandings of government rationality or interests. The transitions of the Soviet bloc and the ending of apartheid in South Africa in the early 1990s seemed to offer strong evidence that subjective and communicative factors were much more impor-tant than material or structural understandings of fixed interests (for example, Black 1999; Harrison 2004; Thomas 2001). The importance given to the agential social construction of meanings, practices, and behaviours in the international sphere reflected a fundamental shift in the study of international relations, which had previously understood the international sphere to be distinct from domestic society precisely because of a lack of shared meanings or interests (for overview, see Bull 1977).

While 'first generation' agency-based theorists often stated that the fact that interests were socially constructed did not make them unimportant, the success of constructivism was based on the understanding that declarations of domestic, state, or national 'interests' could no longer be taken as 'natural' or 'given'. If the structuring ideological interests of Soviet states in their opposition to liberal democracy could seemingly collapse overnight, it was clear that no claim of legitimate interest could withstand the sociological 'interpretivist' critique of rationalism (for example, Hollis and Smith 1990). In this framework, resistance to democratic or human rights norms on the basis of collectivist 'Asian values' was roundly dismissed as illegitimate (for example, Donnelly 1998: 131–35; Parekh 2000; Sen 1997). The prioritizing of international 'sociological' norms over discourses of exogenous state interests was understood as a radical, critical stance toward the traditional framings of the state in international relations theorizing, and this assessment was rarely questioned as the sociological turn to theorizing agential choice became part of the policy and academic mainstream as the 1990s progressed.

AGENCY AND COMMUNICATIVE NORMS

The 'second wave' of social constructivist thinking on communicative knowledge, which developed in the mid- to late-1990s, raised the barrier of problematic agency. However, this was not yet the agency of the vulnerable subject held to lack adequate capacities to adapt to change. Here the barriers to adapting to the new order of global governance were understood to be the rational product of self-interest. Particular emphasis was placed upon the problematic agency of select non-Western state elites, while the understanding of positive or progressive agency shifted to largely Western, nonstate norm entrepreneurs. Martha Finnemore and Kathryn Sikkink developed a model of a 'norm life cycle', stressing the role of policy experts and networks of nonstate actors in the emergence of governance norms and in establishing their broad acceptance: in setting off 'norm cascades' (Finnemore and Sikkink 1998: 902–4). This framework relied on an alternative understanding of a nonatomistic, communicative, rationality, heavily influenced by the work of Jürgen Habermas (see Brown 1994).

This endogenous framing of an emerging and inclusive international society assumed that all state regimes or actors were equally capable of engaging in the communicative global realm and had the rational (and moral) capabilities to choose to follow these emerging liberal global norms.[5] Finnemore and Sikkink referred to the development of 'world time', as increased global interdependence and the spread of communication and transportation links led to an increasing global interconnectedness. This increased connectedness, they suggested, had not just led to the 'homogenization of global norms' but also to the 'speed of normative change' and the success of 'norm entrepreneurs' in their rapid 'cascading' of global norms (Finnemore and Sikkink 1998: 909). It was the intensity of global communicative interaction that enabled liberal norms to spread through persuasion rather than coercion.

Under these assumptions, intersubjective engagement or communicative action enabled the spread of norms as local and parochial understandings become transformed into universal, shared liberal understandings of good governance (Habermas 1997). It was upon this basis that globalization was seen to bring actors into dialogue in ways which enabled global liberal norms to diffuse (see, for example, the World Bank publication, Martinsson 2011). The actions of any state elites, in blocking or opposing liberal reforms, were therefore held to be a product of their illegitimate, mistaken, criminal, or short-sighted perceptions of their self-interests.[6] Despite the condemnation or criminalization of these actions, the agency of blocking state elites was seen as a product of bounded but rational self-interest rather than a vulnerability stemming from a lack of capacity.

Marking the highpoint of liberal internationalist assumptions of an imminent global society with shared, global, liberal frameworks of understanding,

Keck and Sikkink's influential book *Activists beyond Borders* argued that to diffuse liberal understandings of good governance and human rights these illegitimate state-based or interest-based barriers to communicative interaction needed to be removed. These barriers were understood, along similar lines to Habermas; the limit to the diffusion of necessary open and adaptive understandings was the unwillingness of actors to engage in communicative reason (for example, Habermas 1996). For many constructivist theorists, the focus was less on the U.S. resistance to the spread of liberal democratic norms than the alleged reluctance of leaders of non-Western states, which were perceived as being most hostile because they had the most to lose from no longer being able to hide behind the 'impunity' claimed despite their unelected or nondemocratic hold on power (for example, Robertson 1999).

The overcoming of barriers, seen to be at the level of state government resistance, was the work of the 'boomerang effect', which allowed the spread of liberal norms as international actors 'removed the blockage' of the narrow interest-based action of repressive regimes, 'prying open space' for domestic civil society actors which were bearers of these global liberal aspirations (Keck and Sikkink 1998: 12–13):

> Voices that are suppressed in their own countries may find that networks can project and amplify their concerns into an international arena, which in turn can echo back into their own countries . . . networks open channels for bringing alternative visions and information into international debate. . . . At the core of network activity is the production, exchange and strategic use of information. (Keck and Sikkink 1998: x)

In this discourse, all that was needed was the removal of narrow interest blockages of entrenched power elites and the freeing of the agency of the universal rational liberal subject. This framing was perhaps most exemplified by those advocating international intervention in the breakup of Yugoslavia, particularly in the Bosnia War (1992–1995), which was one of the key foreign policy focuses of the mid-1990s. It was held that international interveners were acting in the support of local civil-society actors in seeking to preserve multicultural Bosnia against the machinations of unrepresentative nationalist elites, who were acting in their own narrow and criminal interests (for example, Burg 1997; Fine 1996; Kaldor 1999). Once international intervention had removed the nationalist leaders from power, through prosecutions for war crimes and the oversight of free and fair postwar democratic elections, it was assumed that the population of Bosnia would express their support for universal liberal norms in voting for nonnationalist political representatives.[7]

In the 1990s, the spread of liberal norms was understood on the basis that there were no insuperable barriers to an inclusive global community of communicative interaction and therefore that the only limits to liberal norm diffusion were elite- or state-based barriers to communication. In this way, it was argued that the communicative interactions of transnational activist networks could 'bridge the increasingly artificial divide between international and national realms' (Keck and Sikkink 1998: 4). In many ways, this understanding of the role of Habermasian communicative interaction and the emergence of a global communicative space, mirrored the views and understandings of critical global civil society theorists, such as Andrew Linklater, Mary Kaldor, and John Keane (for example, Acharya 2000; Kaldor 2003; Keane 2003; Linklater 1998), who similarly juxtaposed the counterproductive or irrational understandings of elite self-interest to the progressive spread of an inclusive global communicative rationality.

NORMS AND BEHAVIOURAL MODIFICATION

The 'second generation' of agency-based theorizing claimed to offer a set of explanations for the apparent triumph of liberal internationalist norms in the 1990s. However, they tended to be less able to explain the limits to the agentic dynamic of liberal norm diffusion, which became increasingly apparent in the late 1990s and into the 2000s. From the late-1990s onward, this second generation approach was criticized as positing an idealistic, normative, liberal teleology where it was assumed that 'good' liberal ideas won out through intersubjective discourse (Chandler 2001; 2004; Hopgood 2000; Palan 2000). The concern with the limits of the diffusion of good governance norms reflected an increased disillusionment with liberal internationalism—expressed in the setbacks and extensions to international protectorates in Bosnia (and later in Kosovo) and the disappointing outcomes of the wars fought under the rubric of the global war on terror in Afghanistan and Iraq (for example, Campbell, Chandler, and Sabaratnam 2011; Newman, Paris, and Richmond 2009; Richmond and Franks 2009; Tadjbakhsh 2011). In these states, it seemed that removing elites through war crimes prosecutions or regime change had not freed society's civil or democratic forces, enabling populations to freely make better adaptive choices. The focus inevitably shifted from the elite- or state-level to that of the societal agency itself and the problem of individual and communal capacities and capabilities. [8]

Liberal internationalist understandings assumed the universal rational subject. In this traditional liberal framing, there was no assumption that the subject was vulnerable and lacking in capacities for choice-making and no attention was paid therefore to the social, cultural, or communicative environment as a self-constituted and self-reproduced barrier to the subject's own ability to become self-reflective and adaptive. Neoliberal, societal, or 'third generation' norms research, however, challenged the assumptions previously made by shifting analytical focus to study differential agent-based capabilities and the internal communicative frameworks of states and societies (for example, Acharya 2000). This discussion of the limits of liberal norm diffusion shifted the emphasis from the external diffusion of norms in the communicative space of global civil society to the internal reception of norms in the domestic institutional context, particularly that of the postconflict or fragile or failing non-Western state. Thomas Risse, Stephen Ropp, and Kathryn Sikkink's *The Power of Human Rights* was one of the first books to stake out this shift in sociological perspective (Risse, Ropp, and Sikkink 1999). Rather than celebrating the power of global norms to have a transformative liberalizing impact regardless of the 'geographic, cultural, and political diversity' of the countries studied, they chose instead to focus on the problematic limits to good governance norms in countries where it appeared that the democratic rights situation had worsened in the 1990s (Risse and Sikkink 1999: 3).

Making an important move, Risse, Ropp, and Sikkink argued that the process of norm diffusion was problematic and involved more than just facilitating free communicative links through removing irrational or illegitimate elite blockages.[9] Communicative engagement was not necessarily enough if the institutional frameworks shaping the understanding and behaviour of actors did not enable them to be open to adaptive decision-making. It is within this framing of subjects not able to empower themselves that the concepts of 'vulnerability' become central. Vulnerability was a blockage in understanding and information-processing that needed to be overcome through external assistance. Where this was the case, institutions held to be barriers to freedom, and the understandings and behaviours associated with them, first had to be changed. Risse, Ropp, and Sikkink posed this process in terms of the 'spiral effect': the process through which modes of behaviour and understanding could be changed through external pressure, and the changing of institutional structures, eventually enabling good governance norms to operate through free communicative interaction (Risse, Ropp, and Sikkink 1999).

Rather than the power of good governance norms alone, Risse and Sikkink argued that 'domestic structural changes' were in some cases necessary to enable the spread of liberal norms (Risse and Sikkink 1999: 4). With the shift in emphasis to why liberal 'norms and principled ideas "do not float freely"' (an emphasis largely avoided in earlier discussions of 'global' norms) the focus shifted to the 'very different domestic structures and rationalities of states and societies having problems receiving or taking liberal norms' (Risse and Sikkink 1999: 4). In discussing the limits to liberal norms, there was increasing sensitivity to blockages, not at the level of the state, but at the level of broader societal vulnerability or incapacity. Mere communicative interaction with international liberal norms was no longer adequate for norm diffusion if there was no shared communicative framework due to the lack of adequate 'existing collective understandings' or adequate 'political cultures' (Risse and Ropp 1999: 271).

Here, there was no assumption of freeing the non-Western subject from elite- or state-based constraints: the emphasis was upon the transformation of the capabilities of target societies or populations. External policy intervention, to transform the actions or behaviour of elites, became important only insofar as it was a means to effect state policy changes that sought to overcome vulnerabilities caused by cultural understandings and local communicative interactions. Societal ideational change became the goal rather than changing the behaviour of state elites. [10] In terms of appreciating the centrality of vulnerability to neoliberal understandings of the self-production of society, it is important to highlight the assumption that societal ideational change was not understood to be a matter of engagement in communicative reason—that is, that it was not merely a matter of freeing or liberalizing domestic economic and political frameworks—but rather a matter of enabling behavioural change as the precondition for the later or subsequent free acceptance of global liberal norms:

> we find that a different logic of interaction incrementally takes over and at least supplements strategic behaviour. This logic emphasizes communicative rationality, argumentation, and persuasion, on the one hand, and norm institutionalization and habitualization, on the other. We feel that social constructivism, which endogenizes identities and interests of actors, can accommodate this logic more easily, in conjunction with sociological institutionalism. (Risse and Ropp 1999: 273)

This shift to the emphasis on 'norm institutionalization and habitualization' is of fundamental importance for understanding how social constructivist frameworks have facilitated and legitimated the focus upon the external assistance of data enabling and information-processing capacities on the basis that the local society may be so vulnerable as to be unable to act on, or perceive, its own interests. When endogenously generated norms (at the global level) were understood as progressive and transformative, actor agency was celebrated and seen as morally courageous. However, once endogenously generated societal processes were seen as barriers to progress (at the local level), agency then became problematized and actors were seen to be vulnerable in their lack of capacity for choice-making, resulting in the dangerous choosing and reproduction of 'immoral', 'reactionary' or 'nonliberal' norms and the lack of risk awareness. [11]

In these frameworks, the institutionalization or habituation of problematic communicative interactions necessitates external assistance to inculcate resilience through the removal of vulnerabilities and engineering of different ideational possibilities or subject capabilities. Institutional interventions to change 'everyday' practices and ideas are thus understood as a precondition for changes in agents' receptiveness to adaptive and more open processes of governing. It is only once institutional changes are made, and domestic actors transform their modes of understanding, that good governance norms can become institutionalized as a new habitual practice (Risse and Sikkink 1999: 34). It is at this point that adaptive capacities for peace and progress can be understood as 'sustainable' and self-reproducing. It is important to emphasize this flip side to the constructivist emphasis on the relationship of discursive equality—held to be in play to explain the transmission and spread of liberal norms. This is that the barriers to the spread of these norms are then understood to legitimize a shift from communicative reasoning to external forms of assistance enabling better access to and handling of information to facilitate behaviour modification. [12] This external assistance is not understood to be oppressive but as emancipatory: the basis upon which the postconflict or postcolonial subject can be enlightened and placed in a position of self-liberation. [13]

One clearly formulated example of this approach, arguing for behavioural changing interventions in order to create the conditions for the sustainability of adaptive capacities in the face of rapid change, is that of Roland Paris's conception of 'Institutionalization before Liberalization' (Paris 2004). Paris argued that liberal internationalists have underestimated the societal blockages to reflexive and adaptive choice-making. Rather than liberal frameworks of governance and market social relations freeing the non-Western subject, he argued from the neoliberal perspective that their introduction was highly problematic in societies held to be at high levels of vulnerability and thereby to lack the right ideational and cultural preconditions. In effect, liberal freedoms were held to be problematic and counterproductive in societies understood to be vulnerable. In these cases, the promotion of good governance norms involved the initial limiting of political and economic freedoms. External interventions were held to be necessary to restrict and regulate the political, social, and economic spheres until behavioural and attitude changes allowed the development of more open and adaptive approaches. These dominant discourses of state-building and peace-building thus operated on the basis of a critique of traditional liberal assumptions of the natural subject. Neoliberal discourse privileges difference above universality, and understands the production of difference as the product of agential choice, where those who are vulnerable lack the capacities for adequate choice-making.

This endogenous agency-based approach to the understanding of difference and inequality was influentially articulated in development economics from the early 1970s (Davis and North 1971; North 1990; North and Thomas 1973; Peters 2005). At the international level, endogenous frameworks assert that state institutional arrangements construct vulnerabilities by cutting off their societies from access to the benefits of globalization (Ghani and Lockhart 2008). The need for international state-building as a framework of good governance is largely established on the basis that changes in state institutions can enable the mediation of the domestic and the international so that dysfunctional states can gain from good governance norms and international institutional frameworks rather than being a threat to them. In fact, vulnerable, weak, and failing states are often seen to constitute the major threat to the international order (for example, NSS 2002). Good governance promotion through state-building, as carried out by every major international institution from the European Union (EU) to the UN and the World Bank, is seen to be capable of extending governance norms through institutional behavioural modification with the use of external incentives and conditionalities: including the compacts proposed by a range of authors such as Ashraf Ghani, Clare Lockhart, and Paul Collier (Collier 2010; Ghani and Lockhart 2008).

For neoliberal agency-based understandings, the subject has to be externally constituted before being able to self-govern safely through making efficient adaptive choices. For example, the lessons of the Balkans, the Middle East, and of Africa were increasingly interpreted as the problem of too much democracy rather than too little (for example, Hawksley 2009; Paris and Sisk 2009; Zaum 2007). The title of Paul Collier's 2010 book, *Wars, Guns and Votes: Democracy in Dangerous Places*, sums up the increasing awareness that democracy promotion has to be done gradually and under the guidance of external interveners pursuing the new international state-building agendas of behavioural and ideational change, through extensive processes of societal intervention. Here, international relations theorists often pose the need to join with anthropologists to understand the societal reproduction of particular cultural vulnerabilities as institutional barriers to adaptive choice-making (for example, Fukuyama 1995; Hill 2011; Weldes, Laffey, Gusterson, and Duvall 1999).

Paris's call for extended international assistance to create the conditions for behaviour change highlights the shift in focus from institutional regimes to cultural and social factors that constitute subjects as vulnerable. While Paris still posed assistance in terms of constructing liberal political and economic regimes, neoliberal approaches have increasingly shifted away from posing universalist solutions of liberal markets and democracy as an end goal. From the mid-2000s onward, endogenous understandings of the vulnerable subject have tended to focus much more on the maintenance of the status quo—promoting endogenous awareness and responsiveness to risks and shocks—than on universalist aspirations of socioeconomic transformation. In pluralizing endogenous understandings, neoliberal thinking retreated from claims of global governance or the advocacy of a global governmentality of liberal rule. The work in these framings is much less amenable to universalist liberal understandings and much more orientated around the understanding of the reproduction of difference. Thus, there seems to be an increasing consensus today that the liberal universalist aspirations, so central to international debates in the 1990s, were little more than naïve hubris, merely reflecting a transient historical moment of 'fleeting' Western hegemony (Mayall and Soares de Oliveira 2011: 1).

THE SHRINKING OF THE LIBERAL WORLD

Sociological approaches, bringing a variety of endogenously constructed frameworks of agentic explanation to bear on the reproduction of cultural and ideational barriers to the diffusion of adaptive understandings and behaviours, have increasingly come to dominate the academic and policy agendas in the 2010s. This has particularly been the case in the fields of international peace-building and international state-building, where, as noted, the discourse has shifted from that of freeing the subject from authoritarian regimes of regulation, to the overcoming of vulnerabilities through a broad range of societal interventions under the rubrics of self-empowerment, adaptive capacities, and 'good governance' (Chandler 2010). These multilevel and multistakeholder initiatives are held to be necessary to enable the behavioural and ideational transformation of subjects through their participatory engagement in a wide range of policy activities, enabling a greater self-awareness of economic, political, and ecological risks and challenges at both individual and community levels (Belloni 2008; Chandler 1998; Paffenholz 2009). The need for these understandings to develop endogenously has been highlighted by academic commentators who have focused on the 'hybrid' outcomes when there are attempts to impose global governance policy norms from the outside (for example, Barnett and Zürcher 2009; Mac Ginty 2011; Richmond 2011; Roberts 2008).

The call for more attention to the 'local' and even 'local-local' communicative transactions (for example, Richmond 2010) and to the specific cultural values and 'modes of life' of those in non-Western states and societies (for example, Acharya 2000; Campbell, Chandler, and Sabaratnam 2011; Tadjbakhsh 2011), may seem a radical or critical departure from traditional theorizing in international relations, but constructivist and other agency-based approaches, which eschew rationalist explanations, tend to explain differences in economic wealth or political institutions as the product of agentically constructed ideational structures and choices. In these approaches, the reproduction of difference is more likely to be understood as a product of vulnerable agential social or intersubjective construction than as shaped by material or structural social relations. As Douglass North, John Wallis, and Barry Weingast put it:

> The task of social science is to explain the performance characteristics of societies through time, including the radical gap in human well-being between rich countries and poor as well as the contrasting forms of political organiza-

tion, beliefs, and social structure that produce these variations in performance. (North, Wallis, and Weingast 2009: 1)

For endogenous, agency-based approaches to social differentiation, the operation of market forces is no longer part of any causal explanation because material differences and social relations (though sometimes included) are not, in themselves, adequate for explaining change but are often the product of preexisting social institutional frameworks. Rather than economic orders, endogenous frameworks of thinking understand the world in terms of 'social orders' as they allege that social norms or social institutional frameworks are key to shaping individual behaviours and beliefs which contribute to the perpetuation of differential vulnerabilities and inequalities (for example, Thaler and Sunstein 2008). The key research questions then become the different patterns of social order, which enable theorists to explain the mystery of the reproduction of socioeconomic inequalities and proneness to disaster or, more bluntly: 'why poor countries stay poor' (North, Wallis, and Weingast 2009: 3).

Endogenous approaches argue that culture, values, and communicative and informational frameworks—often agentically framed in the terminology of 'civil society'—are key to understanding the alleged barriers to the spread of governance norms or to adaptive approaches to new threats and risks. Many of these arguments were cohered in the 1990s, in the discussion of the problem of 'transition' in the newly independent states in Central and Eastern Europe, where it was alleged that external assistance for institution-building was necessary to allow democracy and the market to work without conflict and disruption (for example, Fukuyama 1995; Gunther et al. 1996; O'Donnell 1996; Schmitter and Karl 1991). The problems of facilitating change or transition are central to endogenous approaches to international development, where institutional path-dependencies are held to constitute vulnerabilities preventing easy transitioning to liberal 'open-access' adaptive and more resilient social orders (for example, North, Wallis, and Weingast 2009). In this framework, it is the ideas, values, and social institutional, communicative, and informational culture of a society that appears to constitute subjects as vulnerable rather than inequalities of economic wealth or hierarchical socioeconomic relations (Collier 2010; Snyder 2000; Zakharia 2003). As Douglass North argues:

> Culture not only determines societal performance at a moment in time but, through the way in which its scaffolding constrains the players, contributes to the process of change through time. The focus of our attention, therefore, must be on human learning—on what is learned and how it is shared among the members of society and on the incremental process by which the beliefs and preferences change, and on the way in which they shape the performance of economies through time. (North 2005: viii)

As understandings of development increasingly focus upon disaster risk reduction, the focus on 'human learning' and vulnerability comes clearly to the fore. As Jo Scheuer, Coordinator of Disaster Risk Reduction at the UN Development Programme, states, we increasingly understand that 'what we call "natural" disasters are not natural at all' but social products of community vulnerability (Scheuer 2012). Disasters increasingly viewed as subjective or social products, understood in terms of access and use of communicative self-knowledge in relation to a community's embedded relationship with its environment and in terms of how it governs itself. In respect of the environment, disasters are increasingly seen as products of knowable interactive processes, rather than as sudden events: 'Disaster is the culmination of a process and continuum of a disconnect between human beings and their interrelations with the environment' (Cohen 2000). Second, the impact of natural or technological hazards is held to only become a disaster when measures to mitigate impact, such as earthquake resistant buildings, are lacking. For the UNDP: 'We don't have to resign ourselves to the devastation that disasters cause, nor see them as exceptional events that interrupt normal development' (Scheur 2012).

It is important to note that the role of information technology and data access in empowering communities is one of enabling them to cope with disaster through a better understanding of the self. This process of reducing problems to the development of self-orientated knowledge is captured well by Patrick Meier:

> Thanks to [information and communications technologies] ICTs, social media and Big Data, we now have the opportunity to better characterize in real-time the social, economic and political processes . . . this doesn't mean that we have a perfect picture of the road to collapse; simply that our picture is clearer than ever before in human history. In other words, we can better measure our own resilience. Think of it as the Quantified Self movement applied to an entirely different scale, that of societies and cities. (Meier 2013)

The point is that information technology can provide more real-time responsive forms of self-knowledge, critical for adaptation and resilience. Disaster risk reduction thus becomes a way of making communities more self-aware so that they can overcome their own social and ideational barriers to adaptive choice-making. This process of self-monitoring or self-awareness is the essence of some of the UN's Global Pulse projects, for example, using Big Data for real-time awareness of food price changes for famine prevention or providing self-knowledge of social interactions enabling conflict to be prevented or ameliorated (USIP 2013).

Thus, the focus on data empowerment concerns self-reflexive knowledge rather than causal knowledge of external processes. Big Data cannot help explain global warming but it can enable individuals and households to adapt through measuring their own energy consumption through the 'datafication' of household objects and complex production and supply chains. This reflexive approach works to construct a pluralized and multiple world of self-organizing and adaptive processes. The imaginary of Big Data is that the producers and consumers of knowledge and of governance would be indistinguishable; where both knowing and governing exist without external mediation, constituting a perfectly harmonious and self-adapting system: the neoliberal goal of resilient communities and societies. In this discourse, increasingly articulated by governments and policy-makers, knowledge of causal connections is no longer relevant as communities adapt to the real-time appearances of the world, without necessarily understanding them. As Meier states:

> Connection technologies such as mobile phones allow individual[s] . . . to make necessary connections and decisions to self-organize and rapidly recover from disasters. With appropriate incentives, preparedness measures and policies, these local decisions can render a complex system more resilient. At the core here is behaviour change and thus the importance of understanding behaviour change models. (Meier 2013)

Rather than engaging in external understandings of causality in the world, Big Data and other data enabling techniques work on changing social behaviour by enabling greater adaptive reflexivity. If, through Big Data, individuals could detect and manage our own biorhythms and know the effects of poor eating or a lack of exercise, they could monitor their own health and not need costly medical interventions. Equally, if vulnerable and marginal communities could 'datafy' their own modes of being and relationships to their environments, they would be able to augment their coping capacities and resilience without disasters or crises occurring. In essence, the imaginary of Big Data is that of the adaptive and resilient subject. This is why disasters in current forms of resilience thinking are understood to be 'transformative': revealing the unintended consequences of social planning that prevented proper awareness and responsiveness. Disasters themselves become a form of datafication, revealing the existence of vulnerabilities—poor modes of self-awareness and self-governance (ó Súilleabháin 2014).

The idea that the barriers to good governance and adaptive self-awareness are endogenous, subjective, cultural, or communicative products is used to argue that differences cannot be easily overcome. Either this framing results in an apologia for gross inequalities of outcomes or, just as problematically, for gross inequalities of treatment, justifying extensive interventions with the goal of social or ideational engineering. Social constructivism, along with other 'new institutionalist' approaches, has sought to eschew the racialized and culturalized framings of traditional institutionalist sociological and historical approaches of the colonial era, which focused on the endogenous reproduction of societal difference (see Peters 2005: 1–24). However, it seems clear that a complete break with former colonializing approaches, which essentialized difference, is not possible within the framework of endogenous theorizing: the problems with this approach cannot be overcome by substituting the discourses of community empowerment, data enablement or 'agentic norms' for those of race and culture. This is because the problematic of endogenous approaches necessarily involves certain shared methodological assumptions, which are drawn out in the section below.

THE SELF-PRODUCTION OF THE VULNERABLE SUBJECT

The foregoing work has sought to highlight how endogenous frameworks of understanding have constituted the vulnerable subject of neoliberalism. Endogenous approaches share two core attributes, which have enabled social constructivist approaches to cohere neoliberal policy and academic understandings. These attributes are, first, epistemological and, second, ontological.

The epistemological attribute that neoliberal sociological understandings share with other new institutionalist or agent-based approaches, which also lack the foundational grounds of universalist rationalist and materialist approaches, is that they can only work backward to explain the present. Agency-based understandings can easily account for both continuity and for change (Kowert and Legro 1996: 483). This all-purpose explanatory framework may not have seemed so problematic when liberal transformations, perceived as progressive, were being analysed with the fall of the Soviet Union and the 'domino-effect' of democratic change in Central and Eastern Europe (Jervis and Snyder 1991; Macdonald 1995). However, it is certainly much more problematic when dealing with post-hoc communicative and informational-based understandings of the agentic reproduction of different ideas and policy preferences.[14]

Part of this problem is that efforts to identify agency suffer from a bias toward 'the norm that worked' (Kowert and Legro 1996: 485). In the agency-based framings of constructivism, the norm that worked is another way of saying 'the agency that worked'. For this reason, agency was ascribed to nonstate actors and norm-entrepreneurs, well beyond their representative political influence or socioeconomic power. Once the focus shifted to understanding the perpetuation of barriers to self-awareness and adaptive efficiency, the norm that worked gives agential power to those held to be lacking sufficient awareness or information access in order to choose different behavioural responses—often those with the least social, economic, and political weight in non-Western states. In this case, it is not surprising that societies, understood as vulnerable, are seen to be complicit in the reproduction of social and economic inequalities, conflicts or ecological catastrophes.

The ontological attribute shared by both neoliberal constructivist agency-based approaches and other new institutionalist approaches is that they can only explain change (and the limits to change) as endogenous processes (Kratochwil 2000: 97). In early constructivist approaches, this process inevitably marginalized or excluded the 'exogenous' processes taking place outside the global sphere of intersubjective communicative exchange between global actors. The barriers between the domestic and the international were held to be increasingly blurring and this facilitated an understanding of a shared closed system, which increasingly approximated to a dematerialized and discursive global level. From the globalizing of the international into a closed system capable of extending and reproducing global governance norms and values, the problematizing of liberal norm-promotion has led to the construction of a conflicting and differentiated understanding dividing the international into liberal and nonliberal and in neoliberal discourses into resilient and vulnerable worlds.

This subjectivization of the limits of liberalism thus leads theorists to see these vulnerable choices as morally problematic, and thereby an indication of subjective threat to be dealt with through policies of intervention assistance. This endogenous framework of agency-based understanding fits unerringly into the neoliberal framing that political, social, and economic inequalities are a product of problematic information-processing and choice-making: that to paraphrase Wendt (1992), capitalism, democracy, or disasters are what communities make of them.

CONCLUSION

In the neoliberal discourse, we create and institutionalize differences through our own agentic choices, thereby constituting a world that can never be collectively engaged with. Rather than starting from a rationalist position that human subjects are universally rational but that the contexts and the structures in which we make choices and decisions are very different across time and space, the neoliberal gaze sees the individual (or community) constructing their own world through agential choice. The more the explanation for problems and for crises in the world is reduced to the decision-making choices of individuals the less rational or understandable, and the more alien, the world becomes.

As Ralph Waldo Emerson put it, we would be merely living a 'shallow village tale' (1993: 17) if we were not able to find ourselves in the events of our world, both across time and space. We would lack any sense of our common humanity, our understanding of our past or our present, if we could not examine the history of the world and find that: 'There is no age or state of society or mode of action in history, to which there is not somewhat corresponding in [one's] life' (1993: 3). This shared and common world of meaning and understanding is destroyed by the subject-centred approach of neoliberal understandings. Emerson's universalist approach to the reading of history allows us to: 'assume that we under like influence should be like affected and should achieve the like; and we [could] aim to master intellectually the steps, and reach the same height or the same degradation, that our fellow, our proxy, has done' (1993: 4). Under the neoliberal gaze, the problems of the world, from conflict to economic inequality and environmental degradation, become alien to us, because we construct them as products of problematic vulnerable subjects, unable or unwilling to communicate and process information enabling efficient adaptive choice-making.

In giving human agency centre place and in abolishing structures, agent-based understandings of new institutionalism and social constructivism remove the universalist liberal assumptions of rationalist approaches. For the advocates of this shift, the subject is freed or liberated from the constrictions of structural understandings. In this reading, security and sustainable development become possible once it is understood that the subject or agent can resiliently adapt to the natural and societal threats and risks they are confronted with. If, as Wendt argued, 'the world is what agents make of it' the apparent disastrousness of the world appears to indicate that the vulnerable human subject is not capable of very much and there is very little that can be done apart from rejecting the liberal hubris of rationalism and inculcating the necessary capacities for resilience. Once neoliberal framings of the world place vulnerability at the centre of the problematic, even radical agent-centred attempts to improve the world end up reinforcing the neoliberal understanding of limits. Once we start from the problematic of vulnerability—in terms of empowering or capacity-building the subject—we inevitably ignore the external world, reducing the world to the human and the human to informational self-awareness through data processing and the environmental milieu of social institutions, norms and values which are held to influence and shape this process. In the discussion that follows in the concluding chapter of this book I will suggest ways in which we can begin to reinstate the human subject through bringing back the external world as an object of engagement and transformation.

NOTES

1. I follow Wesley Widmaier (2011), although, for heuristic purposes, the analytical framing of these stages differs.
2. A common definition of norms in the international relations literature is that forwarded by Peter J. Katzenstein, as a description of 'collective expectations for the proper behaviour of actors with a given identity' (Katzenstein 1996a: 5).

3. The understanding of classical liberal theory as being blind to social and associative connections has been authoritatively challenged by authors as diverse as C. B. Macpherson (1962) and Amartya Sen (see, for example, 1987; 2009)

4. For more on the problematic of universalism and the overcoming of difference in the Enlightenment conception of 'free' and autonomous subjects, see the treatment by Michel Foucault (2010: 6–39). See also the insightful work of Laura Zanotti (2006; 2011).

5. For example, for the sociologically informed authors of the United Nations instigated 'Responsibility to Protect' Report, the domestic sociopolitical context or preconceived geopolitical interests were no excuse for not choosing to behave according to global liberal norms: 'The behaviour of states is not predetermined by systemic or structural factors, and moral justifications are not merely after-the-fact justifications or simply irrelevant' (ICISS 2001: 129).

6. This was reminiscent of the 'universalist' reasoning of Vitoria, regarding the Spanish conquest of the New World, where refusal to open up to *liberum commercium* and the communicative engagement of Papal missionaries was held to be a violation of Spanish rights justifying suppression (Schmitt 2003: 108–13).

7. For this reason the international administrative mandate was initially intended to last only until the first elections, held in September 1996 (for more information, see Chandler 1999).

8. In shifting policy concerns to the societal rather than the state level, democratic norms discourse followed similar international discourses concerned with security and development, where the emphasis on 'human' individual and social capacities and capabilities was intellectually cohered through the work of Amartya Sen and others (see chapter 5 on adaptation; Sen 1999; the UN Development Reports, published annually from 2004).

9. Previously, Thomas Risse-Kappen had argued that domestic institutional structures had blocking affects, in terms of preventing communicative engagement with international norm-entrepreneurs or transnational nonstate actors from accessing domestic political systems and domestic actors (see, for example, Risse-Kappen 1994; 1995).

10. It is in this context that concerns are often expressed in terms of the limits of the European Union's 'normative power' beyond the periphery of states involved in the accession process (see, for example, Laïdi 2008: 15).

11. There is no methodological necessity for social constructivists to argue for the globalization of liberal norms rather than focus on the barriers to their acceptance—the only difference is the level of focus for the endogenous understanding of the operation of societal intersubjective framings. Whereas earlier norms-based approaches focused on global social interaction, overtly challenging rationalist approaches at the international level, later norms-based approaches have focused on the domestic level of failing or postconflict states and have tended to present endogenous frameworks of understanding in terms of institutionalist frameworks of reasoning, which equally challenge traditional rationalist frameworks of understanding in economic and political social science.

12. This discourse is replicated in domestic discussions of the problems of communicative reasoning and the need for prior behavioural change. See further, the discussion on *Nudge* in chapter 3 on resilience.

13. As Lord Paddy Ashdown, the former international High Representative with administrative ruling responsibilities for Bosnia, explained informally to me in January 2011, external rule was only necessary until the Bosnian people were judged to be capable of freely making their own rational governmental decisions (see also Ashdown 2007).

14. This danger was articulated well by Keohane, in a defence of rationalist understandings that encouraged researchers 'to look beneath the surface', rather than merely focus on 'post hoc observation of values or ideology' (Keohane 1988). Or, as Karl Marx put it: 'all science would be superfluous if the outward appearance and the essence of things directly coincided' (Marx n.d.).

Chapter Eight

Embodiment as Vulnerability

Julian Reid

The shift in the conception of the human within the Western philosophical imagination that I have charted in this book, owes largely to the powers and influences of liberalism in shaping that imagination. In my previous chapters we have seen how this transformation has come about through the promotion of a biologized understanding of the subject in liberal discourses and practices concerned, especially, with increasing the resilience and adaptive capacities of human beings worldwide. However when we look at the theoretical tropes through which the acceptance of a biologized notion of the subject has come about there can be little doubt that one of the most powerful sources of its facilitation has not been liberalism as such, but the biophilosophical movement in France, which in the postwar era, has sought to tear 'the subject from the terrain of the *cogito* and consciousness', and 'root it in life' (Agamben 1999: 221). In other words the very tradition of philosophical thought inspired by Michel Foucault, whose works I am using to denaturalize and politicize this account of subjectivity, is itself complicit with its acceptance. Fundamental to the tradition of philosophical thinking that has developed in Foucault's work is the claim that any theory of subjectivity today has to be able to take into account the embodied nature of subjectivity, and more to the point, the living of the life which embodiment entails. The human subject is a subject that lives, indeed which must live in order to be, and which in living, is a thing that can and must die, and which therefore cannot aspire to the kinds of sovereignty promised to it by the false prophets of Western metaphysics. Sovereignty, once considered in light of the radical dependence and finitude of the human subject, must be dismissed as dangerous fantasy. It is now widely assumed by Foucauldians.

A paradigmatic and contemporarily influential representative of this way of following Foucault on the nature and problem of subjectivity is, of course,

Judith Butler. For Butler, the subject is defined by its embodiment, the vulnerability of its life, the riskiness of its existence, its exposure to death, and dependence on things that exist outside itself in order to get by for the finite time that it is capable of. 'To live is always to live a life that is at risk from the outset and can be put at risk or expunged quite suddenly from the outside and for reasons that are not always under one's control' (Butler 2009: 30). As she states,

> there are no conditions that can fully 'solve' the problem of human precariousness. Bodies come into being and cease to be: as physically persistent organisms, they are subject to incursions and to illnesses that jeopardize the possibility of persisting at all. These are necessary features of bodies—they cannot 'be' thought without their finitude, and they depend on what is 'outside themselves' to be sustained—features that pertain to the phenomenological structure of bodily life. (Butler 2009: 29–30).

Vulnerability in Butler's account is fundamental to the life of the human and places limits on what we can hope to achieve as well as aspire to politically in our worldly existences. 'No amount of will or wealth can eliminate the possibilities of illness or accident for a living body. Although both can be mobilized in the service of such an illusion', she states (Butler 2009: 30). Security, that fundamental predicate of the sovereign subject, which I am interested in reconstituting in alliance with Foucault, is fantasy, Butler argues, while vulnerability is real. Recognizing the vulnerability of the life of the human must mean, Butler argues, searching for a different way of theorizing subjectivity, and in her own words, a different politics. A politics which emerges 'from the fact that we are . . . dependent on what is outside ourselves, on others, on institutions, and on sustained and sustainable environments, and so are, in this sense, precarious' (Butler 2009: 23).[1]

Butler is especially concerned for the circumstances where the condition of vulnerability leads not to a recognition of its fundamentality to all human life but to the targeting of one life by another life, with death or violence, on account of the desire for security of one life from that of another life (Butler 2009: 31). This is a problem that she identifies with the impasses of the Left today whereby, for example, social struggles and movements concerned with achieving protection for sexual minorities are increasingly mobilized to oppose the expansion of rights of protection to immigrant minorities as well as give their support to state violence against vulnerable populations domestically and internationally on behalf of their 'progressive' causes (Butler 2009: 27). Such mobilizations of elements of the Left to do violence to vulnerable populations indicates the failures of the Left, Butler argues, to have developed an 'inclusive and egalitarian way of recognizing' vulnerability (Butler 2009: 13). In light of that failure, she argues for the necessity of a 'new bodily ontology' (Butler 2009: 2), one implying the fundamentality of vulnerability, for the redevelopment of a leftist understanding of political subjectivity. The Left needs to understand vulnerability as 'a shared condition', and leftists ought to aim at developing coalitions between different vulnerable subjects with a view to struggling against the violence by which populations are differentially deprived of the basic resources needed to minimize their vulnerability, she argues (Butler 2009: 32).

There is much that is appealing in Butler's plea for the extension of protection to vulnerable groups not recognized as such. As she states, 'part of the very problem of contemporary political life is that not everyone counts as a subject . . . what is at stake are communities not quite recognized as such, subjects who are living, but not yet regarded as "lives"' (Butler 2009: 31–32). She is right that the determination of the differences between life deemed worthy of protection and life that can be destroyed is a problem of how we 'apprehend a life' as such (Butler 2009: 2). That problem, as she states clearly, is doubly epistemological and ontological, being that of 'the frames through which we apprehend or, indeed, fail to apprehend the lives of others as lost or injured' as well as ontological 'since the question at issue is: *what is a life?*' (Butler 2009: 1). And given that 'the "being" of life is itself constituted through selective means', so she is also right that 'as a result, we cannot refer to this "being" outside of the operations of power, and so must we make more precise the specific mechanisms of power through which life is produced' (Butler 2009: 1). The name that Foucault gave to the mechanisms of power and selective means that produce life today was, "Biopower" (Foucault 1990). Indeed if we want to understand how the wars waged and violence perpetrated in destruction of life are still possible, it is necessary that we understand them through the lens of his concept of biopolitics (Dillon and Reid 2009; Reid 2009; 2006a). Butler is right that this demands that we question the terms of legitimation underwriting war and state violence today, most especially the claims concerning what counts as human life as such and what forms of life it is that are said to be dangerous to our humanity. I agree with much of this and find much consistency with my own appraisals of the biopolitics of state violence and power relations today. But there are some fundamental problems here with respect to the counterontological shift to vulnerability that Butler is proposing and arguing we should build on for a new form of leftism today and which I wish to draw out here.

BUTLER'S LIBERALISM

Let us start with her claims concerning the ontological 'fact' of vulnerability (Butler 2009: 23). Among the many things that Foucault teaches us, one primary lesson is the danger to be had in practicing philosophy by way of what he called 'an imperative discourse' (Foucault 2006: 3). What he meant by this was that rather than engaging in a philosophy which glibly attempts to pronounce *the* facts or truth about life, it is necessary, and in a critical sense truer to the philosopher's vocation, to analyze the 'knowledge effects' produced by the imperative discourses that otherwise circulate and condition the regimes of truth through which life is determined as life as well as how different forms of life are evaluated as worth living. Rather than aspiring to pronounce the truth about life Foucault sought to examine the implications for life of imperative answers to the questions of what life is and what conditions are most amenable to its enablement. Every imperative discourse on life, no matter what its content, entails such effects and implications, which is why we must, if we are to do justice to Foucault, practice circumspection when coming into contact with any text that attempts to circumscribe the reality or facts said to concern life. Imperative discourses are never grounded in facts, no matter how much they may attempt to legitimate themselves on account of 'the facts'. The 'fact' of 'vulnerability' is no different. It is an element within an 'aesthetic discourse' every bit as aesthetic as those political discourses which presuppose the possibility of sovereignty and security, and which Butler critiques for their inauthenticity. Much of this owes to the debased ways in which Butler, along with many others of an antihumanist persuasion, have set about reading Foucault, and the naïve ways in which they have engaged his theory and analysis of biopolitics. Life, as Foucault argued repeatedly, is not an ontological category. Such a way of thinking about subjectivity is so immanently invested within a biopolitical idiom of thought, an idiom that is to say, that Foucault spent so much of his energies attempting to unearth and demonstrate the historical and political contingencies of, that it fails to meet basic criteria of criticality. So, rather than naïvely embracing Butler's argument for the ontological fundamentality of vulnerability for the life of the human, it befalls us, if we are to be true to the Foucauldian remit, to consider what the effects and implications are for life when vulnerability is thus reified, in terms of what forms of life a vulnerable subject discounts as unworthy, deserving sanction, intervention, as well as names dangerous, and indeed which it declares permissible to kill, in order to defend the sanctity of its own account of life as vulnerable.

As it happens this is not an abstract question or problem. Whatever we may like to think about the ontological veracity of Butler's theory of vulnerability as predicate of life and precondition for human subjectivity, it is necessary to note the degree to which this way of thinking about human subjectivity is contemporaneous not with an incipient new leftism, but with the dominant episteme and regime of power relations that a leftism true to its name ought to be set up to combat. The ontology of the social underlying Butler's account of vulnerability is deeply *liberal*. Vulnerability 'implies living socially, that is, the fact that one's life is always in some sense in the hands of the other. It implies exposure both to those we know and to those we do not know; a dependency on people we know, or barely know, or know not at all' (Butler 2009: 14). Such a way of problematizing the relation of the subject to its society in terms of its vulnerability on account of its exposure to an unknowable domain of potential violence and harm partakes of a tradition of thinking about the social and the subject that extends right back to the very foundations of liberalism in the seventeenth century, most significantly to Thomas Hobbes. It is the very foundation on which the liberal state has legitimated itself from the origins of modernity. Foregrounding the vulnerability of the life of the subject on account of its exposure to an unknown and dangerous domain of social relations instantiates the very demand for protection on which liberal governance has always depended for its legitimation in relation with, as well as right to intervene upon, society. One of the major tasks that Foucault took upon himself toward the end of his career was to trace the emergence and development of the political rationality of liberalism within the European state form. In the 1978 lecture series given at the Collège de France, *Security, Territory, Population*, he traced how that rationality grew in accordance with a problematization of the unknowability of the social (Foucault 2007). This unknowability provoked a will to know, and a will to know incited by the desire to secure the life of its subject populations against the vulnerabilities posed at them by social living, not simply on account of some benevolent interest in human well-being, but in order to render the state itself more stable, and less vulnerable to the economic and political costs that arise from social insecurity (Reid 2008). Rather than following Butler, therefore, and naïvely embracing yet another reiteration of liberalism's understanding of the dangers posed to the vulnerable life of subjects by the unknowability of the social, we ought to be more circumspect in receiving her claims as to the authorship of a 'new' ontology. Because it is unclear what exactly is new about it. Instead, we can better pose the questions of why, when, and how it was that the life of the subject came to be so conceived as vulnerable. When we do that we find that we can locate Butler within the very tradition that the left today is pressingly tasked with attempting to think outside of and beyond.

Within the liberal tradition the trope of the vulnerable subject has underwent many shifts and turns. If in the seventeenth century the vulnerability of the subject was said mainly to arise from its exposure to unknowable and potentially dangerous social relations, by the eighteenth century that vulnerability was conceptualized as owing as much to the dependency of the subject on what was now named 'nature'. In his subsequent 1979 lecture series, *The Birth of Biopolitics*, Foucault describes in great depth how liberalism refabricated its understanding of the vulnerable subject in such terms. In the work of the eighteenth-century French liberal, Condorcet, for example, we encounter the idea of a subject which is vulnerable because his interests are 'dependent on an infinite number of things . . . on accidents of nature about which he can do nothing and which he cannot foresee . . . a course of the world that outstrips him and eludes him in every respect' such that 'each is dependent on an uncontrollable, unspecified whole of the flow of things and the world' (Foucault 2007: 277).

One of the definitive outcomes of Foucault's analysis of liberalism is that understanding these ways in which it constitutes a subject of fear and mistrust of the world in which it is embedded requires tracing its continuities with the 'archaic model of the Christian pastorate' (Foucault 2007: 110). The pastorate sketches out and is the prelude, Foucault argued in *Security, Territory, Population*, to liberalism through its constitution 'of a specific subject . . . who is subjected in continuous networks of obedience and who is subjectified through the compulsory extraction of truth . . . a certain secret inner truth', which 'becomes the element through which the pastor's power is exercised, by which obedience is practiced' and by which a 'relationship of complete obedience is assured' (2007: 183–85). That the truth of the pastoral subject was 'internal, secret and hidden' (2007: 184) was of essential importance for Foucault's explanation of the specificity of the pastorate as a form of power, the particularity of the pastoral subject, and its continuities with the biopolitical subject of liberal modernity. Condemned never to be able to know its truth as such, form a 'relationship with a recognized truth', the pastoral subject was likewise condemned to live out a life of permanent obedience, humility, and servitude to a form of spiritual direction that was 'absolutely permanent . . . directed with regard to everything and for the whole of one's life' such that the entirety of his or her life became the object of continuous examination amid pastoral practices of involuntary extraction (2007: 182). The claim as to the specificity of this form of subject called into being by the pastorate and its continuity with the biopolitical subject of liberal modernity was maintained by Foucault throughout his studies of liberalism right up until his death. It was central, certainly, to his explanation of the principle of self-limitation with which he went on to define liberalism in *The Birth of Biopolitics* lectures in 1978 and 1979. No doubt liberal discourses of economy were central, also, to how he arrived at that principle. 'Economics steals away from the juridical form of the sovereign precisely that which is emerging as the essential element of a society's life, namely economic processes' (2008: 282). Beneath its advocacy of the principle of self-limitation Foucault shows us how liberalism rested not simply on a fundamental assumption as to the economic nature of the life of society, but fundamental assumptions as to the hidden nature of the truth of that life, the limits of what can be known of it, and the consequent preoccupation with the permanent surveying and extracting of its forever mutative truths as well as growth from it. The fundamental truth of life understood as economy is, as he explores, 'the unknowability of the totality of the process . . . the economic world is naturally opaque and naturally non-totalizable . . . originally and definitively constituted from a multiplicity of points of view' and 'liberalism acquired its modern shape precisely with the formulation of this essential incompatibility between the non-totalizable multiplicity' of society's life and 'the totalizing unity of the juridical sovereign' (Foucault 2008: 282). Regardless of the atheistic qualities of liberal political economy, its assumptions as to the elusive nature of the economic life of the liberal subject and the inability of the subject to ever know and tell the truth of that life as such, originated in the Christian pastorate and its discourses on the elusive nature of the life of the pastoral subject.

Such reconstituted claims as to the unknowability of the life of the subject, and its vulnerability to the world it inhabits, was, as Foucault reveals, central to the force with which liberalism was able to transform the model of European state sovereignty. It was the basis on which the liberal prohibition on governmental intervention within the economy arose and found its legitimacy. The claim that nature will always elude us, and that if we attempt to control it we will 'only ever see chimeras', was the fabricated truth on which the principal subject of liberal political economy, *Homo Economicus*, was able to proclaim the pointlessness, and impossibility of a sovereign point of view over the totality of the state (Foucault 2007: 281–82). 'You must not attempt to establish sovereignty over the accidents of nature', *Homo Economicus* proclaimed, 'because you cannot achieve such a state, and you cannot because you are powerless in the face of it, and why are you powerless? Because you do not know how to establish such a sovereignty, and you do not know how to because you cannot know how to'. These were the 'imperatives' and 'facts' that *Homo Economicus* wielded against that sovereign subject that would willfully attempt to assert some control, establish some direction, achieve some security, by solving for itself the condition of vulnerability to the accidental nature of the world with which it was otherwise faced.

This is not only the curse that the subject of liberal economy wields at the sovereign that would otherwise seek to remove itself from its condition of vulnerability; it is the very kernel of the concept of economy itself. For what is 'economy', when we look more closely at it, than the name of the nature of the subject itself, *Homo Economicus*? Or to phrase the question differently, what is it for *Homo* to be *Economicus*? Commonly, if we look at classical definitions of what the concept of economy refers to we find that it is identified with forms of activity in which there is involved an 'optimal allocation of scarce resources to alternative ends' (Foucault 2007: 268). To be an economic subject, or indeed *Homo Economicus*, is in that sense to be a subject concerned with utilizing and increasing one's life chances in a context of scarce resources. But what Foucault's interrogation of the biopolitics of the liberal subject reveals is that to be *Homo Economicus* is not simply to be a subject interested in increasing the utility and extent of its biomaterial resources, but more fundamentally a subject in possession of a biomaterial nature, by which is meant a nature reduced to life. A subject that understands itself as a being that lives, indeed that must live in order to be, and that in living, is a thing that can and must die, and that, therefore, cannot aspire to ever achieve security, but can only live in a context of vulnerability to the accidental nature of the world it inhabits. A subject that refuses the authority of a power that claims to be able to act on behalf of its life and secure that life for it, and that proclaims its own superior capacity to seek not security from the sources of its vulnerability, but to live in open relation with them, prospering and growing from them through the continual practice of an entrepreneurial resilience to their abilities to destroy its life.

The whole history of the left has been defined by the struggle with precisely this 'imperative discourse', the subject that speaks it, and the account of the world it presumes. The central problem of the left being that of how to speak back to this curse against the idea of a sovereign capable of intervening in and asserting itself against the contingencies of our worldly existences and afford some transcendence of them. How does Butler's attempt to resituate the politics of the left around the 'apprehension of a common human vulnerability' (Butler 2004: 30) figure within that history of struggle? Butler, unlike liberals as such, does not preach the value of the economic prosperity that can arise from the recognition of the lore of vulnerability. Her project is to extend the franchise of security to populations in need of protection from their sources of vulnerability (Butler 2009: 31). But can that be achieved on the basis on an ontological claim as to the illusion of security and the ontological fact of vulnerability? I don't think so. If anything what Butler's work contributes to is a debasement of the leftist imaginary such that its conception of subjectivity is brought into a situation of alignment with liberalism, thus making it very difficult to challenge liberalism polemologically, by developing a militantly alternative conception of politics. The future of the left, I believe, depends on its ability to reinvest in the hubristic and insane fantasy of a subject that can transcend its experience of vulnerability, by destroying the very sources of its vulnerability, freeing itself from them, not by living in a state of awareness of their fundamentality to its existence, but by eliminating them, cutting itself off from them. The exercise of this expressly political power, a power which can only be exercised from the positionality of the political subject, entails a will to see disappear the biopolitical problem of how to live out a resilient life of perpetual vulnerability to threats and dangers that insecure us to the political problem of how to destroy the biohumanized subject which thinks life in terms of vulnerability, with a view to achieving a substantial state of security. How to condemn the fabricated problem on account of which life is conceived as vulnerability with a view to destroying the enunciator of that problem so that it might realize its difference in kind from the subject that fabricates such a discourse? In other words, not simply a subject that in its conditions of vulnerability is given the life support through which its life is rendered 'sustainable' (Butler 2009: 23). But a subject capable of conceiving a direction upon which to transform those conditions such that its dependency is removed. Vulnerable subjects exist, Butler argues in contrast, in a necessary relation of dependency with their environmental milieus, and as such can only ever live in relations of subjection to them. This is a discourse, in other words, which preaches the impossibility of political subjectivity. As I have already made clear in my previous chapters, political subjects don't live in relations of subjection to the conditions on which they depend and which otherwise structure their lives. They seek to transform them. In contrast Butler preaches the myth of a subject that cannot transform its milieu, but only ever depends on it or its sources of 'life support'. Indeed the Butlerian subject is precisely a subject that lives its life terminally, and for political purposes comatosely, on life support. This is a mode of apprehending the life of the subject that assumes its incapacity, a subject the life of which, as she says, is defined by its vulnerability to injury, loss, destruction, or neglect (Butler 2009: 13). In contrast the left today requires a subject capable of going to war with this very discourse of reduction of life to biological properties and capacities, for this is the episteme and account of subjectivity on which contemporary power relations revolve.

When we look at how, at this moment in time, neoliberal regimes of governance are legitimated, in particular the forms of subjectivity they call into being, we can identify the very traits that Butler claims as new to her ontology. Neoliberalism's account of the relation between the human and its life is one that presupposes the vulnerability of that life, and likewise one which interpellates a subject that is called upon to live out a life of perpetual vulnerability; a subject for whom recognition of one's vulnerability is a required practice without which he or she cannot be trusted to govern others or be governed in its worldly existence. In other words, rather than being simply an ontological aspect of subjectivity, we have to grasp how the concept of vulnerability is functioning within strategies of subjectification on which the regimes that govern us depend for their security. Vulnerability is not something that we can simply claim that we are, but something that we are called upon to demonstrate ourselves as being, individually and collectively, in our relations with ourselves and others. Even if we just take a cursory look at a document as central to the discursive foundations of global liberal governance today as the United Nations' Millennium Declaration we discover that the vulnerable are precisely the population on which world order today is based and on the interpellation of whom the major institution of that police order depends for its authority (UN 2000).[2]

There is an additional point to be made here concerning the politics of 'security'. Every regime of governance invokes its own particular subject of governance, and producing subjects the liberal way has long since been understood to be a game of producing self-securing subjects. Subjects that are capable of securing themselves are less of a threat to themselves and in being so are less of a threat to the governance capacities of their states and to the governance of the global order. What differences are entailed in being a vulnerable subject as opposed to a secure subject? The major condition of possibility for the subject of neoliberalism is, as we have already seen in the contexts of our examinations of discourses on resilience and adaptivity, that it sacrifices its capacity and desire for security. Security, here, is less that which neoliberalism demands of its subjects than what it forbids them. The vulnerable subject is a subject that must permanently struggle to accommodate itself to the world, not a political subject that can conceive of changing the world, its structure, and conditions of possibility, with a view to securing itself from the world, but a subject that accepts the disastrousness of the world it lives in as a condition for partaking of that world.

In this sense the imperative discourse underpinning Butler's 'new bodily ontology' is broadly in alignment with the imperatives that guide the practices for the subjectification of the global poor at work in neoliberal policies of sustainable development. The account of the world envisaged and constituted by neoliberal agencies concerned with promoting sustainable development is one that presupposes the disastrous potential of the biosphere, and likewise one that interpellates a subject that is permanently called upon to bear the risk of that disaster. The sustainable subject is a subject for whom bearing that risk is a required practice without which he or she cannot grow and prosper in the world. This is precisely what is at stake in the discourse of sustainability. The sustainable subject is a subject that must permanently struggle to accommodate itself to the world, not a subject that can conceive of changing the world, its structure, and conditions of possibility, but a subject that accepts the disastrousness of the world it lives in as a condition for partaking of that world. Thus is it that building sustainable subjects involves the deliberate disabling of the political habits, tendencies, and capacities of peoples and replacing them with an acceptance of their ineradicable condition of vulnerability to disaster. Vulnerable subjects are subjects that have accepted the imperative not to resist or secure themselves from threats and dangers they are faced with, but instead adapt to their enabling conditions via the embrace of neoliberalism.

These are elements of the discourses of vulnerability and sustainability that Butler does not recognize or address, refusing even to treat the concepts as discursive, and instead asserting them as crude fact. How can vulnerability be a sufficient condition upon which to base a politics of contestation to the 'mechanisms of power' (Butler 2009: 1) through and by which human lives are framed today, when it is the first presupposition of liberalism, the tradition of thought and governance to which these mechanisms of power owe their principles of formation? How can vulnerability be conceived as the foundation for a counterliberal theory of subjectivity when it is the first presupposition of liberal biopolitics and its biohuman subject? The fact that these questions go unarticulated or answered is precisely why Butler's thesis is so politically debilitating.

Thinking beyond Butler's impoverished ontology, whereby the subject is reduced to its biological life, need not mean an abandonment of life as such. Life, as Foucault teaches us, is not an ontological category, but an expression of changing regimes of practices that are historical and political in formation. Life can be expressed, thought, constituted, and indeed politicized, in many different ways. Discourses on life are subject to revision on account of our capacities for political engagement with the problematic of life and what distinguishes it. The struggle with liberalism requires, therefore, not simply the rejection but contestation of its account of life. If we accept, as I do, that liberalism understands life, fundamentally, in biological terms then obvious-ly it follows that the task of a leftist theory of the subject must be to fabricate an account of the life of the subject in postbiological terms. As a political project the hegemony of neoliberalism depends on its capacities to govern us as subjects who are incapable of conceiving our life in anything more than merely biologized terms. It requires making us believe, in other words, in the impossibility of being anything more than biohuman subjects. For liberalism to legitimate itself the horizons that determine our ways of living must be successfully biologized, which is why the political discourses of global poli-tics are so replete today with values deriving from biological sources. The contemporary valorization of capacities for connectivity, adaptation, emer-gence, and informationalization, nationally and internationally, are sympto-matic expressions of this strategy.

Captured as she is within the biological limits of liberal discourse, Butler produces an account of a subject dependent on a milieu without which it cannot survive and the powers of protection that it must continually strive to maintain. Thus it is akin to the subject of psychoanalysis, a subject defined by that which it lacks, relations with an environment of objects without contact with which it cannot be complete. Of course the experience of lack and dependency are elements of subjectivity, but they do not encompass the entirety of subjectivity, nor merely its life, and certainly not its capacities for politics (Sloterdijk 2010: 13–19). In contrast the task of a leftist theory of the subject today has to be to rediscover the other side to subjectivity which entails not its experience of lack but the ways by which it decides and takes what it wants, asserts what it possesses, and celebrates what it is able to do. This is what I refer to as the hubristic or mad dimension of the subject. Hubris and madness have, of course, negative connotations, the former de-scribing the arrogance of the human who dares to act against the gods, the latter the irrationality of the human that does not think and act within reason-able limits. Today we might observe that hubristic is he or she who acts against the monarchy of life, challenging his reduction to a status of dependency on a milieu of things outside himself, sacrificing that on which he has hitherto depended, taking that which he wants not just because it secures him but because it thrills him; and mad he or she who reasons in ways that support such a regime of action. Confidence, ambition, courage, absence of fear, these are the sources of the political subject. It is not, as Butler would have it, that we are by necessity dependent on what lies outside ourselves, our milieus, or life supports, but that to become apolitical as opposed to a merely vulnerable subject we have to be able to engage freely with them, proving to ourselves and our peers that we are not dependent on them. That is the political problem of the subject; how to establish its autonomy from the things which others would have it be dependent on. The problem of vulnerability is not ontological but epistemological, and subjective not universal.

RESOURCING POLITICAL SUBJECTIVITY

There are two particular sources in Foucault's works that I think might serve us in this task. The first is his journal writings from Iran in 1978 just prior to the Iranian Revolution, which he called 'the first great insurrection against global systems, the form of revolt that is the most modern and the most insane'. There he speculated on how Islam was working to transform the discontent, hatred, misery, and despair of Iranians into what he described as 'a force'. Islam was not for Foucault well understood as a religion. It was much better understood as a force, a mysterious current, a way of being together, a way of speaking the truth and listening to truth, something that allows one to be listened to by others, and to yearn for something with them at the same time as they yearn for it. It was the *spirit* that bound a people together, constituting a shared regime of truth more powerful than the simple biological fact of their being members of the same species, giving them the courage with which to risk their own lives in order to achieve the revolutionary change that they sought and dreamt about. He speculated on the major differences between the Islamic Modernity being sought through revolutionary means in Iran and the liberal modernity that Iranian Muslims saw as archaic and were rising up to overthrow in 1978. While liberal modernity produces a subject preoccupied by a fear of its vulnerability, the death and damage that can be done to its biological life, for the Muslim, Foucault argued, death is what attaches him or her to life. And while for the liberal subject the fear of death and damage initiates an ethic of constant care for life to ensure its well-being for the finite time of which it is capable, death gives him or her the courage to fight and ultimately act without care for his or her life. Not out of obedience to a law or authority but in renewal of a fidelity, to the eventality of a truth greater than life itself. A truth which cannot be coded by law, nor which belongs to a prophet, or other representatives, but to the people which that truth inhabits.

The second resource is his very last lecture, given at the College de France in 1984, only three months before his death, and recently published in English under the title *The Courage of Truth*. The lecture was on the topic of the use of the term 'parrhesia' or 'truth telling' in early Christian texts. There Foucault described 'the opposition between two major frameworks, two major cores of Christian experience'. On the one hand, the experience specific to the very earliest forms of Christianity, of the 'parrhesiac', a being possessed with an openness of heart, immediate presence, and direct communication of the soul with God that gave him or her the confidence, ability to speak the truth, to know the truth, and courage to act, be careless with their life, risk their life, to the point of martyrdom (2011: 332). Parrhesia as such was the courage to assert the truth that one is confident of knowing and to which one wishes to bear witness regardless of every danger, and, on the other hand, the experience of the fear of the parrhesiac in the subsequent and institutionalized forms of Christianity which diagnosed parrhesia as a kind of disease, an excess and danger to be prevented, and which sought and succeeded in regrounding the project of Christianity in a completely other principle: that of trembling obedience, fear of God, recognition of the necessity to submit to His will and the will of those who represent him. This obedient subject did not, and could not, have confidence in him or herself. He or she had to operate on a principle of mistrust of oneself. He or she must not, it was understood within this other far more influential framework of Christian experience, believe, imagine or be so arrogant as to think that he or she can secure their own truth and find a way of opening to God by him or herself. He or she must be the object of their own mistrust, an attentive, scrupulous, and suspicious vigilance. And only by renunciation of self and the putting of this general principle of obedience into practice will he or she be able to secure salvation, it was understood in this second framework of Christian experience described by Foucault. So you have, as Foucault demonstrated, two very different ways of conceiving how to fulfill the eschatological promise in Christianity. On the one hand through obedience, renunciation of self, care for life, and blind submission of the will, and on the other through confidence, truth telling, risk of life, and courage.

Now, it seems to me, if we consider these two texts together, written at different times, and to entirely different audiences, and never conjoined thematically, that Foucault saw a significant resonance between the very earliest historical forms of Christianity and the Political Islam of his present. Likewise, we see that he saw in the later more institutionalized forms of Christianity the seeds of liberal modernity, biopolitics, and liberal subjectivity. And, it seems to me, what Foucault is describing when he describes the experience of subjectivity in early Christianity and Political Islam is a form of experience that can only posit itself in hostility to liberal modernity and its biopolitical subject, a form of experience which liberalism itself can only comprehend as threatening and fearful to its biopolitical project. So, if we want to found a politics beyond liberalism it may be that we can learn something from these examples. Political subjects do not merely live in order to fit in with and adapt to existing times, or desire the sustainability of the conditions for their living the lives they do. In contrast they resist those conditions, and where successful, overcome them, transforming time into that which it was not, a new time in succession of an old and destroyed time. The task is to affirm the eschatological confidence of the subject, which entails not its experience of vulnerability to injury and fear of death, but the hubristic trust in itself and others with whom it decides what it wants, asserts what it possesses, and celebrates what it is able to do, in accordance with truths that transcend its existence as a merely living entity. If the temporal limit of biopolitical modernity promises an infinite horizon of finite possibility, the temporality of properly political modernity promises an end to present time and the beginning of a new time. Not the infinity of finite possibilities on which promise the liberal imaginary rests, but the finitude of liberal governance in context of the irreducibility of revolt. Of course, liberalism possesses its own eschatology, being itself a product of a profound religiopolitical nexus (Dillon 2011). But it is a mistake to think that liberalism's promise to secure an 'infinity of finite possibility' is the only political eschatology.

THE BEYOND OF BIOPOLITICS

The eschatological confidence of the political subject arises in response to the question of its disposition in the face of seeming disaster and consequently the way in which the disaster in question is received and named. As Evan Calder Williams describes, there is a vast difference, for example, between the subject which names its disaster 'apocalypse' to that which reads disaster in terms of 'catastrophe' (Williams 2011: 1–13). Slavoj Zizek's recent analysis of the 'apocalypticism' and 'catastrophism' of our 'end times' more or less effaces these differences (Zizek 2010: 315–52). Apocalypse like so much of the discourse of disaster has a conceptual history irrevocably tied up, also, with the historical development of Christianity. An apocalypse, traditionally understood, is an end, but one that occurs with the important addition of revelation, a 'lifting of the veil', which in turn constitutes a conception of 'a beyond'. In that sense it is different from catastrophe, which is an end without escape, removal, or road leading to a world beyond (Williams 2011: 4–5). The concept has a history within a specific literature called apocalyptic literature. In a brilliant book written in the mid-twentieth century, *Occidental Eschatology*, the political theologian, Jacob Taubes told that history, detailing the historicity of the very concept of 'the beyond', including its political importance for militancy, and the modern revolutionary tradition. In it, and through his analysis of the very first example of apocalyptic literature to come down to us in its complete form, the Apocalypse of Daniel, Taubes described in concise terms the elements that compose what he called 'the structure of apocalypse' (Reid 2014; Taubes 2009: 43). 'The belief in providence, the outline of world history, the cosmic horizon against which world history is set, visions of a dreamlike nature, the concealment of the writer, a seething eschatology, the computation of the End Time, the apocalyptic science, a symbolism of numbers and secret language, the doctrine of angels' and confidence in an afterlife. All of these comprise the elements of the structure of the apocalypse within apocalyptic literature which in turn created the conditions of possibility for a politics of the beyond (Taubes 2009: 43).

Among these elements of the structure of apocalypse I am interested particularly in one: the dreamlike visions of the authors of apocalypses Taubes mentions. Every apocalypse, as Taubes describes, required its seer, its visionary, and its truth teller. The seer of the apocalypse saw into the obscurity of the decrees of fate, the evil deeds of a monster that passed in front of its eyes, and then bore witness to the figure of a man, or manlike figure, who the seer told would finally triumph over the monster and thus begin his never ending rule of the world. Apocalypticism entails, therefore, a fundamentally benevolent disposition toward disasters, underpinned by an understanding of their necessarily conflictual and divisive nature. It is a mode of prophetic truth telling, but an avowedly political form, which assumes the benevolence of the division to come between times present and future. The apocalyptic prophet, in contrast with other forms of prophet, does not merely warn human beings of what is hidden from them concerning their future, but encourages them to engage with and ultimately welcome it, on account of the change it will bring, rather than thinking they have to change their ways in order to be prepared for or able to adapt to it. The concept of apocalypse has had a profound influence on the political development of humanity ever since its first articulation by Daniel. Taken up by the Zealot movement in the Jewish revolt against the Roman Empire, apocalyptic prophesy has nourished and stoked the flames of revolution and social transformation ever since. Christianity was not something new in this regard, and Jesus himself emerged out of the apocalyptic movement in Israel, fitting into the succession of itinerant preachers that came before him. Each of those preachers had essentially one thing to say: "I am a divine spirit. I have come because the world is about to come to an end and an element of Humanity will be carried away because of their injustices. But I will save you and you will see me come again with the power of heaven" (Taubes 2009: 48).

I have no interest in the religious content of such prophetic modes of truth telling. What interests me are how they may alert us to the preconditions for political subjectivity, as well as the extent to which such preconditions have become foreign to us in the context of liberal governance. Fundamental to the writing of apocalypse was this imaginative consciousness, this confidence, this absolute resolve, and certitude of possession of the power to be able to welcome disaster as a precondition for access to a beyond. Today, in the context of the widespread and deep-seated belief in the inescapably catastrophic nature of the world we inhabit, such an imagination and confidence in the abilities to welcome it is liable to be diagnosed as a form of, what we moderns have learnt to name madness. But perhaps that is the point. The apparent extremity of not just belief, but imagination, confidence, and even certainty in the possibility of apocalyptic division between worlds and between times, of present and future, is a sign of how detached we have become from this particular mode of truth telling.

Of course, the life of the neoliberal subject is not itself bereft of imagination or images. Consider the proliferation of pictorial images enabled by the forms of social media discussed in the previous chapter; the 'image-charged' relation with our worlds which we in the technologized 'Functioning Core' now inhabit and have possessed for some time now (Auge 1994: 64–65), the density of image-environments made a reality by social media, and the endless proliferation of technological devices with which photographic images are now made and circulated. Guy Debord's concept of spectacle famously described 'the means by which our experiences are constantly mediated by images that produce their own forms of alienated social relations' (Murray 2011: 166). It is not merely 'a collection of images, but a social relation among people, mediated by images' (Debord 2010: 4). For Debord the spectacle is aimed at controlling, not the means of production, but the entire social and cultural infrastructure, through the deployment of images; a deployment of images that works to destroy a public's very abilities to see, for it 'concentrates all gazing and all consciousness' (Debord 2010: 3), while finding vision to be the sense through which human subjugation can best be obtained (Debord 2010: 18). It is both the affirmation of appearance and the affirmation of human life as mere appearance (Debord 2010: 10). 'It says nothing more than "that which appears is good, that which is good appears"' (Debord 2010: 12). If earlier phases of the domination of capital over human life degraded their being into having, the contemporary phase has led to a shift from having into appearing, 'from which all actual "having" must draw its immediate prestige and its ultimate function' (Debord 2010: 17). The spectacle is by definition immune from human activity, inaccessible to any political intervention. It is the opposite of dialogue (Debord 2010: 18). It seduces us into believing we are communing with it and its images, yet works tirelessly to prevent us from accessing it and to maintaining a nondialogical relation between power and public (Murray 2011: 166). Images function for the spectacle to maintain an illusion of dialogue, while our imaginations become the source of our subjection. As such the task of critique, Debord maintained, is to expose the spectacle as the 'visible negation of life, as a negation of life which has become visible' (2010: 10), which is to render capital itself into the form of the visible, for 'the spectacle is capital to such a degree of accumulation that it becomes an image' (Debord 2010: 34).

Research into the life cycle of photographic images conducted by the Hillman Photography Initiative at the Carnegie Museum of Art suggests that the average networked individual currently encounters around five thousand photographic images a day (Hillman Photography Initiative 2014). The consequence of these media and their utilization is that the spectacle is no longer a property of states or top-down regimes of economy but an everyday practice, which neoliberal subjects practice upon themselves. Our imaginations are said to be governed by the pictorial images that are circulated through these media, facilitating a sense of false intimacy with our worlds, as we become used to discussing images as if they were realities (Auge 1994: 65). Even our basic capacities for memory, it is said, are being outsourced to digital devices such as the camera phones on which so many photographic images are made and circulated every day (NPR 2014). No wonder that neoliberal regimes see in these forms of media the sources of the governability of their subject populations.

Certainly Foucault thought that the relations between political subjectivity, imagination, religious experience, and madness were crucial for us to understand. To recall, 'the first great insurrection against global systems, the form of revolt that is *the most modern and the most insane*' was how he described the Iranian Revolution. That concatenation of madness and modernity which he thought he saw in the Iranian Revolution demands much further consideration than has been afforded to date. The idea that it is not in the domain of the subject's capacity for reason but its madness, or in other words its distance from reason, that a politics beyond biopolitics lies. Indeed if we look back at the history of struggles with liberalism we discover that practically every nonliberal politics that has ever emerged has been subject to a discourse which renders it fanatical, deviant, extreme, irrational, and mad (Colas 1997; Toscano 2010). But if we take Foucault seriously, then we have to understand madness not simply as a discourse or subject position of relative distance from reason, but a power, and source of revolt itself. In this sense his thinking certainly dovetailed with the directions that the work of Gilles Deleuze and Felix Guattari moved in the 1970s, for whom delirium was also a profound power and source of revolutionary force misunderstood and improperly pathologized by the Marxist left (Deleuze 2004).

Madness itself is of course a multiplicity. And the obvious question that then arises is which madness? The madness of the subject which possesses this hubristic confidence, this absolute resolve, and ability to welcome disaster for the confrontation with time that it beckons toward is much closer to the paranoiac pole which Deleuze and Guattari identified with fascism than the schizophrenic pole to which they assigned a hitherto unexplored revolutionary potential (Deleuze and Guattari 2000: 9–15). But that may say more about the relative limits of their exploration of the dualistic sources of fascism and revolutionary politics. Certainly if we examine, as Dominic Colas has in her brilliant study, the history of fanatical revolts we find that the psychopolitical sources of antiliberal struggles have tended to bear the tendencies as well as being subject to the diagnosis of paranoia much more than they have schizophrenia. The paranoiac prophet is directly plugged into the truth, 'the absolute, or knowing subject, who reveals its secrets to him, lets him in on the plan. Separation or exile are over, and the creature is reintegrated into the word of the great knower, who makes truth flow from the prophet's mouth' (Colas 1997: 217). Such a paranoiac-prophetic relation with truth was what Colas identified in, for example, the remarkable Camisard rebellion against Louis XIV in the Languedoc region of France in the early eighteenth century in which unarmed Camisard peasants, including men, women, and children of all ages defeated the troops of the French state in circumstances of open battle, where they were outnumbered on a ratio of ten to one. 'The Military exploits of the Camisards were founded in their certitude of being . . . contempt of death and capacity for self-sacrifice' (Colas 1997: 203–17). 'Paranoia works. It works where common sense would fail and hysteria wouldn't even try' (Colas 1997: 217).

To reiterate, the question Foucault's concatenation of madness, imagination, modernity, and revolution poses is not one of how to recover the content of such militantly religious experience as evinced in the history of the Camisards or the Iranian Revolution, but one of a recognition of the peculiarity of such regimes of truth, founded as they were on a resolve and certitude of being rendered unimaginable and labeled pathologically dangerous on account of its foreignness to the limits of liberal reason. The enthusiasm with which Foucault greeted the Iranian Revolution, and the generosity with which Deleuze and Guattari gave hospitality to psychotics, were each expressions of a shared sense that it is in that concatenation of relations that a beyond to liberal biopolitical modernity will find its expression.

VULNERABLE VIOLENCE

Every account of subjectivity entails its own account of violence, and cannot avoid riffing on the questions of who it is desirable to kill and how. Does the age-old problem of political violence get any better if we invest in vulnerability as contrasted with hubris or madness as the foundation for political subjectivity? I don't think so. Vulnerability breeds its own violence, and Butler herself is not shy about endorsing forms of political and indeed state-led violence, for example in situations of imminently declared 'genocide' (Butler 2009: 37) to protect 'the vulnerable'. But the weaknesses of Butler's understanding of the utility of stressing a 'common human vulnerability' (Butler 2004: 31) as a means of challenging the violence of the United States owes as much to her understanding of the nature of subjectivity underpinning U.S. foreign policy and national identity. On this problem Butler follows a familiar and well-trodden leftist path of misperceiving U.S. foreign policy as an expression of an 'arrogant politics' born out of its supposedly classical imperialist ambition (Butler 2009: 37; 2004: 11). It is a subject, she argues, produced not only to conceive its own violence as righteous but to conceive its own destructibility as 'unthinkable' (Butler 2009: 47). As she expresses it, 'the notion of the subject produced by the recent wars conducted by the US, including its torture operations, is one in which the US subject seeks to produce itself as impermeable, to define itself as protected permanently against incursion and as radically invulnerable to attack' (Butler 2009: 47). Is this true? Butler's argument is devoid of analytical or empirical support, but when we examine the discourses underpinning the legitimation of the reassertion of the sovereign power of the United States to wage war since the declaration of its 'War on Terror', what do we see? A sovereign subject convinced of its indestructibility? Or a vulnerable subject preoccupied obsessively with its own weaknesses and openness to injury? A subject that conceives itself deploying violence strategically with a view to achieving a 'permanent' condition of security, or one that no longer believes in the possibility of such a security, and is committed to a policy of an endless war without ends?

Of course it is the latter. We only have to look at the hysterical discourse within the United States around the cited 'vulnerability' of the 'national infrastructure' (Dillon and Reid 2009: 127–46). In the United States, infrastructure is defined as the 'various human, cyber, and physical components that must work effectively together to sustain . . . quality of life' and the U.S. War on Terror has become organized around the protection of the conditions for 'quality of life' (DHS 2004: 63; Reid 2011). The compatibility between the U.S. State Department account of U.S. vulnerability to 'terrorism' and Butler's demand that we reconceive political obligation as the obligation 'to the conditions that make life possible' because 'there can be no sustained life without those sustaining conditions, and those conditions are both our political responsibility and the matter of our most vexed ethical decisions' (Butler 2009: 23) is startling. It reveals the lie on which her representation of the subjectivity whose violence she is concerned with contesting as well as the claim to originality and newness on which her own account of the subject rests. The vulnerable subject today, par excellence, is the United States and its violence flows from its own biopoliticized self-understanding of itself as a living entity whose very survival as a living entity as well as capacity to care for life tout court is at stake in a war with an enemy dedicated to the destruction of the conditions for the flourishing of life (Reid 2006a).

CONCLUSION

So where else can the left go from here? Now that we have lain to rest the issue of the potential of Butler's account of vulnerability for the future theorization of political subjectivity it befalls us to repose the question of what the preconditions of a leftist account of subjectivity may be. The major task facing the left today is that of reconceptualizing the human subject in terms of its capacities for politics so that it may free itself from hegemonic and stultifying accounts of its being, which revolve around the fears of what can be done to its biological properties and capacities: the reduction, in other words, of political subjectivity to biopolitical subjectivity, and that of the human to the biohuman (Dillon and Reid 2009: 147–56). For this is a way of conceiving subjectivity peculiar to the very regimes of subjectivation that it is the pressing task of the left today to combat. A politics to supersede the conditions of biopolitical modernity is a politics which must be capable of thinking within an idiom not of the corporeal life of bodies but what Felix Guattari once named 'incorporeal species' (Guattari 2000: 43–44). Incorporeal species live, but they do not die. They can be forgotten or lost, cease to exist, but die as such they cannot. The friend whose life expires does not stop being your friend just because he no longer lives. Love, solidarity, friendship: in the existence of these incorporeal species and their practices lies the possibility of the reinvigoration of the political animal known as human. Likewise the political subject, whose existence as political does not depend on his life as such, but on the deeds and bonds of which he is capable, some of which will compromise his mere life, and the very livability of his subjectivity. Political subjects do not merely depend on their milieus, or desire the sustainability of the conditions for their living the lives they do, much rather they resist those conditions, and where successful, overcome them and transform them into that which they were not, in the process establishing new conditions by which to live differently. Hubris, imagination, and madness are the constitutive powers through which political subjects come into existence: the fantasy of the possibility of another life, another existence. This is not to deny the illusional quality of fantasy but to underline the claim that illusion is the fundamentally human capacity. Liberalism is what is finite. It will die. The question is how and when. And the eschatological confidence of peoples, while challenged by liberal modernity, remains evident, outside of Europe largely, but in Europe too—just look at the recent riots in London and growing uprisings in the Southern European countries largely. These insurrections give us confidence in a future beyond liberalism. And the renewal of such an eschatological confidence—that these times will be succeeded by a new time—is a singular precondition for human resistance and revolt in the world.

NOTES

1. While the two concepts have different resonances in her works, Butler uses 'precariousness' and 'vulnerability' in a thoroughly interchangeable manner as far as I have been able to ascertain. For the sake of consistency I will use the concept of vulnerability in interpretation of her use of 'precariousness'.

2. 'As leaders we have a duty therefore to all the world's people, especially the most vulnerable and, in particular, the children of the world, to whom the future belongs' (UN 2000).

Conclusion

Interview with Gideon Baker

We agree about many aspects of the neoliberal subject and the discourses of vulnerability, adaptation, and resilience, which to us seem to close off possibilities of exploring and expanding what it could mean to be human, along with the possibilities of politics, critique, and collective projects of resistance, change, and transformation. The purpose of this book was to explore together the critique of the neoliberal subject without blunting the edges of our approach on the basis of articulating merely our shared grounds and shared normative conclusions. By way of conclusion then, we have decided to explore a little more the differences in our approaches and the stakes involved, through a discussion with our colleague and friend, Gideon Baker.

Gideon: Although the two positions set out here focus on the neoliberal subject, the underlying objective is clear: to ask whether another subject, another subjective path is conceivable, and to pursue this question because of the poverty of the neoliberal subject, a subject reduced to the many and varied ways in which it is embedded in, rather than potentially transcendent of, its world. What appears particularly important to me in your intervention, David and Julian, is the (re)appearance of the question of the relationship of subjects to truth. By and large, this is not a question that Anglophone international or political thought seem very interested in, and I think I agree with you both that, partly as a result of this, the 'subjects' that emerge in these discourses are 'debased', or certainly highly depoliticized. So there is an out-of-joint quality to your engagement which makes it particularly fresh and interesting. But there is also something timely here. Whether in Alain Badiou's theory of the subject as subject precisely to and for truths, or in the

167

recovery of the late Foucault's truth-telling subject (a subjectivity cut off by the disaster that was and is the Christian pastorate in its still mutating forms), now is clearly the moment for a move beyond the post-Cartesian subject by way of an idea of a subject that can know (and thereby act). For as you both helpfully illuminate, the death of the subject in post-structuralist or constructivist thought is mirrored in the neoliberal recasting of subjects as ever doubtful, as subjects that can never move beyond charting their dependencies and vulnerabilities, knowing only the inter- of their inter-subjectivities.

So I would like to explore this question of the subject further. This is where there is both common ground between you (we must find a more potent vision of the subject), and yet also the most fundamental disagreement (where does this subject come from and what does it look like?). The first thing that struck me was that the genealogies of your two subjects diverge significantly. David: Your subject seems strongly identified with the classical liberal subject, with the Enlightenment in short. Julian: Your 'mad' or 'paranoid' subject renews its ancient eschatological hope in a new world to come. On each account there is a Janus-faced temporality that involves looking at once into past and future, whether to the event of eschatology as the historical condition for radical political subjectivity in the future or to the historically given Enlightenment subject, which, though no doubt neither universal nor necessary, is capable of refurbishment (otherwise why recover it at all?). Whence my first question, which attempts to draw you each into a more explicit encounter with the other's position:

David: Given your emphasis on the rational subject, can you see any use for a subject sourced in the reveries of ancient apocalypse? Julian: Is recuperation of the Enlightenment subject for you a bridge too far in the rethinking of anti-humanism that you call for?

David: I do not really know what it would mean to 'source a subject'. I wish it was really just a matter of picking up some encyclopedic history of the subject, flicking through and picking out one which we fancied—whether it is the Enlightenment subject or any other and arguing which is somehow 'best'. This is not really my approach. First, before we have any discussion of 'alternatives', I think it is important to engage with what we understand as the neoliberal subject, and its conditions of possibility. I have suggested that the neoliberal subject is a construct of governance practices and an effect of the exhaustion of the Enlightenment project or of the progressive content of liberalism. Rather than humanizing the world or liberalizing, securing, and democratizing the international sphere—the liberal telos of progress—there is an inversion: the world of meaning, of progress, is shrinking. This seems more than clear in the discourses covered in my chapters and their themes of security, development, and democracy.

I have tried to suggest that in this shrinking of the liberal world, the subject is also shrunk, degraded, or erased. I have also tried to argue that there is a material basis to this diminished engagement with our world, a material basis of defeats of political struggles for progress, which gave liberalism its progressive content. To my mind, the only alternative is one which can give expression to the revival of these aspirations, one which thereby enables an imposition of a collective framework of practical meaning upon the world. Without this material struggle, 'another world' would not be meaningfully thinkable. I do not think that any alternatives will come from accepting the world as it is and retreating into subjective imagination or 'the reveries of ancient apocalypse'. This could only create diverse, atomizing, subjective worlds drawing us further apart, undermining collective meaning further, and discouraging transformative material possibilities.

Where I disagree fundamentally with Julian (and with what is conceived in my chapters as the interpellated subject of neoliberalism) is over the alleged progressive potential of 'agent-centred' or individualistic understandings of the subject. Where both neoliberal framings and Julian's alternative come unstuck is in the view that freedom or progress can be possible at the level of the individual, which seemingly needs to be 'freed' from the intersubjective constraints upon their reason (or in Julian's case, their imagination). To me this is, in both cases, pure subjectivism. The world remains exactly as it was. I don't want to get all Marxist about this, but for me the problems are in the world, not in our heads. However, this does not mean that subjectivity is not important. The alternative to the inward looking atomized subjectivity of neoliberalism—one which necessarily can only see contingency, which needs to be responded or adapted to—is a collective, plural, understanding of the human subject; one which is capable of constructing shared frameworks of meanings, managing contingency, and engaging as a subject in the world (this, of course, is where the connection to the Enlightenment comes in). It is only in this practical engagement with the world, rather than in seeing 'freedom' as a retreat from the world, that collective subjectivities are formed.

I would argue that, in the project of recovering the human as a political subject, Kant and Arendt are useful sources of inspiration, because they help us draw a political line of struggle against neoliberalism. They do this because in distinction to contemporary neoliberal approaches, they encourage us to remake the world rather than to remake the human. However, as I have said, the precondition for remaking the world is that humans aspire to social and political progress and act as humanly as they can in the cause of the human, in terms of struggling to build human collective institutions of meaning and action. Building or socially constructing the human scaffolding of laws and structures enables us to act as fully as subjects in the external world as is humanly possible. Rather than demonstrating the problem of the human, through holding up the world as a mirror, Kant and Arendt suggest to us, in different ways, that the problem can be understood in terms of the collective constitution of the subject and practical political struggle. I would argue that building on this problematic today can enable us to posit the necessity of the transformative human subject in order to resist and critique the neoliberal concerns of ethical reflectivity, resilience, adaptation, and external limits.

In our neoliberal world, ethical understandings start from the position of the world as it appears rather than from the perspective of human collectivities with goals orientated to transforming the external world. As Alain Badiou noted, this orientation reflects an ethics that 'designates above all the incapacity . . . to name and strive for a Good' (2001: 30). Necessity is welcomed as an ethical imperative that allows us to feel at ease with a world in which human freedom appears to be responsible for the disastrous nature of the world. In this way, ethics and necessity displace the space of politics. For Hannah Arendt, the appearance of necessity was always based on working backward from the status quo, whereas working forward with a future-based orientation (acts of will) depended on the collective social and political frameworks of human meaning and organization that could enable us to cope with contingency:

> the Will's impotence persuades men to prefer looking backward, remembering and thinking, because, to the backward glance, everything that is appears necessary. The repudiation of willing liberates man from a responsibility that would be unbearable if nothing that was done could be undone. (1978: II, 168)

For Arendt, only as political subjects could we construct a meaningful human world in which politics was possible. Using this framework, or reading Arendt in terms of today, it is possible for neoliberal approaches to be understood as a way of thinking that both internalizes and externalizes the human condition. Neoliberal approaches understand the problems of plural and interactive humanity as either being an internal problem of the limited rationality of individuals or of the unknowability of the external world. Instead of living with contingency with the plural clash of wills and aspirations and the creative processes generated through this, we thereby seek to remove or to naturalize contingency. Neoliberal approaches do both, asserting that contingency is a part of our external world—a product of globalization—and therefore natural, but also that the effects of contingency can be minimized through being aware of the problems of rationalist thinking and therefore continually working upon our own ethical self-reflectivity and upon that of others.

Rather than constituting the problem, or understanding contingency as a problem per se, for Arendt, human agency is the solution to the problem of coping with contingency. Contingency, as a fact of the world, can be managed through an appreciation of the human capacity for politics, for conscious intervention and organization. This is precisely where politics becomes important. By acting as rational and responsible citizens we come together to bind ourselves to each other and to collective projects of meaning, through our promises, contracts, treaties, and constitutions. The sphere of politics—of self-determined goals—for Arendt, was something that could not exist independently of practice:

> The space of appearance comes into being wherever men are together in the manner of speech and action, and therefore predates and precedes all formal constitution of the public realm and the various forms of government, that is, the various forms in which the public realm can be organised. Its peculiarity is that, unlike the spaces which are the work of our hands, it does not survive the actuality of the movement which brought it into being, but disappears . . . with the disappearance or arrest of the activities themselves. (1998: 199)

Our ability to construct our world as a human one, one which is amenable to human understanding and intervention, is therefore contingent on our subjective constructions of political collectivity, which in turn shape our subjectivity and understanding of ourselves in relation to our external world. In this way, our neoliberal understanding of the imposition of necessity over freedom is neither a trick of ideology, nor a product of the external world, but rather the real, but contingent, reflection of our lack of human activity and engagement in constructing a human world. The loss of world and the internalized understanding of transformative agency are products of a broader problematic of real material political and ideological defeat of struggles to construct a human world.

Contingency becomes a problem because we have lost a sense of public reason and public power as a way of managing contingency. If we are unable to cope with uncertainty and contingency, the inevitable result is that:

> All this is reason enough to turn away with despair from the realm of human affairs and to hold in contempt the human capacity for freedom, which by producing the web of human relationships, seems to entangle its producer to such an extent that he appears much more the victim and the sufferer than the author and doer of what he has done. Nowhere . . . does man appear to be less free than in those capacities whose very essence is freedom and in that realm which owes its existence to nobody and nothing but man. (1998: 233–34)

In a world dominated by neoliberal understandings, man appears to be unfree and the presuppositions of the political and public sphere seem to be hubristic and false. Neoliberal approaches reflect this disappearance of man, charted by Arendt in terms of the natural and social sciences, whereby 'man began to consider himself part and parcel of the two superhuman, all-encompassing processes of nature and history' both of which produced contingencies 'without ever reaching any inherent telos or approaching any preor-dained idea' (1998: 307). In these framings, rather than humans as active and creative subjects, the understanding of the human becomes one of the pro-cesses in which they are embedded subjects, open to the understandings of behaviouralist and natural sciences. The solution to the problems of the world then becomes sought inside the human head and in the processes within which the human is embedded, with the serious danger 'that man may be willing and, indeed, is on the point of developing into that animal species from which, since Darwin, he imagines he has come' (Arendt 1998: 322).

Arendt presciently noted that when the social displaces the public politi-cal sphere, there is no longer personal responsibility for deeds and words (action) and people are judged according to their behaviour. She noted the development of 'the all-comprehensive pretension of the social sciences which, as "behavioural sciences", aim to reduce man as a whole, in all his activities, to the level of a conditioned and behaving animal' (1998: 45), perhaps even more pertinently noting that: 'through society it is the life process itself which in one form or another has been channelled into the public realm' (1998: 45). The realm of necessity, of the natural, then predom-inates over the human. In this world, it seems that our sciences of the social and the political lag far behind our achievements in the natural sciences; that the human is the problem despite science and technology. Arendt argued:

> this criticism concerns only a possible change in the psychology of human beings—their so-called behaviour patterns—not a change of the world they move in. And this psychological interpretation, for which the absence or pres-ence of a public realm is as irrelevant as any tangible, worldly reality, seems rather doubtful in view of the fact that no activity can become excellent if the world does not provide a proper space for its exercise. (1998: 49)

She suggests the resurrection of the public realm as an alternative to the current insistence that politics be reduced to the administration of 'behaviou-ral change'. The removal of the public sphere means that we live together in the world without bonds of connection. The public sphere may be a con-structed and artificial world but it is one which is common to all of us, as a human construction or artifice, which brings us together as equals by virtue of separating us from our private lives and existences but at the same time makes us separate and individuated as responsible actors (Arendt 1998: 52–53). Without a public realm, human life really is embedded in overlap-ping complex adaptive systems within which the human is reduced to a fleeting individual life.

Julian: It's wrong to think we can distinguish between the real and the imaginary. There is no hard and fast distinction, even though the fact that we speak of the real and the imaginary indicates that they are different. We perceive and make sense of the real through images. And the maps we construct to navigate the real are composed of images. Are images dependent on the real? That I find harder to say. But the world exists in our heads every bit as much as our heads are in the world. Images and reality are ceaselessly interchanging such that the two are forever interfused. What we have learnt to call 'the world' is the manifestation of that interfusion.

Politics is an art of worldly transformation, and transformation demands, first of all and fundamentally, a subject capable of conceiving the possibility of worldly transformation. A subject that sees the intolerability of the world as it is presently arranged and demands the seemingly impossible: the creation of a new one, a subject which affirms and follows the paths opened up to it by the visions which the play of images creates for it, a subject that affirms the reality of the existence of different worlds, their antagonisms, as well as tangibility and reachability, so to say. I call this the political subject, and it is closely related to the prophetic subjects of eschatological thought and practice. I think David is searching for something similar, but he's searching in the wrong places. Maybe he needs to read more Kant. If you want to understand Kant, the degradation of the human world he and his cronies are responsible for, you need to read his *Anthropology from a Pragmatic Point of View*. It's all in there. Foucault wrote his PhD thesis on it, and it is a fundamental text for understanding everything that he said about liberalism subsequently. The Kantian enlightenment, if we want to give it that absurdly paradoxical name, gave license to human beings to speculate on the possibility of other worlds, but always with the insistence that this world, as it is supposedly known, is the only world that can be. The possibility of another world is thinkable only within this world we inhabit, Kant said, and thus the possible has to always be suborned to the actual. The corollary of the possibility of me or you conceiving another world is the impossibility of me moving beyond this world, the world, as it is known and said to be. In that sense it was and still is a powerful and demeaning discourse on limits, one which forces us to accept our sense of the limits of this world as an imperious necessity without which we cannot think or act or indeed, imagine. Its influence goes some way to explaining why the world we live in has become so depoliticized, so absent of any sense of tangible alternatives, and crucially, subjects capable of creating and establishing them. When one reads back through the history of liberal thought what's striking is the extent to which this project of constituting a subject of limits required a wholesale pathologization of the human imagination. Kant was a very sober man for a reason. He feared the intoxicating powers of drink, its abilities to incite the imagination, the wildness of what we see and feel, the freedom from care it gives us, and the sense of increased vital force which leads us to follow the trajectories it opens up for us. We all know, or should know, the experience of intoxication, and the ways in which it enables us to see the world differently, as well as act and speak differently, on account of the images it induces us. Stuff happens, collectively and individually, under the influence of drink. It's not that different from the ways in which subjects are seized in states of madness. And I think politics today requires a subject that is able to become not just a little more, but a lot more, drunk on itself, delirious with the sense of its own capabilities, free from the care that attends states of sobriety, sanity, and good mental and physical health. Of course we all know drunks who are bores, who use drink as a path to sadness and cretineity, who induce sadness in us by their slobbering presence. There has to be an art to these practices of the subject and we have to be able to discern the differences between the subjective states we encounter in ourselves and each other under their influence. And that is politics too, obviously. There's no easy way of deciding beforehand. That's what makes politics worthwhile, the risk of getting it all badly wrong, of becoming a botched piece of work, but the equal possibility of pulling something off worth acclaiming, of saying something worth saying, doing something which might be proclaimed an event, and an opening to new worlds worth living in.

The war on the imagination which Kant and others inaugurated was, of course, also an attempt to govern truth, practices of truth telling, and human relations to truth. It is not, of course, that the Enlightenment forbids us to tell truth, but that it sought to govern its production, and to subject it to a new regime of biopolitical power relations. For truth to be truth, Kant said, it had to be allied not simply to the world, but to the life of the world, or better understood, a world which itself is finite and living, requiring care and protection, vulnerable to the destructive potential of the maps and trajectories human beings impose on it on account of the power of their visions of what it can become. Today the name we give to that Kantian conception of the world as a living being is the biosphere. Biospheric life is the vulnerable guide of the Kantian subject of liberal modernity. As living beings, so the story goes, our time cannot be indifferently dispersed and scattered. We have not just a path to follow, but a movement by which we might learn to follow life along that path, by accepting the reality that we owe our life, its sustenance and survival, finitely, to the world on which our paths are inscribed. Sustainable development is the name we give, today, to the Kantian conception of truth. The discourse on worldliness, and the prescription of the limits of the human imagination, is underwritten by a claim as to the infinite debt of all finite beings to the biosphere. The truths we can tell of this world and those to come have to be said in recognition of our debt and responsibility to it in all its finitude, vulnerability, and limits.

Now it seems to me that this original investment of Kant and others in biospheric life is what accounts for the fundamental antinomy between political and liberal subjectivity. An antinomy that continues to shape the antagonism between the neoliberalism analysed here in this book, the subject it calls into being globally today, and the erstwhile political subject of a modernity I am attempting to recover the entrails of. Because the telling of political truth demands an affirmation of the conflict between worlds, a breaking through, without due care for what the implications will be for the world we inhabit and believe we somehow possess, a violence unto life which dispossesses the world we inhabit of the life which preserves it, a severing of the life-support systems which make the world we know possible. Political truth cannot be told simply out of care for life. That idea is the great conceit of liberal modernity, and has been manifestly proven wrong by the long history of war and violence done unto life supposedly out of care for life. I have written on that extensively. We need an entirely different way of apprehending the relations between truth, life and death if we are to recover the politics of subjectivity. Political truths are told by subjects that risk life, their own, that of others, and the world itself, in telling the truths which they do. They respect not the truth of life that Kant insists on, its being a phenomena of finitude and vulnerability, but the life of truth. For truth has life only insofar as it outlives me while being spoken by me. Its vitality has to outstrip me for it to be worth telling. Fundamentally the Kantian enlightenment understands none of these categories and their relations; life, world, death, politics, truth. Not only does it not understand them, but it is responsible for the installation of a world in which their miscomprehension continues to reverberate power-fully. Neoliberalism is the manifestation of the power of that miscomprehension. So, more fundamentally still, the war against neoliberalism is in essence a war against the legacies of the Kantian enlightenment. Obviously that declaration is not an incitement to 'forget Kant'. Kant is not understood or read well enough. But the idea that we could somehow go back to Kant to tool up in order to do battle with the subject he is in the first place, philosoph-ically speaking, the inaugurator of, seems daft to me. We need other textual resources. There is a rich tradition of thought which explores and affirms the imagination, which I have only been able to reference cursorily in this book, but which can be made much more useful for political purposes. It's pointless sticking with the canon.

Gideon: Both of your political subjects are proud, even hubristic—certain of their truths and capable, thereby, of changing the world rather than only ever adapting to it. But the truths your subjects hold to, which constitute them, are very different indeed. One is a rational subject and one 'mad'; one must recover its reason while the other must keep reason at bay, or at least not succumb to the injunction: 'be reasonable!' David: Your rational subject can and must know its world in order to change it. Julian: Your hubristic subject can know its mad truth, the truth of the time to come. So while there is a shared orientation here toward truth and the capacity of truths to produce subjects that can know and thereby act, there is a very different knowing at stake. On the one hand, David's political subjects need first to know their objective world and the subjective worlds they produce in their heads are the very problem to be overcome. Julian's political subjects, on the other hand, are defined precisely by the subjective world in their heads—the imagination is that facility by which the human as a political being transcends its mere animal status as a being determined like any other. But, David, surely the Enlightenment subject didn't discover its world so much as posit a new one that didn't previously exist? The bourgeoisie produced a world in its own image, and is not a new imagination of the subject required if 'world' is to be produced differently. Surely this prioritization of subjective over objective world is at least in part what Marx is driving at in his famous aphorism about the point being not to interpret the world, but to change it? As the reverse of this, however, and this time to Julian, if the eschatological subject is to successfully bridge this world and the world to come, then surely it needs to get 'this' world, its 'objective' conditions, right? The failure of Jewish apocalypticism to inspire successful political revolt against the Roman Empire meant that 'Jerusalem' only triumphed over 'Rome' centuries later, by way of Christian accommodation with empire. (If ever there was a Pyrrhic victory, surely this was it?) So there seems here to be a problem with each emphasis, taken on its own. This leads me on to my second question:

What is the relationship between knowing our world and knowing our truths? On the one hand: To what extent can knowledge of this world foster political subjects in the absence of truths from 'another' world? On the other hand: to what extent can 'other-worldly' truths dispense with knowledge of 'this world'?

David: I am pretty sure that there is no link between knowledge, the search for truth (which is not the same), and political subjectivity. Even the search for truth does not necessarily make us political subjects; however, as theorists as diverse as Socrates and Foucault are often understood to have argued, the questioning of truths, even if not a political act in itself, develops the possibility of independent and critical thinking, the prerequisites for political subjectivity. As Arendt has argued, it is thinking, not the quest for truth, which is the most dangerous and challenging activity for power (2003: 176). However, as suggested earlier, I do not think that the production of an alternative subject is a purely philosophical question, but rather one of practical politics and collective engagement. My only concern is therefore with regard to the 'practical' philosophical truths that might clarify or facilitate such a project. These 'truths' are neither objective facts to be discovered or unveiled in the world, but nor are they truths from another world, another time, or some subjectivist imagining. The truths called for are those that provide a framework for practical political struggle: truths for our world and our time.

I have spoken about Arendt at some length, so now might be a good time to bring in the importance of Kant, alluded to earlier in the discussion. I think that it is in the work of Immanuel Kant that we find indications of what this approach to practical philosophical truth might entail. Here I don't entirely agree with Julian's reading of Kant as limiting us to the world that exists in the present and closing off future alternative possibilities, although these do remain at the level of ideals. Kant was a product of his time, but nevertheless he argued powerfully for human reason *and* human imagination, understanding that these were not opposed concepts but mutually dependent, and could be articulated in ways that enabled us to take responsibility for our actions without suborning ourselves to the contingent appearances of the world.

Kant rightly argued that we cannot assert as empirical fact anything that exists in the conceptual world of philosophy, politics, and political theory. The necessary idea that humans are rational subjects confronting an external world amenable to human control and dominion is not a fact: 'It is in fact merely an idea of reason, which nonetheless has undoubted practical reality' (Kant 1970: 79). For Kant, for example, there was no original social contract, in which individuals in a state of nature constituted a sovereign, however, as political subjects we nevertheless need to act as if this act had occurred: 'it is the Idea of that act that alone enables us to conceive of the legitimacy of the state' (Kant 1999: 146). It is an act of a priori reasoning which allows us to posit the 'Idea' of the political subject: the universal rational subject.

The fundamental point is that if we live in a world of political defeat—a neoliberal world—we cannot merely assert the empirical existence or future existence of the transformative human subject. It seems entirely possible that with the historical defeat of the social and political struggles that gave content and meaning to the Enlightenment project, even the empirical growth of organized labour in China, or elsewhere, could not be expected to reproduce previous subjective understandings or claims with regard to the human subject. It seems that, at present, it is not possible to empirically indicate an alternative political force with programmatic aspirations reasserting the transformative political power of the subject.

Today, therefore, we do not appear to live in a 'Marxist' world, where there is an emerging transformative subject, we seem to live in a 'Kantian' one. We face the problems that Kant faced, of deriving the human subject, qua subject, from the philosophical idea rather than the concrete and material reality. We need a philosophical conception of the human as a political subject in order to keep alive even the possibility of critique. The possibility of the return of the human as a real political subject in the world is not something that can be purely addressed as an academic or philosophical question, but is one of practical politics. However, maintaining the stance of the critique of neoliberal approaches seems a fundamental requirement (whether or not the subject does, in fact, revive or return). Without an existing political movement stressing the transformative and creative possibilities of the human subject, all that remains is a critique based on practical political reasoning: on the positing of the necessary Idea of the human subject.

In this world, as Kant argued: 'experience cannot provide knowledge of what is right' (1970: 86). It is only through starting with a set of a priori assumptions, which assume the possibility of the existence of the human subject, that political critique can be possible. In Kant's own day, his view of the possibilities for human reasoning and progress were roundly critiqued on the basis of the chaotic, irrational, and conflict-filled empirical world around us. Kant argued that his perspective was based not upon empirical fact or the truths of the world as it existed but upon his:

> inborn duty of influencing posterity in such a way that it will make constant progress (and I must thus assume that progress is possible), and that this duty may be rightfully handed down from one member of the species to the next . . . And however uncertain I may be and may remain as to whether we can hope for anything better for mankind, this uncertainty cannot detract from the maxim I have adopted, or from the necessity of assuming for practical purposes that human progress is possible . . . It is quite irrelevant whether any empirical evidence suggests that these plans, which are founded only on hope, may be unsuccessful. (1970: 88–89)

For Kant, we had to act as human subjects with an a priori set of assumptions of what that would mean, in order to construct ourselves as humans in reality. This is why Kant held fast to the teleology of human progress, suggesting that this truth did not depend on the actions or even the beliefs of individuals in the present. Today, of course, teleological assumptions of the inevitability of human progress—the metaphysical assumptions of Enlightenment idealism—can only be empty assertions, more likely to encourage fatalism than critical thinking. As Arendt noted in her Kant lectures, the problem of how to deal meaningfully with the present is evaded in Kant's resort to the metaphysics of history or progress (Arendt 1982: 77). The philosophical assumptions we need are those which ground the possibility of the alternative subject in the present and enable us to constitute practices as if this subject existed even if, like the social contract, it may not have literally existed as an empirical fact.

The alternative, future, human subject may not make much sense from the scientific or sociobiological perspective, but it is not a product of nature but an artifice, a social construction, of man. The same could be said regarding even the distinction between humans and nonhumans or living beings and inanimate matter. While it is possible to follow new materialist or object-based theorists in their deconstruction of these subject/object binaries (for example, Latour 1993; Coole and Frost 2010; Harman 2010) the political consequences of such a shift are rarely fully drawn out. More worryingly, for authors like Jane Bennett, it is important to consciously 'elide the question of the human' (2010: 120) and 'to question the question: Why are we so keen to distinguish the human self from the field?' (Bennett 2010: 121). The existence of the alternative, human, subject is not a 'truth' in terms of sociological or biological knowledge, it is not something 'out there', hidden and to be revealed by a priest, a prophet, or a political scientist. The human subject is a necessary, practical, political truth, which can only be given concrete content through struggle. Say what we like about the sobriety and lack of personal lifestyle experimentation of 'the great Chinaman of Königsberg' (Nietzsche 1997: 82), he stands out as an example of how to undertake critique as a practical philosophical project in the absence of a strong sense of the human subject.

The tasks of critique from the standpoint of the political subject pose specific questions of our time, in terms of what this act of practical reasoning would involve. What are the moral or practical truths that are essential in today's political context? I would like to suggest three, interlinked, practical truths that may be crucial for critique on the basis of the possibility of the future political subject.

First, neoliberal approaches abolish the distinction between structure and agency. In freeing individuals from the truths of structures, the world is reduced to human agency as a product of past human agency (Wendt 1992). Structure and agency are enfolded together as we seek to understand problematic and bounded choice-making in a world structured by previous problematic and bounded choice-making. In the neoliberal world, we make our own capitalism; we make our own conflicts and our own catastrophic disasters. Without structures as practical political ideas we cannot begin to distance ourselves from the world and to socially construct the space in which we begin to act on it according to our self-chosen goals and aspirations. Politics cannot exist as the contestation of ideas if we have no conception of humans as agents and collective actors able to freely decide on their goals and thereupon to shape their circumstances.

In the neoliberal world, structure and agency are reduced to process, in fact to endogenous or self-reproducing processes. These processes have no director and no centre of power. They are multiple and overlapping and, as process-based thinking is an approach, can be understood to operate at all levels, from the individual, to peer groups, communities and states to the global level. In a world reduced to processes, there is only agency; however, without structures this agency is no longer the conscious agency of a political subject transforming an external object. The neoliberal world removes structures and therefore can only work on the behaviour and choices of individuals, understood as producing and reproducing problematic outcomes. A precondition for critique in a world with such a diminished idea of the human subject is the upholding of the idea that it is possible to exert conscious transformative power upon the external world.

Second, neoliberal approaches dissipate the liberal formal world of law and politics, rights and freedoms, into the informal world of the inequalities of the social sphere. In order to defend the artificial sphere of autonomy and rights perhaps we need to discursively separate the sphere of public contestation, requiring the fullest freedoms of speech and organization, from the world of social and economic inequality. Posing economic and social questions as problems of empowerment, of a lack of democracy and a lack of capacity, does not give agency to the marginalized and excluded rather it places upon them the moral responsibility for the problems of the world.

Radical and participatory democracy suggests that our lives in the economic and social sphere become empowering; that our choice-making, our democracy, is about the informed choices we make and the information we receive as individuals in our everyday lives and relationships. In this case, our public lives, our good and active citizenship, would concern our everyday private decision-making in the social sphere. This extension of democracy to the social sphere, through the granting of 'empowerment rights', features strongly in the work of academics keen to expand the sphere of democracy from the formal sphere (for example, Held 1995). It seems that a precondition for critique without a strong sense of the subject is the idea of a distinction between the political and the social: we can only equalize our social and economic power by transforming the external world not through transforming ourselves.

Third, for neoliberal approaches there is no such thing as a shared or universal reality outside the intersubjective contexts of our consciousness. In this world, theorizing is reduced to the study of human consciousness, based upon the individual's relationship to social consciousness. Instead of theories of human subjectivity, capable of relating consciousness to dynamics of material and scientific progress, neoliberalism poses the problems of the psychosciences at the centre of our analysis. Starting from the individual as actor and decision-maker, neoliberal frameworks can only operate with mid-range theory or approaches attuned to the analysis of difference and complexity. These theories with no a priori assumptions can only work backwards to analyze the path-dependencies, norms and knowledge gaps, which can explain events after the fact. These theories are practice-based, micro-theories, relational theories, actor-based theories and knowledge distribution theories. For neoliberalism, there is not and cannot be anything beyond the world of appearances.

There can be no critique without a practical philosophical construction of humanity as a collectivity, with universal and rational attributes. The struggle to raise the importance of practical political truths has been generally ignored by critical thinkers, especially those focused more upon the destruction of truths than the construction of them. It seems perhaps that our starting point today, if we do indeed wish to consider the possibility of politics after neoliberalism, rather than merely affirm the morality and truth of the neoliberal world, is a reconsideration of our political and philosophical tradition from the standpoint of today's crisis of the political subject. This reevaluation, as intimated above, would force us to reconsider positions that appeared to have been made redundant by radical critiques of classical liberalism.

A precondition for critique in a world with a diminished sense of the human subject is the practical assertion of human universality, the phenomenological construction of meaning beyond the finite life of the individual. However, rather than a metaphysical assertion of human progress or an understanding of history as a teleology, the claim for the human subject has to be informed by the materialist understanding of humanity as a collectively constituted subject continually making and remaking itself through practical engagement in the world. When we approach the world not from the neoliberal standpoint of the consciousness of the individual—where it appears that we come into the world where understandings and discourses preexist us, standing externally to us as much as the sun, seas, or mountains—but from the perspective of the collective historical subject, the processes through which we learn and engage and progress become clearer (see the excellent treatment in Ilyenkov 1982).

The human project, as a practical political truth, has to be always an open and contingent one; always open to new problems and new situations and new solutions and new ways of thinking. In the discourses of neoliberalism, the human project is assumed to be dead, a mistake, a hubristic error. In problematizing the subjectivity of the human subject, the human is continually being reduced to the biological, to its environment, in the same way that the political is reduced to the social and psychological. There can be no sharper distinction than that between the critical humanist project of problematizing the givenness of the world—and thus developing humanity's transformative capacities—and the neoliberal project which starts from problematizing the human subject—assumed to lack the adaptive capacities of resilience—thus suborning the human to the world as it appears.

Julian: It's a good question. It would be daft of course to want to wish away reason and the forms of knowledge it provides, or even to think that one could dispense with it, should one want to. It is reason that tells you when you are being fucked over, it is reason that tells you the life you are living is limited, the laws you are subject to are unjust, the disciplines you are made to conform to silly, the power relations you are captured within suffocating, and so on. The conditions of suffering out of which political subjects emerge are not imaginary, they are real, material, known, and felt. Kant did not invent reason. It does not belong to the Enlightenment. It is an archaic instrument of

human struggle and intelligence, honoured and celebrated in Western literature, thought and art, going back at least to Homer. It is also a discourse unto
itself; a multiplicity and practice, constantly reinvented and redeployed to
serve different purposes and signify different forms of intelligence at different times, as well as in different ways at the same time. Kant effectively
degrades reason, limiting it, trying to draw boundaries around it, deploying it
discursively to signify the limited, finite nature of the human, and in process
limiting and degrading human understandings of the potentiality of progress
and politics. We have to reappropriate it, once more. It would be an insult to
those who suffer to suggest that they have to exercise their imagination to
experience the cold-blooded anger and hate out of which political subjectivity emerges. You know when you are being shafted because reason speaks to
you and tells you that 'this is how it is here'. But when it comes to the
question of 'what is to be done?' about your suffering, the limitations of your
form of life, reason will do little for you. Of course it will try to help you if
you ask it, carefully calculating for you the particular ways and means by
which you might proceed out of your conditions of injustice and subjection
on the basis of what it knows and can tell you of this world, but on that basis
it will only ever lead you back, one way or another, to this world, and forms
of life conditional to this world. That is the story of reason which Homer's
Odyssey told us more than two thousand years ago. If you want to be Odysseus, go round in circles, and back to the wife and kids, then reason is your
very best friend. To paraphrase Oscar Wilde, the reasonable subject always
knows where he is going and he always gets there because he ends up going
nowhere in particular but here. He clings to the life that he possesses, and the
world he inhabits, being very successful in navigating the twists and turns of
this world, forever adapting its form of life to the challenges and obstacles
the world throws at it, but when it comes to the question of giving you access
to another life, and another world, he cannot help you. That requires the
taking of a subjective path and the transformative powers of the imagination.
Reason imagines nothing. It cannot create and thus it cannot transform. And,
of course, reason also knows that. It is reason which tells you that these are
its limits. It is not made for opening up new worlds, but enabling us to
survive present ones. That is all it is tasked with and intended for. So don't
ask it to do or perform that which it is not crafted for, even if it will try to
help, should you ask it. There are plenty of problems in the course of life for
which reason is perfectly adequate, but collective political transformation is
not one of them. For that we need to turn to the imagination. Reason itself
tells us thus. It says, 'I am Reason, ask me to help you, and I will do my best,
because I am reasonable, but know that in being reasonable, I am also limited, and know that there is another power, different to myself, defined indeed
by everything which I am not, and which you should ask, if the transformation of the limits of this world is your problem. Its name is the Imagination'.

That turn, from reason to imagination, is itself founded upon rational knowledge of the limits of reason, and thus it is a product of the evolution of reason, its maturity, capacity to disincline itself, and abdicate responsibility for political subjectivity and action. We owe it to reason and its own self-deprecation to follow the path of imagination.

There is a further utility to reason that I want to highlight here, and that is important to respond to Gideon's question and reiterate the point he makes, essentially, about the danger of eschatological pyrrhicism. What fascinates and disturbs me, when we look today at so-called radical political thought, is not just the poverty, but the inadequacy of its imaginaries, the emptiness of the visions of what new forms of political subjectivity and ways of being together it provides for us, and thus the weakness of new fronts being opened up, in conditions of struggle. These are I think strategic mistakes being made today by the left, which can only lead, indeed, to pyrrhic victories. The inadequacy of those visions is also something which we can only recognize through the deployment of reason. We can see, through the deployment of a higher more savvy form of political reason, the extent to which our imaginations remain governed, complicit with dominant liberal epistemologies of power. In a sense that's precisely what my chapters in this book have been aimed at doing: showing us how discourses of vulnerability, resilience, and adaptivity cannot provide for a form of political subjectivity capable of going to war, meaningfully, with the neoliberal subject. And yet it is precisely these discourses, these ways of imagining what the human is fundamentally, and can become, that are fuelling the so-called imagination of counterliberal thought. Mere talk of the imagination, imaginaries, and visions is cheap. We have to deploy the coldness of reason to sort out the good from the bad prophets, and govern, ourselves, the circulation of cliché in the dream life of the subject, such that the imagination can be quality controlled. Every idiot dreams and imagines; the question is which image works, such that it is capable of decretinization, the destruction of cliché, and the production of new worlds and new forms of life. And that is a strategic problematic for which reason is indispensible; we have to know back to front, and inside out, the subject against which we are struggling, such that we do not merely recuperate it. There has to be a kind of constant frenetic audit, and analysis even, of the function of the imagination. We have to know ourselves back to front and inside-out. The risk is that we place a blind faith in what goes by the name of imagination, but which is all too reasonable in its conformity with dominant and disempowering images of the human. The hyper rationality of paranoia, fear of the bad prophet, is necessary, if we are to imagine well.

And this is what I hear David arguing, in effect, and in a circular and ultimately self-defeating way: that in lieu of an actually existing political subject, we need to imagine (or 'construct' to use that more Anglo-American architectural metaphor) the possibility of one. In the ways that Kant imagined his subject back in the eighteenth century, to such influential effect within Western philosophical thought. I think Gideon is right that liberalism itself, including its idea of the rational subject, is a product of the imaginary. We are still inhabiting its nightmarish effects, but I don't think the problem of politics today is a question of constructing, philosophically, an alternative image of the human, replete with political potentiality, in the practical reality of its absence.

The liberal image of the human, degraded and incapable of action and meaning creation, is the real chimera. Liberal regimes put so much effort into imagining the necessity and possibility of the neoliberal subject, equipped with vulnerability, resilience, and adaptive capacity because in reality the real world is a human one, replete with politics, hubris, creativity, action, imagination, and transformative potential. Liberalism imagines the possibility of a world where humans are stripped of their imaginations, and led to live merely adaptive lives. But the reality is that life is not led that way, anywhere, by anyone. Odysseus, as he himself said, is 'no-one' and 'nothing'. He does not exist and cannot be found anywhere. We are living out the final scenes of the liberal nightmare. It's obvious that its images are imploding and that the idea of the liberal subject is dying. One would have to believe political philosophers to think otherwise. Think practically, pay attention to the realities of the world we live in, the struggles that are building, the new forms of human life and politics that are erupting, and you will see the conceit on which the image of the human still sheltered in the Anglo-American academy rests. Who takes seriously posthumanism? And why? It's just liberalism by another name. Behind Jane Bennett and William Connolly crouches Kant with the Vaseline.

Bibliography

Acharya, A. (2000). 'How Ideas Spread: Whose Norms Matter? Norm Localization and Institutional Change in Asian Regionalism', *International Organization*, 2(1): 65–87.

Adger, W. N. (2000). 'Social and Ecological Resilience: Are They Related?', *Progress in Human Geography*, 24(3): 347–64.

Agamben, G. (1999). 'Absolute Immanence' in Giorgio Agamben, *Potentialities*, 220–42. Stanford CA: Stanford University Press.

———. (2009). 'What Is an Apparatus?' in Giorgio Agamben, *What Is an Apparatus? And Other Essays*, 1–24. Stanford, CA: Stanford University Press.

———. (2011). *The Kingdom and the Glory: For a Theological Genealogy of Economy and Government*. Stanford, CA: Stanford University Press.

Ahrens, J., and Rudolph, P. M. (2006). 'The Importance of Governance in Risk Reduction and Disaster Management', *Journal of Contingencies and Crisis Management*, 14(4): 207–20.

Althusser, L. (2008). 'Reply to John Lewis', in *On Ideology*, 61–139. London: Verso.

Annan, K. (2005). *In Larger Freedom: Towards Development, Security and Human Rights For All*. New York: United Nations Publications.

Arendt, H. (1978). *The Life of the Mind*. New York: Harcourt.

———. (1982). *Lectures on Kant's Political Philosophy*. Brighton: Harvester Press.

———. (1998). *The Human Condition*, 2nd ed. Chicago: University of Chicago Press.

———. (2003). *Responsibility and Judgement*. New York: Schocken Books.

———. (2005). *The Promise of Politics.* New York: Schocken Books.

Ashdown, P. (2007). 'The European Union and Statebuilding in the Western Balkans', *Journal of Intervention and Statebuilding*, 1(1): 107–18.

Auge, M. (1994). *An Anthropology for Contemporary Worlds*. Stanford, CA: Stanford University Press.

Bachelard, G. (2005). *On Poetic Imagination and Reverie*. New York: Spring.

Badiou, A. (2001). *Ethics: An Understanding of Evil*. London: Verso.

Barbier, E. B., and Markandya, A. (1990). 'The Conditions for Achieving Environmentally Sustainable Development', *European Economic Review*, 34(2–3): 659–69.

Barnett, M. (2008). 'Social Constructivism', in J. Baylis, S. Smith, and P. Owens (eds.), *The Globalization of World Politics: An Introduction to International Relations*. Oxford: Oxford University Press, pp. 160-173.

Barnett, M., and Zürcher, C. (2009). 'The Peacebuilder's Contract: How External Statebuilding Reinforces Weak Statehood', in R. Paris and T. D. Sisk (eds.), *The Dilemmas of Statebuilding: Confronting the Contradictions of Postwar Peace Operations*, 23–52. London: Routledge.

Barnett, Thomas P. M. (2009). *America and the World after Bush*. New York: Putnam.

Beck, U. (1992). *Risk Society: Towards a New Modernity.* London: Sage.

Belloni, R. (2008). 'Civil Society in War-to-Democracy Transitions', in A. K. Jarstad and T. D. Sisk (eds.), *From War to Democracy: Dilemmas of Peacebuilding*, 182–210. Cambridge: Cambridge University Press.

Ben-Ami, D. (2006). 'Who's Afraid of Economic Growth', *Spiked* (4 May). Available at http://www.spiked-online.com/articles/0000000CB04D.htm.

Benn, H. (2004). 'A Shared Challenge: Promoting Development and Human Security in Weak States', Center for Global Development (23 June, Washington). Available at http://www.dfid.gov.uk/Documents/pdf_misc/sp-weakstatesbenn.pdf.

Bennett, J. (2010). *Vibrant Matter: A Political Ecology of Things.* Durham, NC: Duke University Press.

Berger, P., and Luckmann, T. (1991). *The Social Construction of Reality: A Treatise in the Sociology of Knowledge.* London: Penguin Books.

Berlin, I. (1969). *Four Essays on Liberty.* Oxford: Oxford University Press.

Birch, K., and Mykhnenko, V. (2010). *The Rise and Fall of Neoliberalism: The Collapse of an Economic Order.* London: Zed Books.

Black, D. (1999). 'The Long and Winding Road: International Norms and Domestic Political Change in South Africa', in T. Risse, S. C. Ropp and K. Sikkink (eds.), *The Power of Human Rights: International Norms and Domestic Change.* Cambridge: Cambridge University Press.

Brassett, J., and Vaughan-Williams, N. (2011). 'Performative Ecologies of Resilience and Trauma: A Critical Analysis of UK Civil Contingencies'. Paper presented at the Open University, Centre for Citizenship, Identities and Governance workshop 'Resisting (In)Security, Securing Resistance', Camden Town, London, 12 July.

Briggs, R. (2010). 'Community Engagement for Counterterrorism: Lessons from the United Kingdom', *International Affairs*, 86(4): 971–81.

Brown, C. (1994). '"Turtles All the Way Down": Anti-Foundationalism, Critical Theory and International Relations', *Millennium: Journal of International Studies*, 23(2): 213–36.

Bull, H. (1977). *The Anarchical Society: A Study of Order in World Politics.* London: Macmillan.

Bulley, D. (2011). 'Producing and Governing Community (through) Resilience'. Paper presented at the 'Resilient Futures: The Politics of Preventive Security' workshop, Department of Politics and International Studies, University of Warwick, 27–28 June.

Burchell, G. (1991). 'Peculiar Interests: Civil Society and the "System of Natural Liberty,"' in G. Burchell, C. Gordon, and P. Miller (eds.), *The Foucault Effect: Studies in Governmental Rationality*, 119–50. London: Harvester Wheatsheaf.

———. (1996). 'Liberal Government and Techniques of the Self', in A. Barry, T. Osbourne, and N. Rose (eds.), *Foucault and Political Reason: Liberalism, Neo-Liberalism and Rationalities of Government*, 19–36. London: University College London Press.

Burg, S. L. (1997). 'Bosnia Herzegovina: A Case of Failed Democratization', in K. Dawisha and B. Parrot (eds.), *Politics, Power, and the Struggle for Democracy in South-East Europe*, 122–45. Cambridge: Cambridge University Press.

Burgess, A. (1997). *Divided Europe: The New Domination of the East.* London: Pluto.

Burke, A. (2007). *Beyond Security, Ethics and Violence: War against the Other.* London: Routledge.

Butler, J. (1997). *The Psychic Life of Power: Theories in Subjection.* Stanford: Stanford University Press.

———. (2004). *Precarious Life: The Powers of Mourning and Violence.* London and New York: Verso.

———. (2009). *Frames of War.* London and New York: Verso.

Campbell, D. (1998). *Writing Security: United States Foreign Policy and the Politics of Identity.* Manchester: Manchester University Press.

Campbell, S., Chandler, D., and Sabaratnam, M. (eds.). (2011). *A Liberal Peace? The Problems and Practices of Peacebuilding.* London: Zed Books.

Carothers, T. (2004). *Critical Mission: Essays on Democracy Promotion.* Washington, DC: Carnegie Endowment for International Peace.

Carter, J. A., Maher, S., and Neumann, P. (2014). 'Greenbirds: Measuring Importance and Influence in Syrian Foreign Fighter Networks (ICSR)'. Available at http://icsr.info/wp-content/uploads/2014/04/ICSR-Report-Greenbirds-Measuring-Importance-and-Infleunce-in-Syrian-Foreign-Fighter-Networks.pdf.

Castells, M. (2006). 'The Network Society: From Knowledge to Policy', in Manuel Castells and Gustavo Cardoso (eds.), *The Network Society: From Knowledge to Policy*, 3–21. Washington, DC: Center for Transatlantic Relations.

CGG. (1995). *The Report of the Commission for Global Governance: Our Global Neighbourhood.* Oxford: Oxford University Press.

Chakrabortty, A. (2010). 'Cameron's Hijacking of Nudge Theory Is a classic Example of How Big Ideas Get Corrupted', *Guardian*, 7 December.

Chandler, D. (1998). 'Democratization in Bosnia: The Limits of Civil Society Building Strategies', *Democratization*, 5(4): 78–102.

———. (1999). *Bosnia: Faking Democracy after Dayton.* London: Pluto.

———. (2001). 'Universal Ethics and Elite Politics: The Limits of Normative Human Rights Theory', *International Journal of Human Rights*, 5(4): 72–89.

———. (2004). *Constructing Global Civil Society: Morality and Power in International Relations.* Basingstoke: Palgrave-Macmillan.

———. (2007). 'The Security-Development Nexus and the Rise of "Anti-Foreign Policy,"' *Journal of International Relations and Development*, 10(4): 362–86.

———. (2009). *Hollow Hegemony: Rethinking Global Politics, Power and Resistance.* London: Pluto Press.

———. (2010). *International Statebuilding: The Rise of Post-Liberal Governance.* London: Routledge.

Checkel, J. (1998). 'The Constructivist Turn in International Relations Theory', *World Politics* 50(2): 324–48.

Chimni, B. (2008). 'The Sen Conception of Development and Contemporary International Law Discourse: Some Parallels', *The Law and Development Review*, 1(1): 1-22.

Chomsky, N. (1998). *Profits Over People: Neoliberalism and the Global Order.* New York: Seven Stories Press.

Clark, D. A. (2005). 'The Capability Approach: Its Development, Critiques and Recent Advances', Global Poverty Research Group, Working Paper 32, November. Available at http://www.gprg.org/pubs/workingpapers/pdfs/gprg-wps-032.pdf.

Clarke, J., and Nicholson, J. (2010). *Resilience: Bounce Back from Whatever Life Throws at You: Practical Solutions for Taking Control and Surviving in Difficult Times.* Surrey: Crimson Publishing.

Coaffee, J., and Rogers, P. (2008). 'Rebordering the City for New Security Challenges: From Counter-Terrorism to Community Resilience', *Space and Polity*, 12(1): 101–18.

Coaffee, J., Wood, D. M., and Rogers, P. (2009). *The Everyday Resilience of the City: How Cities Respond to Terrorism and Disaster.* Basingstoke: Palgrave Macmillan.

Cohen, M. P. (2000). 'Risk, Vulnerability, and Disaster Prevention in Large Cities', *Lincoln Institute of Land Policy Working Paper*. Available at http://www.alnap.org/pool/files/1348-666-perlo00pc1-final.pdf.

Colas, D. (1997). *Civil Society and Fanaticism: Conjoined Histories.* Stanford, CA: Stanford University Press.

Collier, P. (2010). *Wars, Guns and Votes: Democracy in Democracy Places.* London: Vintage.

Commons, J. R. (1936). 'Institutional Economics', *American Economic Review*, 26(Supplement): 237–49.

Condorcet, A.-N. (2009). *Outlines of an Historical View of the Progress of the Human Mind (1795).* Chicago: G. Langer.

Coole, D., and S. Frost. (2010). *New Materialisms: Ontology, Agency, and Politics.* Durham, NC: Duke University Press.

Cooper, M. (2008). *Life as Surplus: Biotechnology and Capitalism in the Neoliberal Era.* Seattle: Washington University Press.

Cortell, A. P., and Davis, J. W. (2000). 'Understanding the Domestic Impact of International Norms: A Research Agenda', *International Studies Review*, 2(1): 65–87.

Coyle, D., and Meier, P. (2009). *New Technologies in Emergencies and Conflicts: The Role of Information and Social Networks*. Washington, DC: United Nations Foundation and Vodafone Foundation). Available at http://www.globalproblems-globalsolutions-files.org/pdf/ UNF_tech/emergency_tech_report2009/Tech_EmergencyTechReport_full.pdf.

Curtis, P. (2011). '"Nudge Unit" Not Guaranteed to Work, Says Oliver Letwin', *Guardian*, 20(February). Available at http://www.theguardian.com/politics/2011/feb/20/nudge-unit-oliver-letwin.

Cyrulnik, B., and Macey, D. (2009). *Resilience: How Your Inner Strength Can Set You Free from the Past*. London: Penguin.

Davis, L. E., and North, D. C. (1971). *Institutional Change and American Economic Growth*. Cambridge: Cambridge University Press.

Day, E. (2011). 'Julia Neuberger: "A Nudge in the Right Direction Won't Run the Big Society,"' *Observer*, 17 July.

Dean, M. (2010). *Governmentality: Power and Rule in Modern Society*, 2nd ed. London: Sage.

———. (2011). 'Resisting the Irresistible Event'. Paper presented at the Open University, Centre for Citizenship, Identities and Governance workshop 'Resisting (In)Security, Securing Resistance', Camden Town, London, 12 July.

Debord, G. (2010). *Society of the Spectacle*. Detroit: Black & Red.

Deleuze, G. (2004). 'Five Propositions on Psychoanalysis', in Gilles Deleuze, *Desert Islands and Other Texts, 1953–1974*, 272–82. New York: Semiotext.

Deleuze, G., and Guattari, F. (1999). *What Is Philosophy?* London: Verso.

———. (2000). *Anti-Oedipus: Capitalism and Schizophrenia*. London: Athlone Press.

Dillon, M. (1996). *Politics of Security*. London and New York: Routledge.

———. (2007a). 'Governing Terror: The State of Emergency of Biopolitical Emergence', *International Political Sociology*, 1(1): 7–18.

———. (2007b). 'Governing through Contingency: The Security of Biopolitical Governance', *Political Geography*, 26(1): 41–47.

———. (2011). 'Specters of Biopolitics: Finitude, *Eschaton*, and *Katechon*', *South Atlantic Quarterly* 110(3): 780–92.

Dillon, M., and Reid, J. (2009). *The Liberal Way of War: Killing to Make Life Live*. London: Routledge.

Donnelly, J. (1998). *International Human Rights*. Boulder, CO: Westview Press.

Doucet, M. G., and de Larrinaga, M. (2011). 'Human Security and the Securing of Human Life: Tracing Global Sovereign and Biopolitical Rule', in D. Chandler and N. Hynek (eds.), *Critical Perspectives on Human Security: Rethinking Emancipation and Power in International Relations*, 129–43. London: Routledge.

Duffield, M. (2001). *Global Governance and the New Wars: The Merging of Development and Security*. London and New York: Zed Books.

———. (2007). *Development, Security and Unending War: Governing the World of Peoples*. Cambridge: Polity.

———. (2008). *Development, Security and Unending War: Governing the World of Peoples*. Cambridge: Polity.

———. (2011a). 'Total War as Environmental Terror: Linking Liberalism, Resilience, and the Bunker', *South Atlantic Quarterly*, 110: 757–69.

———. (2011b). 'Liberal Interventionism and the Crisis of Acceptance: From Protection to Resilience'. Annual Lecture, Centre for the Study of Global Security and Development, Queen Mary University of London, 19 May.

Edkins, J., and Pin-Fat, V. (1999), 'The Subject of the Political', in Jenny Edkins, Nalini Persram, and Veronique Pin-Fat (eds.), *Sovereignty and Subjectivity*, 1–18. Boulder, CO, and London: Lynne Rienner.

Edwards, C. (2009). *Resilient Nation*. London: Demos. Available at http://www.demos.co.uk/ files/Resilient_Nation_-_web-1.pdf?1242207746.

Edwards, E. (2009). *Resilience: Reflections on the Burdens and Gifts of Facing Life's Adversities*. New York: Broadway Books.

Emerson, R. W. (1993). 'History', in R. W. Emerson, *Self-Reliance and Other Essays*, 1–17. New York: Dover Publications.

Esposito, R. (2008). *Bios: Biopolitics and Philosophy*. Minneapolis and London: University of Minnesota Press.

Evans, B. (2013). *Liberal Terror: Global Security, Divine Power and Emergency Rule*. London: Routledge.

Evans, B., and Reid, J. (eds.). (2013). *Deleuze and Fascism: Security, War, Aesthetics*. London and New York: Routledge.

Fine, K. (1996). 'Fragile Stability and Change: Understanding Conflict during the Transitions in East Central Europe', in A. Chayes and A. H. Chayes (eds.), *Preventing Conflict in the Post-Communist World*, 541–81. Washington, DC: Brookings Institution.

Finnemore, M. (1996a). 'Norms, Culture and World Politics: Insights from Sociology's Institutionalism (A Review Essay)', *International Organization*, 50(2): 325–47.

———. (1996b). 'Constructing Norms of Humanitarian Intervention', in P. Katzenstein (ed.), *The Culture of National Security: Norms and Identity in World Politics*, 153–85. New York: Columbia University Press.

Finnemore, M., and Sikkink, K. (1998). 'International Norm Dynamics and Political Change', *International Organization*, 52(4): 887–917.

Folke, C., Carpenter, S., Elmqvist, T., Gunderson, L., Holling, C. S., and Walker, B. (2002). 'Resilience and Sustainable Development: Building Adaptive Capacity in a World of Transformations', *Ambio*, 31(5): 437–40.

Folke, C., and Kautsky, N. (1989). 'The Role of Ecosystems for a Sustainable Development of Aquaculture', *Ambio*, 18, 4: 234–243

Forest, J., and Mehier, C. (2001). 'John R. Commons and Herbert A. Simon on the Concept of Rationality', *Journal of Economic Issues*, 35(3): 591–605.

Foucault, M. (1981). *The History of Sexuality, Volume 1: An Introduction*. London: Penguin.

———. (1984). 'What Is Enlightenment?', in P. Rabinow (ed.), *The Foucault Reader*, 32–50. New York: Pantheon Books.

———. (1991). *Discipline and Punish: The Birth of the Prison*. London: Penguin.

———. (1997). *The Order of Things*. London: Routledge.

———. (2001). 'Risks of Security', in Michel Foucault, *Power: The Essential Works 3*, 365–81. London: Allen Lane.

———. (2003). *Society Must Be Defended: Lectures at the Collège de France 1975–1976*. London: Allen Lane.

———. (2007). *Security, Territory and Population: Lectures at the Collège de France 1977–1978*. Basingstoke: Palgrave.

———. (2008). *The Birth of Biopolitics: Lectures at the Collège de France 1978–1979*. Basingstoke: Palgrave.

———. (2010). *Government of the Self and Others: Lectures at the Collège de France 1982–1983*. Basingstoke: Palgrave.

———. (2011). *The Courage of Truth: Lectures at the Collège de France 1983–1984*. New York: Palgrave Macmillan.

Fukuyama, F. (1995). 'The Primacy of Culture', *Journal of Democracy*, 6(1): 7–14.

Furedi, F. (2007). *Invitation to Terror: The Expanding Empire of the Unknown*. London: Continuum.

Galison, P. (1994). 'The Ontology of the Enemy: Norbert Wiener and the Cybernetic Vision', *Critical Inquiry* (21): 228–26.

Geuss, R. (2005). *Outside Ethics*. Princeton, NJ, and Oxford: Princeton University Press.

Ghani, A., and Lockhart, C. (2008). *Fixing Failed States: A Framework for Rebuilding a Fractured World*. Oxford: Oxford University Press.

Giddens, A. (1984). *The Constitution of Society: Outline of the Theory of Structuration*. Cambridge: Polity.

———. (1994). *Beyond Left and Right: The Future of Radical Politics*. Cambridge: Polity Press.

———. (1998). *The Third Way: The Renewal of Social Democracy*. Cambridge: Polity.

———. (2000). *The Third Way and Its Critics*. Cambridge: Polity.

Gladwin, T. N., Kennelly, J. J., and Krause, T. S. (1995). 'Shifting Paradigms for Sustainable Development: Implications for Management Theory and Research', *The Academy of Management Review* 20(4): 874–907.

Gordon, C. (1991). 'Introduction', in G. Burchell, C. Gordon, and P. Miller (eds.), *The Foucault Effect: Studies in Governmental Rationality*, 1–51. London: Harvester Wheatsheaf.

Grist, M. (2009). *Changing the Subject: How New Ways of Thinking about Human Behaviour Might Change Politics, Policy and Practice*. London: Royal Society for the Arts.

———. (2010). *STEER: Mastering Our Behaviour through Instinct, Environment and Reason*. London: RSA.

Guattari, F. (1995). *Chaosmosis*. Indiana: Indiana University Press.

———. (2000). *The Three Ecologies*. London: Athlone.

Gunther, R. et al. (1996). 'Debate: Democratic Consolidation: O'Donnell's "Illusions": A Rejoinder', *Journal of Democracy*, 7(4): 151–59.

Habermas, J. (1996). *The Divided West*. Cambridge: Polity Press.

———. (1997). *Between Facts and Norms: Contributions to a Discourse Theory of Law and Democracy*. Cambridge: Polity Press.

Hall, S. (2007). 'The West and the Rest: Discourse and Power', in T. Das Gupta et al. (eds.), *Race and Racialization: Essential Readings*, 56–63. Toronto: Canadian Scholars' Press.

Han-Pile, B. (2010). 'The "Death of Man": Foucault and Anti-Humanism', in Timothy O'Leary and Christopher Falzon (eds.), *Foucault and Philosophy*, 118–42. Oxford, Blackwell.

Handmer, J. W., and Dovers, S. R. (1996). 'A Typology of Resilience: Rethinking Institutions for Sustainable Development', *Organization and Environment* (9): 482–511.

Haraway, D. (1991). *Simians, Cyborgs and Women: The Reinvention of Nature*. New York: Routledge.

Harman, G. (2010). *Towards Speculative Realism: Essays and Lectures*. Winchester: Zero Books.

Harrison, E. (2004). 'State Socialization, International Norm Dynamics and the Liberal Peace', *International Politics*, 41(4): 521–42.

Harvey, D. (2005). *A Brief History of Neoliberalism*. Oxford: Oxford University Press.

———. (2007). 'Neoliberalism as Creative Destruction', *The ANNALS of the American Academy of Political and Social Science* 610: 22–44.

Hawksley, H. (2009). *Democracy Kills: What's So Good about Having the Vote?* London: Pan Macmillan.

Hay, C. (2006). 'Constructivist institutionalism', in R. A. W. Rhodes, S. A. Binder, and B. A. Rockman (eds.), *The Oxford Handbook of Political Institutions*, 56–74. Oxford: Oxford University Press.

Hayek, F. (1952). *The Sensory Order: An Enquiry into the Foundations of Theoretical Psychology*. Chicago: University of Chicago Press.

———. (1960). *The Constitution of Liberty*. London: Routledge.

Hayles, N. K. (1999). *How We Became Posthuman: Virtual Bodies in Cybernetics, Literature, and Informatics*. Chicago and London: University of Chicago Press.

Heidegger, M. (1977). *The Question Concerning Technology and Other Essays*. New York: Harper & Row.

Held, D. (1995). *Democracy and the Global Order*. Cambridge: Polity.

Hill, M. A. (2011). *Democracy Promotion and Conflict-Based Reconstruction: The United States and Democratic Consolidation in Bosnia, Afghanistan and Iraq*. London: Routledge.

Hillman Photography Initiative (HPI). (2014). 'About Hillman Photography Initiative'. Available at http://www.nowseethis.org/about (accessed May 21, 2014).

Hollis, M., and Smith, S. (1990). *Explaining and Understanding International Relations*. Oxford: Clarendon Press.

Hopgood, S. (2000). 'Reading the Small Print in Global Civil Society: The Inexorable Hegemony of the Liberal Self', *Millennium: Journal of International Studies*, 29(1): 1–25.

Howell, A., and Neal, A. (2012). 'Human Interest and Humane Governance in Iraq: Humanitarian War and the Baghdad Zoo', *Journal of Intervention and Statebuilding*, 6(2): 213-232.

Ilyenkov, E. V. (1982). *Lennenist Dialectics and the Metaphysics of Positivism*. London: New Park.

Institute for Government (IfG). (2010). *Mindspace: Influencing Behaviour Through Public Policy: The Practical Guide*. London: Cabinet Office.

Intergovernmental Panel on Climate Change (IPCC). (2007). 'Climate Change 2007: Impacts, Adaptation and Vulnerability' (Brussels).

International Commission on Intervention and State Sovereignty (ICISS). (2001). *The Responsibility to Protect: Research, Bibliography, Background*. Ottawa: International Development Research Centre.

Jackson, R. H., and Sorensen, G. (2010). *Introduction to International Relations: Theories and Approaches*. Oxford: Oxford University Press.

Jaeger, H-M. (2013). 'Governmentality's (Missing) International Dimension and the Promiscuity of German Neoliberalism', *Journal of International Relations and Development*, 16(1): 25–54.

Jepperson, R. L., Wendt, A., and Katzenstein, P. J. (1996). 'Norms, Identity, and Culture in National Security', in P. J. Katzenstein (ed.), *The Culture of National Security: Norms and Identity in World Politics*, 33–75. New York: Columbia University Press.

Jervis, R., and Snyder, J. (eds.). (1991). *Dominoes and Bandwagons: Strategic Beliefs and Great Power Competition in the Eurasian Rimland*. Oxford: Oxford University Press.

Kaldor, M. (1999). *New and Old Wars: Organized Violence in a Global Era*. Cambridge: Polity.

———. (2003). *Global Civil Society: An Answer to War*. Cambridge: Polity.

Kant, I. (1970). *Kant: Political Writings*. Cambridge: Cambridge University Press.

———. (1999). *Metaphysical Elements of Justice*, 2nd ed. Indianapolis, IN: Hackett.

Katz, J. (1997). 'The Digital Citizen', *Wired* (December).

Katzenstein, P. J. (1996a). 'Introduction: Alternative Perspectives on National Security', in P. J. Katzenstein (ed.), *The Culture of National Security: Norms and Identity in World Politics*, 1–32. New York: Columbia University Press.

———. (1996b). 'Conclusion: National Security in a Changing World', in P. J. Katzenstein (ed.), *The Culture of National Security: Norms and Identity in World Politics*, 498–537. New York: Columbia University Press.

Katzenstein, P. J., Keohane, R. O., and Krasner, S. D. (1998). '*International Organization* and the Study of World Politics', *International Organization* 52(4): 645–85.

Kauffman, S. (2000). *Investigations.*, Oxford and New York: Oxford University Press.

Kavalski, E. (2008). 'The Complexity of Global Security Governance: An Analytical Overview', *Global Society*, 22(4): 423–43.

Kay, L. E. (1993). *The Molecular Vision of Life: Caltech, the Rockefeller Foundation, and the Rise of New Biology*. New York and Oxford: Oxford University Press.

———. (2000). *Who Wrote the Book of Life: A History of the Genetic Code*. Stanford, CA: Stanford University Press.

Keane, J. (2003). *Global Civil Society?* Cambridge: Cambridge University Press.

Keck, M. E., and Sikkink, K. (1998). *Activists beyond Borders: Advocacy Networks in International Politics*. Ithaca, NY: Cornell University Press.

Kennelly, D. (2003). 'Q&A With . . . Thomas P. M. Barnett', *Doublethink* (Summer Issue): 17–21.

Keohane, R. O. (1988). 'International Institutions: Two Approaches', *International Studies Quarterly*, 32(4): 379–96.

———. (1989). *International Institutions and State Power*. Boulder, CO: Westview.

Khagram, S., Clark, W. C., and Raad, D. F. (2003). 'From the Environment and Human Security to Sustainable Security and Development', *Journal of Human Development*, 4(2): 289–313.

Kiersey, N. (2009). 'Neoliberal Political Economy and the Subjectivity of Crisis: Why Governmentality is not Hollow', *Global Society*, 23(4): 363–86.

Kottow, M. H. (2002). 'The Vulnerable and the Susceptible', *Bioethics*, 17(5–6): 460–71.

Kowert, P., and Legro, J. (1996). 'Norms, Identity, and Their Limits: A Theoretical Reprise', in P. J. Katzenstein (ed.), *The Culture of National Security: Norms and Identity in World Politics*, 451–97. New York: Columbia University Press.

Krasner, S. D. (ed.). (1983). *International Regimes.* Ithaca, NY: Cornell University Press.

Kratochwil, F. (2000). 'Constructing a New Orthodoxy? Wendt's Social Theory of International Politics and the Constructivist Challenge', *Millennium: Journal of International Studies*, 29(1): 73–101.

Lacy, M. (2008). 'Designer Security: Control Society and MoMA's SAFE: Design Takes on Risk', *Security Dialogue*, 39(2–3): 333–57.

Laïdi, Z. (2008). 'European Preferences and their Reception', in Z. Laïdi (ed.), *EU Foreign Policy in a Globalized World: Normative Power and Social Preferences*, 1–20. London: Routledge.

Larner, W. (2000). 'Neo-Liberalism: Policy, Ideology, Governmentality', *Studies in Political Economy*, vol. 63: 5-26.

Latour, B. (1993). *We Have Never Been Modern.* Cambridge, MA: Harvard University Press.

Lentzos, F., and Rose, N. (2009). 'Governing insecurity: contingency planning, protection, resilience', *Economy and Society*, 38(2): 230–54.

Linklater, A. (1998). *The Transformation of Political Community.* Cambridge: Polity.

Lipshutz, R. (2005). 'Power, Politics and Global Civil Society', *Millennium: Journal of International Studies*, 33(3): 747–69.

Locke, J. (1967). *Two Treatises of Government.* Cambridge: Cambridge University Press.

Lugard, Lord. (1923). *The Dual Mandate in British Tropical Africa.* Abingdon: Frank Cass.

Lynch, M., and Freelon, D., Aday, S. (2014). 'Syria's Socially Mediated Civil War', *Peaceworks* 91. Washington, D.C.: United States Institute of Peace.

Macdonald, D. J. (1995). 'Communist Bloc Expansion in the Early Cold War: Challenging Realism, Refuting Revisionism', *International Security*, 20(3): 152–88.

Mac Ginty, R. (2011). *International Peacebuilding and Local Resistance: Hybrid Forms of Peace.* Basingstoke: Palgrave.

Macpherson, C. B. (1962). *The Political Theory of Possessive Individualism: Hobbes to Locke.* Oxford: Oxford University Press.

Maddi, S. R., and Khoshabba, D. M. (2005). *Resilience at Work—How to Succeed No Matter What Life Throws At You.* New York: Amacom.

Mahoney, J., and Thelen, K. (eds.). (2010). *Explaining Institutional Change: Ambiguity, Agency, and Power.* Cambridge: Cambridge University Press.

Martinsson, J. (2011). *Global Norms: Creation, Diffusion, and Limits* (World Bank/Communication for Governance and Accountability Program). Available at http://siteresources. worldbank.org/EXTGOVACC/Resources/FinalGlobalNormsv1.pdf.

Marx, K. (1954). *Capital: Volume One.* London: Lawrence and Wishart.

———. (n.d.). 'The Trinity Formula', Chapter 48. *Capital Vol. III.* Available at http://www. marxists.org/archive/marx/works/1894-c3/ch48.htm.

Masten, A. S., and Powell, J. L. (2003). 'A Resilience Framework for Research, Policy and Practice', in S. S. Luthar (ed.), *Resilience and Vulnerability: Adaptation in the Context of Childhood Adversities*, 1–27. Cambridge: Cambridge University Press.

Mayall, J., and Soares de Oliveira, R. (2011). 'Introduction', in J. Mayall and R. Soares de Oliveira (eds.), *The New Protectorates: International Tutelage and the Making of Liberal States*, 1–29. London: Hurst.

McFaul, M. A. (2004). 'Democracy Promotion as a World Value', *Washington Quarterly* 28(1): 147–63.

Meier, P. (2013). 'How to Create Resilience through Big Data', *iRevolution*, 11 January. Available at http://irevolution.net/2013/01/11/disaster-resilience-2-0/.

Menkhaus, K. (2004). 'Vicious Circles and the Security Development Nexus in Somalia', *Conflict, Security and Development*, 4(2): 149–65.

Miller, P., and Rose, N. (2008). *Governing the Present: Administering Economic, Social and Personal Life.* Cambridge: Polity.

Mitra, S. (2005). 'Self Organising Systems for Mass Computer Literacy: Findings From the 'Hole in the Wall' Experiments', *International Journal of Development Issues*, 4(1): 71–81.

Mitra, S., and Rana, V. (2001). 'Children and the Internet: Experiments with Minimally Invasive Education in India', *British Journal of Educational Technology*, 32(2): 221–32.

Mondzain, M-J. (2005). *Image, Icon, Economy: The Byzantine Origins of the Contemporary Imaginary*. Stanford, CA: Stanford University Press.

Moore, B. (1978). *Injustice: The Social Bases of Obedience and Revolt*. New York: Macmillan.

Murray, A. (2011). 'Beyond Spectacle and the Image: The Poetics of Guy Debord and Agamben', in Justin Clemens, Nicholas Heron, and Alex Murray (eds.), *The Work of Giorgio Agamben: Law, Literature and Life*, 164–80. Edinburgh: Edinburgh University Press.

Nakamura, J., and Csikszentmihalyi, M. (2009). 'Flow Theory and Research', in C. R. Snyder and S. J. Lopez (eds.), *Oxford Handbook of Positive Psychology*, 2nd ed., 195–206. Oxford: Oxford University Press.

Narvaez R. W. M. (2012). *Crowdsourcing for Disaster Preparedness: Realities and Opportunities*. Unpublished dissertation, Graduate Institute of International and Development Studies, Geneva. Available at https://www.academia.edu/2197984/Crowdsourcing_for_ Disaster_Preparedness_Realities_and_Opportunities.

Navarro, V. (2000). 'Development and Quality of Life: a Critique of Amartya Sen's Development as Freedom', *International Journal of Health Services: Planning, Administration and Evaluation*, 30(4): 661–74.

Neenan, M. (2009). *Developing Resilience: A Cognitive Behavioural Approach*. London: Routledge.

Neocleous, M. (2008). *Critique of Security*. Edinburgh: Edinburgh University Press.

Newman, E., Paris, R., and Richmond, O. P. (eds.). (2009). *New Perspectives on Liberal Peacebuilding*. New York: United Nations University Press.

Nietzsche, F. (1997). *Beyond Good and Evil: Prelude to a Philosophy of the Future*. New York: Dover.

———. (2006). *The Gay Science*. New York: Dover.

North, D. C. (1990). *Institutions, Institutional Change and Economic Performance*. Cambridge: Cambridge University Press.

———. (2005). *Understanding the Process of Economic Change*. Princeton, NJ: Princeton University Press.

North, D. C., and Thomas, R. P. (1973). *The Rise of the Western World*. Cambridge: Cambridge University Press.

North, D. C., Wallis, J. J., and Weingast, B. R. (2009). *Violence and Social Orders: A Conceptual Framework for Interpreting Recorded Human History*. Cambridge: Cambridge University Press.

NPR. (2014). 'Overexposed? Camera Phones Could Be Washing Out Our Memories', http://www.wbur.org/npr/314592247/overexposed-camera-phones-could-be-washing-out-our-memories?ft=3&f=314592247 (accessed May 24, 2014).

NSS. (2002). *National Security Strategy of the United States of America*. Available at http://www.au.af.mil/au/awc/awcgate/nss/nss_sep2002.pdf.

Nussbaum, M. C. (2011). *Creating Capabilities: The Human Development Approach*. Cambridge, MA: Harvard University Press.

O'Brien, R., Goetz, A. M., Scholte, J. A., and Williams, M. (2000). *Contesting Global Governance: Multilateral Economic Institutions and Social Movements*. Cambridge: Cambridge University Press.

O'Donnell, G. (1996). 'Illusions about Consolidation', *Journal of Democracy*, 7(2): 34:51.

O'Malley, P. (2004). *Risk, Uncertainty and Government*, London: Routledge.

———. (2010). 'Resilient Subjects: Uncertainty, Warfare and Liberalism', *Economy and Society*, 29(4): 488–509.

ó Súilleabháin, A. (2014). 'Building Urban Resilience in Bangkok: Q&A with Apiwat Ratanawaraha', *Global Observatory*, 13 August. Available at http://theglobalobservatory.org/interviews/801-building-resilience-in-bangkok-apiwat-ratanawaraha.html.

Owens, P. (2011). 'Human Security and the Rise of the Social', *Review of International Studies*. Available on First View. 38(3): 547-567.

Paffenholz, T. (2009). *Civil Society and Peacebuilding: A Critical Assessment*. Boulder, CO: Lynne Rienner.

194

Bibliography

Palan, R. (2000). 'A World of their Making: An Evaluation of the Constructivist Critique in International Relations', *Review of International Studies*, 26(4): 575–98.

Parekh, B. (2000). *Rethinking Multiculturalism: Cultural Diversity and Political Theory.* Basingstoke: Macmillan.

Paris, R. (2004). *At War's End: Building Peace after Conflict.* Cambridge: Cambridge University Press.

Paris, R., and Sisk, T. D. (eds.) (2009). *The Dilemmas of Statebuilding: Confronting the Contradictions of Postwar Peace Operations.* London: Routledge.

Parkin, D. M. (2011). 'The Fraction of Cancer Attributable to Lifestyle and Environmental Factors in the UK in 2010', *British Journal of Cancer* 105, S2–S5. Available at http://www.nature.com/bjc/journal/v105/n2s/pdf/bjc2011474a.pdf.

Peet, R., and Watts, M. (1993). 'Development Theory and Environment in an Age of Market Triumphalism', *Environment and Development*, 69(3–4): 227–53.

Pender, J. (2001). 'From "Structural Adjustment" to "Comprehensive Development Framework": Conditionality Transformed?', *Third World Quarterly*, 22(3): 397–411.

Peters, B. G. (2005). *Institutional Theory in Political Science: The New Institutionalism*, 2nd ed. London: Continuum.

Pingali, P., Alinovi, L., and Sutton, J. (2005). 'Food Security in Complex Emergencies: Enhancing Food System Resilience', *Disasters*, 29(51): S5–S24.

Pinto, K. C. (2004). 'Intersections of Gender and Age in Health Care: Adapting Autonomy and Confidentiality for the Adolescent Girl', *Qualitative Health Research*, 14(1): 78–99.

Plato. (1960). *Georgias.* London: Penguin.

Polit, D. F., and Beck, C. T. (2004). *Nursing Research: Principles and Methods.* Philadelphia: Lippincott, Williams & Wilkins.

Prozorov, S. (2007). 'The Unrequited Love of Power: Biopolitical Investment and the Refusal of Care', *Foucault Studies*, 4: 53–77.

Pupavac, V. (2007). 'Witnessing the Demise of the Developing State: Problems for Humanitarian Advocacy', in A. Hehir and N. Robinson (eds.), *State-Building: Theory and Practice.* London: Routledge.

Reid, J. (2006a). *Biopolitics of the War on Terror: Life Struggles, Liberal Modernity and the Defence of Logistical Societies.* Manchester and New York: Manchester University Press.

———. (2006b). 'Life Struggles: War, Disciplinary Power and Biopolitics in the Thought of Michel Foucault', *Social Text*, 86 (1) (Spring): 127-152.

———. (2006c). 'Re-appropriating Clausewitz: The Neglected Dimensions of Counter-Strategic Thought', in Beate Jahn (ed.), *Classical Theory and International Relations: Critical Investigations.* Cambridge, University of Cambridge Press, pp. 277-295.

———. (2009). 'Politicizing Connectivity: Beyond the Biopolitics of Information Technology in International Relations', *Cambridge Review of International Affairs*, 22(4): 559–75.

———. (2010). 'Of Nomadic Unities: Gilles Deleuze on the Nature of Sovereignty', *Journal of International Relations & Development*, 13(4): 405–28.

———. (2011). 'The Vulnerable Subject of War', *South Atlantic Quarterly* 110(3).

———. (2012a). 'The Disastrous and Politically Degraded Subject of Resilience', *Development Dialogue* (April).

———. (2012b). 'The Neoliberal Subject: Resilience and the Art of Living Dangerously', *Revista Pleyade* (10).

———. (2013). 'Towards an Affirmative Biopolitics: On the Importance of Thinking the Relation between Life and Error Polemologically', in Jakob Nilsson and Sven-Olov Wallenstein (eds.), *The Politics of Life.* Stockholm: Sodertorn University Press, pp. 91-104.

———. (2014). 'Fighting States of Subjection: The Liberal Biopolitics of the War on Terror' in Alex Houen (ed.), *States of War.* London and New York: Routledge.

Reivich, K., and Shatte, A. (2003). *The Resilience Factor: 7 Keys to Finding Your Inner Strength and Overcoming Life's Hurdles.* New York: Broadway Books.

Reus-Smit, C. (2001). 'Constructivism', in S. Burchill et al., *Theories of International Relations*, 209–30. Basingstoke: Palgrave.

Richards, D., and Smith, M. (2011). 'Good Governance and Civil Service Reform', written evidence submitted to the UK Parliament Public Administration Select Committee,

2010–2011 session. Available at http://www.publications.parliament.uk/pa/cm201011/cmselect/cmpubadm/writev/goodgov/gg14.htm.

Richmond, O. P. (2005). *The Transformation of Peace*. Basingstoke: Palgrave.

———. (2010). 'Resistance and the Post-Liberal Peace', *Millennium: Journal of International Studies*, 38(3): 665–92.

———. (2011). *A Post-Liberal Peace: The Infrapolitics of Peacebuilding*. London: Routledge.

Richmond, O. P., and Franks, J. (2009). *Liberal Peace Transitions: Between Statebuilding and Peacebuilding*. Edinburgh: Edinburgh University Press.

Riddell, R. (2007). *Does Foreign Aid Really Work?* Oxford and New York: Oxford University Press.

Risse, T., and Ropp, S. C. (1999). 'International Human Rights Norms and Domestic Change: Conclusions', in T. Risse, S. C. Ropp, and K. Sikkink (eds.), *The Power of Human Rights: International Norms and Domestic Change*, 234–78. Cambridge: Cambridge University Press.

Risse, T., Ropp, S. C., and Sikkink, K. (eds.). (1999). *The Power of Human Rights: International Norms and Domestic Change*. Cambridge: Cambridge University Press.

Risse, T., and Sikkink, K. (1999). 'The Socialization of International Human Rights Norms into Domestic Practices: Introduction', in T. Risse, S. C. Ropp, and K. Sikkink (eds.), *The Power of Human Rights International Norms and Domestic Change*, 1–38. Cambridge: Cambridge University Press.

Risse-Kappen, T. (1994). 'Ideas Do Not Float Freely: Transnational Coalitions, Domestic Structures, and the End of the Cold War', *International Organization*, 48(2): 185–214.

——— (ed.). (1995). *Bringing Transnational Relations Back In: Non-State Actors, Domestic Structures, and International Institutions*. Cambridge: Cambridge University Press.

Roberts, D. (2008). 'Hybrid Polities and Indigenous Pluralities: Advanced Lessons in State-building from Cambodia', *Journal of Intervention and Statebuilding*, 2(1): 63–86.

———. (2011). 'Over 40% of Cancers Due to Lifestyle: Says Review', *BBC News*, 7 December. Available at http://www.bbc.co.uk/news/health-16031149.

Robertson, J. (1999). *Crimes Against Humanity: The Struggle for Global Justice*. London: Allen Lane.

Rose, N. (1999a). *Governing the Soul: Shaping of the Private Self*. London: Free Association.

———. (1999b). *Powers of Freedom: Reframing Political Thought*. Cambridge: Cambridge University Press.

Rosenau, J. (1992). 'Citizenship in a Changing Global Order', in J. Rosenau and E. Czempiel (eds.), *Governance without Government: Order and Change in World Politics*, 272–94. Cambridge: Cambridge University Press.

———. (1998). 'Governance and Democracy in a Globalization World', in Daniele Archibugi, David Held and Martin Kohler, eds., *Re-imagining Political Community: Studies in Cosmopolitcan Democracy*. Stanford: Standford University Press. 28-57.

———. (2002). 'Information Technologies and the Skills, Networks and Structures That Sustain World Affairs', in James N. Rosenau and J. P. Singh (eds.), *Information Technologies and Global Politics: The Changing Scope of Power and Governance*. Albany: SUNY Press.

———. (2008). *People Count! Networked Individuals in Global Politics*. Boulder, CO, and London: Paradigm Press.

Saad-Philo, A., and Johnston, D. (2004). *Neoliberalism: A Critical Reader*. London: Pluto Press.

Said, E. (1995). *Orientalism: Western Conceptions of the Orient*. London: Penguin.

Samaddar, R. (2006). *Flags and Rights*. Kolkata: Mahanirban Calcutta Research Group/Timir Printing Works.

———. (2010). *Emergence of the Political Subject*. New Delhi: Sage.

Scheuer, J. (2012). 'What We Call "Natural" Disasters Are Not Natural At All', *United Nations Development Programme*, 12 October. Available at http://www.undp.org/content/undp/en/home/ourperspective/ourperspectivearticles/2012/10/12/what-we-call-natural-disasters-are-not-natural-at-all-jo-scheuer/.

Schmitt, C. (2003). *The Nomos of the Earth: in the International Law of the Jus Publicum Europaeum*. New York: Telos.

196   *Bibliography*

Schmitter, P. C., and Karl, T. L. (1991). 'What Democracy Is . . . and Is Not', *Journal of Democracy*, 2(3): 4–17.
Scott, W. R. (2008). *Institutions and Organizations: Ideas and Interests.* London: Sage.
Sen, A. (1987). *On Ethics and Economics.* Oxford: Blackwell.
———. (1992). *Inequality Reexamined.* Oxford: Oxford University Press.
———. (1997). 'Human Rights and Asian Values', *New Republic*, July 14–21.
———. (1999). *Development as Freedom.* Oxford: Oxford University Press.
———. (2006). *Identity and Violence: The Illusion of Destiny.* London: Penguin Books.
———. (2009). *The Idea of Justice.* London: Allen Lane.
Sloterdijk, P. (2010). *Rage and Time.* New York: Columbia University Press.
Snyder, J. (2000). *From Voting to Violence: Democratization and Nationalist Conflict.* New York: W. W. Norton.
Staats, S. J. (2009). 'Sen. Kerry Champions Development in Knock-Out Speech'. Available at http://blogs.cgdev.org/globaldevelopment/2009/05/sen-kerry-champions-development-in-knock-out-speech.php.
Steger, M. B., and Roy, R. K. (2010). *Neoliberalism: A Very Short Introduction.* Oxford: Oxford University Press.
Steinmo, S., Thelen, K., and Longstreth, F. (1992). *Structuring Politics: Historical Institutionalism in Comparative Analysis.* Cambridge: Cambridge University Press.
Stewart, F. (2004). 'Development and Security', *Conflict, Security and Development*, 4(3): 261–88.
Tadjbakhsh, S. (ed.). (2011). *Rethinking the Liberal Peace: External Models and Local Alternatives.* London: Routledge.
Tandon, N. (2007). 'Biopolitics, Climate Change and Water Security: Impact, Vulnerability and Adaptation Issues for Women', *Agenda*, 73: 4–20.
Taubes, J. (2009). *Occidental Eschatology.* Stanford, CA: Stanford University Press.
Thaler, R. H., and Sunstein, C. R. (2008). *Nudge: Improving Decisions about Health, Wealth and Happiness.* New York: Yale University Press.
Thomas, D. C. (2001). *The Helsinki Effect: International Norms, Human Rights, and the Demise of Communism.* Princeton, NJ: Princeton University Press.
———. (2011). *Making EU Foreign Policy: National Preferences, European Norms and Common Policies.* London: Palgrave-Macmillan.
Todorova, M. (1997). *Imagining the Balkans.* New York: Oxford University Press.
Toscano, A. (2010). *Fanaticism: On the Uses of an Idea.* London and New York: Verso.
Touraine, A. (2001). *Beyond Neoliberalism.* Cambridge: Polity Press.
UK Cabinet Office. (2011a). 'UK Resilience'. Available at http://www.cabinetoffice.gov.uk/ukresilience.
———. (2011b). *Strategic National Framework on Community Resilience*, UK Cabinet Office, March. Available at http://www.cabinetoffice.gov.uk/sites/default/files/resources/Strategic-National-Framework-on-Community-Resilience_0.pdf.
United Kingdom Joint Doctrine Publication. (2007). *Operations In the UK: The Defence Contribution to Resilience* (Development, Concepts and Doctrine Centre). Available at http://defenceintranet.diiweb.r.mil.uk/DefenceIntranet/Library/AtoZ/DevelopmentConceptsAndDoctrineCentrePublications.htm. United Nations. (2000). 'United Nations Millennium Declaration', Resolution 55/2. Available at http://www.un.org/millennium/declaration/ares552e.htm.
———. (2004). *Living with Risk: A Global Review of Disaster Reduction Initiatives.* New York: UN Publications.
———. (2014). 'Independent Expert Advisory Group on a Data Revolution for Sustainable Development', *A World That Counts: Mobilising the Data Revolution for Sustainable Development: Report Prepared at the request of the United Nations Secretary-General.* Available at http://www.undatarevolution.org/report/.
UNDP. (1990). *Human Development Report 1990: The Concept and Measurement of Human Development.* New York: United Nations Development Programme.
United Nations Environment Programme (UNEP). (2004). *Exploring the Links: Human Well-Being, Poverty & Ecosystem Services.* Nairobi: UN Publications.

United Nations Office for Disaster Risk Reduction (UNISDR). (2014). *Progress and Challenges in Disaster Risk Reduction: A Contribution Towards the Development of Policy Indicators for the Post-2015 Framework for Disaster Risk Reduction.* Geneva, Switzerland: UNISDR.

UNPEP. (2008). 'Poverty, Health and Environment: Placing Environmental Health on Countries', Development Agendas. Available at http://issuu.com/undp/docs/pov-health-env-cra/15.

United States Institute for Peace (USIP). (2013). *Sensing and Shaping Emerging Conflicts.* Washington, DC: National Academies Press.

Urry, J. (2003). *Global Complexity.* Cambridge: Polity Press.

Walker, R. B. J. (1997). 'The Subject of Security', in K. Krause and M. C. Williams (eds.) *Critical Security Studies: Concepts and Cases.* London: UCL Press, pp. 61-81.

Walker, J., and Cooper, M. (2011). 'Genealogies of Resilience: From Systems Ecology to the Political Economy of Crisis Adaptation', *Security Dialogue*, 42(2): 143–60.

Weldes, J., Laffey, M., Gusterson, H., and Duvall, R. (eds.). (1999). *Cultures of Insecurity: States, Communities, and the Production of Danger.* Minneapolis: University of Minnesota Press.

Welsh, I. (1996). *Trainspotting.* New York: W. W. Norton.

Wendt, A. (1992). 'Anarchy Is What States Make of It: The Social Construction of Power Politics', *International Organization*, 46(2): 391–425.

———. (1999). *Social Theory of International Politics.* Cambridge: Cambridge University Press.

Widmaier, W. (2011). 'Taking Stock of Norms Research—From Structural, Cognitive and Psychological Constructivisms to Intellectual Irony and Populist Paradox', Participant Write-Up, IPS working group on Norms, International Studies Association, Annual Convention 2011, Montreal, Canada, 15–19 March. Available at http://www.isanet.org/isa_working_groups_ips/2011/03/ips-working-group-widmaier-write-up.html.

Wiener, N. (1954). *The Human Use of Human Beings: Cybernetics and Society.* Boston: Da Capo Press.

Williams, E. C. (2011). *Combined and Uneven Apocalypse.* Winchester and Washington, DC: Zero Books.

Wolf, G. (2009). 'Know Thyself: Tracking Every Facet of Life, from Sleep to Mood to Pain, 24/7/365', *Wired* 17(7), 22 June. Available at http://archive.wired.com/medtech/health/magazine/17-07/lbnp_knowthyself.

Wolff, L. (1994). *Inventing Eastern Europe: The Map of Civilization on the Mind of the Enlightenment.* Stanford, CA: Stanford University Press.

World Bank. (2006). *World Development Report 2007: Development and the Next Generation.* Washington, DC: World Bank.

World Commission on Environment and Development (WCED). (1987). *Our Common Future.* Oxford: Oxford University Press.

WRI. (2008). *World Resources 2008: Roots of Resilience—Growing the Wealth of the Poor* Washington, DC: World Resources Institute.

Youngs, R. (2002). *The European Union and the Promotion of Democracy: Europe's Mediterranean and Asian Policies.* Oxford: Oxford University Press.

Zakharia, F. (2003). *The Future of Freedom: Illiberal Democracy at Home and Abroad.* New York: W. W. Norton.

Zanotti, L. (2006). 'International Security, Normalization and Croatia's Euro-Atlantic Integration', *European University Institute Working Papers*, SPS No. 2006/02.

———. (2011). *Governing Disorder: UN Peace Operations, International Security, and Democratization in the Post-Cold War Era.* University Park: Pennsylvania State University Press.

Zaum, D. (2007). *The Sovereignty Paradox: The Norms and Politics of International Statebuilding.* Oxford: Oxford University Press.

Zebrowski, C. (2009). 'Governing the Network Society: A Biopolitical Critique of Resilience', *Political Perspectives*, 3(1). Available at http://www.politicalperspectives.org.uk/wp-content/uploads/2010/08/Vol3-1-2009-4.pdf. Last accessed 10 February 2012.

Zizek, S. (2010). *Living in the End Times.* London and New York: Verso.

Index

Acharya, Amitav, 130, 131, 136
adaptive capacity-building, 78, 88–91, 94
Adger, Neil W., 61, 101
Agamben, Giorgio, 48n1, 60, 145
agency-based approaches to International
    Relations, 126, 127, 128, 131, 134, 136,
    140, 140–141
Ahrens, Joachim and Rudolph, Patrick M.,
    46
Althusser, Louis, 47
Arendt, Hannah, 16, 46–47, 48n1,
    169–172, 176–177, 178
Aristotle, 60
Augé, Marc, 160–161
autonomy and human subjectivity, 1, 22,
    108, 110, 117, 155; and rationality, 2, 3,
    9, 10, 35, 81, 83, 125; as threat to life,
    1, 4, 33, 100, 103, 107, 109, 110, 116;
    as diminished capacity to connect, 9,
    70, 100, 114–115; pathologization of,
    100
autotelic self. *See* autotelic subject
autotelic subject, 32, 33, 45, 48

Bachelard, Gaston, 18, 20–21
Badiou, Alain, 167, 170
Barbier, Edward and Markandya, Anil, 55
Barnett, Michael, 127
Barnett, Michael and Zürcher, Christoph,
    136
Barnett, Thomas P.M., 115, 118n4

Beck, Ulrich, 4
Ben-Ami, Daniel, 79
Benett, Jane, 178, 183
Berger, Peter and Luckmann, Thomas, 40,
    49n5, 127
Berlin, Isaiah, 100, 110
Big Data, 33, 45–46, 47, 76, 138–139
biomateriality, 151
biopolitical framework of analysis, 53, 61
biopolitical imaginary, 21, 70, 174
biopolitics and ecology, 61, 69
biopolitics and development, 59
biopower, 147
Biospheric catastrophe. *See* ecological
    catastrophe
Birch, Kean and Mykhnenko, Vlad, 2
Black, David, 128
Blake, William, 20
Bosnia war, 130
Brasett, James and Vaughan-Williams,
    Nick, 30
Briggs, Rachel, 29
Brown, Chris, 129
Bruntland Commission report 'Our
    Common Future', 57
Bulley, Dan, 29
Burchell, Graham, 10
Burg, Steven L., 130
Burgess, Adam, 86
Burke, Anthony, 105, 117